MAESTRO

DAVID TOSSELL

MAESTRO

A PORTRAIT OF

GARRY SOBERS

CRICKET'S GREATEST ALL-ROUNDER

pitch

First published by Pitch Publishing, 2025

1

Pitch Publishing
9 Donnington Park,
85 Birdham Road,
Chichester, West Sussex,
PO20 7AJ
www.pitchpublishing.co.uk
info@pitchpublishing.co.uk

ISBN 978 1 83680 194 8

Typesetting and origination by Pitch Publishing

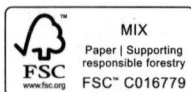

MIX
Paper | Supporting
responsible forestry
FSC
www.fsc.org   FSC™ C016779

Printed and bound on FSC® certified paper in line with
our continuing commitment to ethical business practices,
sustainability and the environment.

Printed and bound in India by Replika Press Pvt. Ltd.

CONTENTS

INTRODUCTION

Garry Sobers, when you call his name
He's the one and only
He's the maestro of the cricket game
Be proud of this great West Indian
Hold him in esteem
He's the greatest cricketer the world has ever seen

'Garry Sobers' by The Merrymen. (Emile Straker,
Merry Disc, 1973)

THE MERRYMEN were singing about one of their own. While they were establishing themselves as one of the leading calypso and folk groups on the island of Barbados, so Garry Sobers was dominating his sport. Yet the claims they made on behalf of their countryman met with no dispute from any corner of the world. Even Sir Donald Bradman described Sobers as the greatest all-round cricketer he had laid eyes upon.

When Sobers was named as one of *Wisden*'s Five Cricketers of the 20th Century the only inexplicable thing about his selection was that ten of the 100 voters on the panel found a reason to overlook him, in spite of his record in 93 Test matches: 8,032 runs, 26 centuries, 235 wickets and 109 catches. If the World XI matches that Sobers skippered in England in 1970 and Australia in 1971/72 had not been denied full Test status you could add almost 1,000 runs, three more centuries and 30 wickets.

In 2007, *Wisden* assembled 16 judges to retrospectively identify the 'Leading Cricketer in the World', an award the publication had introduced in 2004. Only Bradman, with ten nominations, was given the honour more often than Sobers, who was chosen for 1958, 1960, 1962, 1964, 1965, 1966, 1968 and 1970.

Yet while it is possible to validate the greatness of Sobers with averages and accolades, mere numbers could never fully capture its essence. In his Players of the Century citation in *Wisden*, Ian Wooldridge highlighted 'a vibrancy, nobility of spirit and versatility of accomplishment that transcended all statistics'.[1]

With bat in his left hand, Sobers loped to the crease with a casualness that disguised the approaching menace. Collar upturned; his stooped stance served to exaggerate the impact of seeing him uncurl into shots with a swing so full that the follow-through of his bat would sometimes be halted only by his backside. A predominantly back-foot player, he was described by the great South African, Barry Richards, as 'the only 360-degree player in the game' at a time when he achieved such versatility without the ramps and reverse sweeps of the 21st century. The mind boggles at the invention Sobers might have brought to the modern Twenty20 leagues, and the millions he could have earned as a charismatic force in the Indian Premier League.

'If there was a superman of cricket it was Garry Sobers,'* is the verdict of Australian fast bowler Dennis Lillee, who was on the wrong end of one of his most famous innings. 'There is no chance there has been, or will be, anyone who will be a better or more complete all-rounder.'[2]

His greatest deeds are among those that have shaped cricket history: from his breaking of Len Hutton's Test record to his series-winning brilliance in England in 1966; from the then-mythical achievement of six sixes in an over to the breathtaking 254 he scored for the World team against Lillee's Australia – rated by Bradman as the greatest of all innings. He maintained his productivity throughout his career, including a brilliant Lord's century in his final Test in England.

As a bowler, Sobers could deliver with pace or swing the ball both ways. Then he could return to spin it off his fingers or with his wrist. Throw in his ability to catch anything in any position and you have what Australian writer Ray Robinson called 'evolution's ultimate specimen in cricketers'.[3]

Even members of the great generation of all-rounders that followed him, Ian Botham, Kapil Dev and Richard Hadlee, only once achieved a feat that Sobers managed three times: that of 300 runs and 20 wickets in a series. Imran Khan never did it at all. In later years, South African Jacques Kallis was the all-rounder most frequently mentioned in the same breath and for a while he maintained a higher differential between batting and

---

* For much of his career, the shortened form of Sobers's first name appeared in most places as 'Gary'. As the years progressed, Garry became the accepted version and was the form he used himself.

bowling average – often a guide to effectiveness – than Sobers. By the time Kallis played his final Test in 2013, Sobers was even leading in that category, by 23.75 to 22.72, and he betters any of the game's recognised all-rounders at the time of writing.

And, as Richards proposed, 'There will always be this comparison with Kallis and, don't get me wrong, both were geniuses, both in the top echelon. But if you wanted to win a game then Garry was more likely to do it for you and Jacques was more likely to save it for you. That is the best way I can describe it.'[4]

Former England bowler Mike Selvey also spoke for the older generation when he wrote, 'Those who had never seen Sobers play may query how anyone could play the game with greater all-round efficiency than Kallis, but then only those who have seen Sobers as well can truly make that judgement. It is not just about the sheer versatility of Sobers ... but the manner in which he changed matches. And charisma. And star quality.'[5]

Sobers founded his game on natural instinct rather than the MCC manual or extensive coaching. Perhaps that is why there were doubts about his captaincy, the one area of the game in which he never excelled. He was not a natural or analytical leader, not one for planning, strategy, discipline or motivation. He left his men to their own devices on tour while he played golf, and struggled to get the best out of lesser players because he was used to carrying them with his own talent. 'He was too great a cricketer to be captain because he always expected everyone to perform as he did, and that was not possible,' observed Clyde Walcott, former team-mate turned administrator.[6]

In his history of West Indian cricket, Michael Manley concluded that Sobers 'possessed every asset save that indefinable quality that enables some leaders to lift the team out of adversity by making it more than the sum of its parts'.[7]

* * *

The fifth of seven children, one of whom died in infancy, Sobers was born and raised in the parish of St Michael in Barbados, enduring the loss of his father at five years old. Sport, especially cricket, consumed him to the point of a lack of interest in most of what went on around him, creating a naivety and absence of curiosity and insight that appeared to accompany him into adulthood – not without consequence.

His appointment as West Indies Test captain in 1964 was, it could be argued, every bit as significant as that of Frank Worrell to lead the side in Australia in 1960/61. Worrell was the first black man to be entrusted permanently with the job, but it was Sobers who more closely reflected the people he represented. Worrell was educated at an English university and belonged to the Freemasons; Sobers was raised in a shack. West Indian historian Hilary Beckles called his rise 'a signal of hope for collective redemption'.[8]

In 1998, he was given the official status of National Hero of Barbados, yet he was loved in every corner of the globe where cricket is played, as well as having an ability to unite the often-fractured Caribbean cricketing community. And no one could doubt that he was a proud West Indian. He held dear the success of the national team and took exception to the image he felt English fans and media held of his side as happy-go-lucky players who lacked professionalism and killer instinct.

Paradoxically, however, Sobers did not always wear his mantle as representative of the people comfortably. He didn't see defeat in a Test match as cause for national mourning, certainly not if the game had been approached in the right way. His insistence that 'I always saw cricket as a noble sport and I tried to play in the true spirit of the game' was what informed his decision in Trinidad in 1968 to offer England an opportunity to make 215 to win. 'When things pay off you are great and when they don't you are a darn idiot,' he said as his effigy was being hanged.[9]

Perhaps more serious, and more difficult for those in his region to understand, was his acceptance in 1970 to contest a double-wicket competition in Rhodesia at a time when that country was banned from global sport because of the white minority government's apartheid policies. After calls for his resignation from influential Caribbean voices, Sobers salvaged his status with an apology of sorts.

Sobers had claimed he 'knew nothing of politics at the time'. That cut little ice with someone such as Viv Richards, a man whose dream of emulating Sobers had driven him through his formative professional years. Richards saw playing cricket as a political act in itself. It is instructive that Sobers described Tony Greig's infamously ill-judged comment about making West Indies 'grovel' in 1976 as a 'throwaway line', while Richards described it as a 'racist dig'. Even in later years, when Sobers discussed turning down an offer to play in South Africa, it was not because he acknowledged his countrymen's concerns or had opened his eyes to the social injustices. He couldn't be bothered with a repetition of the hullabaloo that had accompanied the Rhodesia expedition.

When Sobers took his strongest stance, it was personal rather than political. For example, he threatened not to accept his invitation for the West Indies tour of England in 1963 because the fee of £800 was less than he could have earned in league cricket. He turned up for the tour only after warnings from Worrell, Bradman and Richie Benaud not to let down his country. They were aware that West Indian cricket fans were not yet prepared for a player who recognised his commercial worth.

Sobers conceded that cricket gave him a good lifestyle, but he had to play year-round to capitalise upon his value. He once expressed regret during a television interview that he had not excelled in a sport such as golf, where earnings were more substantial and down to individual achievement rather than the whim of employers.

In retirement, he supported the financial claims of his successors, especially when it allowed him to bolster his own pension fund. He was engaged, at the suggestion of Tony Greig, as an ambassador for Kerry Packer's anti-establishment World Series Cricket in 1977, arguing, 'I wanted to see the leading players earn more money from the game.' He sympathised with the West Indies players who went on rebel tours to South Africa in the 1980s because he recognised the financial opportunity. And, embarrassingly as it turned out, he was one of the West Indian cricket legends who allowed themselves to be hoodwinked into supporting Allen Stanford, whose patronage of West Indies cricket in the 2000s was revealed to have been funded by a crooked financial empire.

Despite his supernatural ability, Sobers was human and flawed. Australian writer Gideon Haigh noted, 'In what one might call the Jamesian chain of cricket heroes – linking Constantine, Headley, Worrell, Sobers and Richards – Sobers is an unusual presence, one who did all things on the cricket field with ease but who encountered the difficulty of having to be all things to all men.'[10] It makes him a compelling biographical subject, and meant he was even more relatable to the mere mortals who could only dream of his sporting prowess.

He liked to socialise, even on the night before a big game, causing Sunil Gavaskar to recall, 'We once went to a nightclub and I was astonished at the way he could knock back a drink. He kept on having a dig at me for drinking Coca-Cola and said that it was more harmful to the intestines than liquor.'[11] His love of competition, meanwhile, meant that he was quick to accept any kind of gamble, whether it was on his beloved horses or taking risks on the field.

Sobers also had a complicated private life. After an early engagement to an Indian actress, his marriage to a white Australian – itself a ground-breaking act for its era – ended in divorce. And he suffered his darkest hours in 1959 after the car he was driving in Staffordshire was involved in a crash that killed friend and West Indies team-mate Collie Smith. Sobers – who, according to the tone of the coroner's summation, might have been lucky to face charges only for reckless driving

– carried the responsibility for the tragedy on to the field with him. 'For most of my international career I was playing for two,' was how he described it in the opening line of one of his autobiographies.[12]

It is now more than two decades since the last Sobers-penned book, and half a century since the biography written by the former England all-rounder Trevor Bailey, a friend who adopted a less than objective approach. For such a monumental figure in his sport, Sobers has not been particularly well served by literature. His numerous memoirs offer a flavour of the man, but the awed tones of contemporaneous writings by team-mates, opponents and observers are more instructive in placing his achievements in context – something Sobers was too modest and too uninterested to worry about.

By the time he approached the latter years of his life, he'd had enough of talking about himself. 'Why do you all ask the same questions? All you journalists want to hear about is my six sixes,' he told writer Will Buckley in 2001, prior to the release of his final autobiography – although it was far from the only time he expressed such weariness. Buckley concluded, 'It is always a surprise to come across someone who doesn't like talking about himself. And Sir Garry, both modest and shy, really doesn't like talking about his achievements. It is his curse that, so great were those achievements, everyone wants to talk to him about them.'[13]

The publications bearing the name of Sobers were, it is apparent, born of financial opportunity rather than any great desire to share his story. My hope is that this book illuminates and properly frames his career, perhaps introducing him in detail to some for the first time, and supports his legacy as the greatest all-round cricketer the world has ever seen.

1

LIFE AFTER DEATH: BOY FROM THE BAY

'There are few successful adults who were not first successful children.'

American author Alexander Chase

THE SPOTLIGHTS pierced the dark Atlantic waters, shooting ominously from the silhouette of the submarine and finding their mark on the hull of SS *Lady Hawkins*. The ship's carpenter, William Burton, was the first to spot the German U-boat poised for its deadly strike. 'It was a big one,' he said. 'It came up about 100 yards off us and just lay there with two white lights on us.'[1]

An 8,000-ton steam turbine ocean liner, part of the Canadian merchant navy fleet in the Caribbean, *Lady Hawkins* was one of a group of ships built in the 1920s to carry mail, passengers and perishable cargo. It had set off from Montreal for Bermuda earlier in the month and was carrying 2,900 tons of cargo; vital provisions that Germany and its Second World War allies knew would be badly missed if they failed to reach their destination.

It was only five days since the Panamanian tanker *Norness* had been sunk by two torpedoes 60 miles off Long Island, marking the beginning of a campaign of similar attacks on passenger and cargo ships that would see German submarines sink 12 vessels in the Atlantic in little over two weeks, costing almost 350 lives.

Blacked out, but unescorted and possessing only one small gun, *Lady Hawkins* had been ordered by Captain Huntley Giffin to follow a zig-zagging course to make it more difficult to track and hit. It was 150 nautical miles off North Carolina's Cape Hatteras when, at around 2 a.m. local time on 19 January 1942, Burton made his sighting.

Most of the 212 passengers and 109 crew were in their cabins and quarters, among them General Servant Shamont Sobers, a 34-year-old father of six from Barbados. A handsome man, good at sport and leader of a YMCA scout troop, Shamont was known for his zest for life and for always being well dressed. Awaiting his return after this voyage were his wife, Thelma, and a brood of offspring whose four boys included a five-year-old known as Garry.

Barely a minute elapsed after Burton's discovery before Korvettenkapitän Robert-Richard Zapp, commander of IXC class submarine U-66, gave the order to fire. A stern-launched torpedo exploded into *Lady Hawkins*' number two hold. Bellboy Leo Riveira, another Barbadian, had been asleep alongside a colleague under a table in the first-class dining room, believing it was safer there than in his berth below. 'The ceiling of the dining room started to fall in, so we got up and out of there,' he recalled.

The ship began to keel over, throwing everyone on deck into the sea. Lights went out, leaving passengers and crew to begin a panic-stricken grope towards the upper deck, the stench of cordite burning their nostrils. Then a second torpedo ripped into hold number three, continuing its course of destruction into the engine room; also taking out two lifeboats. 'We got on to the promenade, but the ship was listing fast, and there was only one lifeboat ready for use,' Riveira continued. 'The chief officer said, "All right, boys, jump for it!" And we did.'[2]

Less than 30 minutes after the first strike, *Lady Hawkins* had sunk. Shamont Sobers perished with it.

It was nine days before the ship's fate was fully understood, when the 21 crew and 50 passengers picked up by New York liner SS *Coamo** – having been adrift in a lifeboat for five days – arrived in San Juan, Puerto Rico. Only then could the families of the 245 victims be told what had happened to their loved ones.

'I remember a messenger coming to our house and my mother Thelma sobbing and crying. She told us that his boat had been torpedoed,' Garry recounted. Initial hopes that another two lifeboats might have made it to safety proved unfounded. 'After a few days and then the weeks passed, we came to realise that Dad would never be coming back.'[3]

The subsequent issue of *Canada-West Indies* magazine announced, 'Shocked by the ruthlessness of this deed, it is only natural that we should cry for vengeance on the cowardly Nazi

---

* *Coamo* was sunk by a U-boat attack later in the year off the coast of Ireland, with the loss of all 186 on board.

rat who cold-bloodedly committed this murder. As surely then as night follows day, that submarine commander, here, or in the hereafter must answer … for his act.'

Such sentiment might have been shared by Thelma, but it offered no practical help for a mother whose husband had died while serving in a civilian, rather than military, role. It would not be until 2000, the year before Thelma's death, that the Canadian government announced details of a $50 million compensation package for 7,300 merchant seamen and widows.

* * *

The home where the Sobers family lived, and where Garry was born, was a small, shambling single-storey wooden construction on Walcott's Avenue, a tidy but unaffluent street in Bay Land. Part of the St Michael's parish in the south-west of Barbados, the two-square-mile area had been developed for plantation workers after the abolition of slavery in the region almost a century earlier and its chief claim to fame was rivalling nearby Oistins for the island's largest fish market.

'A depressed place for persons of his origins,' was how Barbadian lawyer and historian Guyson Meyers described it. 'Like most people around him, [Garry] would have been acquainted with poverty and little expectation. Living conditions then were not far removed from what existed a hundred years earlier. Prospects for a significant life were not good for a black boy born in the Bay Land during that period. We know of nothing which would have suggested that the young Garfield

Sobers would have had a life different from what was common for boys like him at that time.[4]

It did not need any kind of formal policy of apartheid to make the majority black population aware of their status. By the end of the 1930s, not much more than three per cent of the population, most of them white, were eligible to vote, while the vast majority of white-collar jobs were closed off to the black community. Charlie Griffith, born in Barbados two years after Sobers and destined to become a West Indies team-mate, recalled that 'life was simple and uncomplicated'. But he added, 'Opportunities were few and horizons seemed very restricted. No one ever dared look beyond the next meal or the bare necessities of life.'[5]

Since the 1920s, Barbados's population had been expanding, economics having reversed the trend for workers to head to the United States and South America for greater opportunities. But wages were now failing to keep pace with the cost of living as the worldwide depression reached its shores. In 1937, the year after Garry's birth, 14 people on the island were killed and 47 injured in protests and rioting that was mirrored throughout the Caribbean. Such events were the spur for Grantley Adams, who had attended Oxford University, to found the Barbados Labour Party.

According to Mary Chamberlain in her historical study of Barbados:

The Great Depression of the 1930s had hit the West Indies like a hurricane, devastating the already precarious national economies in its wake and with it the even more precarious household economies of its workers. Migration – the great safety valve of the region – had come to a standstill. Work was intermittent or non-existent, wages were low, malnutrition rife, housing deplorable. Apart from the privileged few, West Indians were poorly educated and in many cases illiterate. Child labour was common.[6]

In the third decade of a new century much has changed in Bay Land, now known as Bayville. Four-storey apartment blocks have been built in some of the bigger streets; two-bedroom, one-bathroom houses in the neighbourhood can fetch upwards of BD$300,000 (well over £100,000); and Garry's old school in Bay Street became a ministerial building.

But Walcott's Avenue retains enough of its character and construction to make it easy to imagine Garry and his brothers playing on the single-track road or in the narrow passages between brightly painted houses. As you complete a mile's walk north from the Garrison Savannah racetrack, the pink boards of a small general store and the green-painted house at opposite corners of the south end of the street offer a warm welcome to the tentative visitor.

Keith Sandiford, a schoolmate of Garry's, said of Bay Land, 'Its residents shared strong community bonds and a sense of belonging, neighbours were generally very kind and helpful, and crime was rare, probably in part because few of the inhabitants had anything worth stealing. With the exception of a small number of larger houses with guard dogs, almost all houses were left unlocked.'[7]

Most of the houses have been replaced or modernised over the decades. Garry's status in the sport might not have afforded the luxury to which the modern Test and IPL stars are accustomed, but it did allow Thelma, determined to remain in the family home, to have it extended and updated in stone.

Born on 28 July, 1936, and given the full name Garfield St Aubrun Sobers, the new arrival was Shamont and Thelma's fifth child, after George, Greta, Elise and Gerald. Another son, Cecil, followed. There was even a seventh child, a boy, who died very young. The way the adult Garry would refer to this early brush with tragedy is instructive. Remarkably, he addresses it in his 1988 autobiography with the most jarring of throwaway lines. 'The seventh child died in infancy, the victim of an accident with a kerosene lamp.'[8] No elaboration, no suggestion of the horror it must have inflicted upon his family.

It is indicative of several things: Garry's young age when it happened, of course; the family's preference, hardly untypical of the time, to move forward with stoicism and not to speak of such things; and a lack of curiosity, or need for insight, that would continue to manifest itself throughout Sobers's life – whether analysing the brilliance of his cricket or exploring his background. In discussing the origins of his unusual name, he thought that both Garfield and St Aubrun might have been derived from distant relatives in the US, or 'there was a suggestion I was named after John Garfield, the American actor'. The latter was untrue, given that Garfield had not made his movie debut at the time of Sobers's birth, nor had he yet adopted his professional surname. 'I do not bother looking into how names were handed down,' Sobers shrugged.[9] Similarly, he believed he was born at 3.30 in the morning, but 'I couldn't tell you. I never troubled to go into it that deeply.'[10]

Shamont's salary as a merchant seaman put his family nowhere near the island's lower-middle class bracket of teachers, policemen and civil servants, but it was higher than the average plantation or domestic worker, the jobs occupied by the majority of his peers. There was rarely spare cash for luxuries, but enough for the necessities. His children were properly clothed and always had full bellies. If they were poor, his family were happy because they knew no different. They were popular figures in the neighbourhood; the sight of the boys playing cricket in the street a familiar one.

Yet Garry's relationship with his father was one of ambivalence. When friend and former opponent Trevor Bailey wrote his 1976 book on Sobers – as much personal memoir as biography – he suggested that Shamont nurtured his sons' cricket and he painted a picture of domestic bliss. 'When home on leave he would spend hours playing with them,' Bailey wrote.[11]

It was true that Sobers senior was a keen sportsman, although football was closer to his heart than cricket, and he would play the latter with his boys alongside their house or on a patch of land behind known as Bay Pasture, then the home of Wanderers Cricket Club. But Garry was fearful enough of his father to describe his death as 'a blessing in disguise'. Garry recalled Shamont as a 'very strict man'. If he and his siblings were playing in the neighbourhood when news arrived that his father's ship had docked, they would rush home and pretend they had been inside the whole time. 'He didn't like us going outside to play with the other children,' recalled Garry, who didn't understand the reasons at the time and, typically, 'never bothered inquiring as a I grew older'. He said, 'It wasn't the sort of thing to bring up and question my mother about after the tragedy.'[12]

Instead, he got on with enjoying childhood under the less rigid regime of his mother, who, despite early misgivings about letting her sons wander too far from home, was happy for them to be playing cricket outside because at least she knew what they were up to. She even tolerated some indoor games, played with marbles, when darkness brought close of play, although a shot that endangered furniture or ornaments meant instant dismissal. Other sports were staged indoors, even the high jump until one of their friends, Harcourt Lewis, broke a leg.

The trade-off for Thelma's tolerance was to accompany her to church every Sunday, sitting in the same pew at St Paul's Anglican Church and listening to the sermons of the Rev. Barlee, who they nicknamed 'Bup'. Attendance at Sunday school was also required – at least until they were old enough to plead that they had other things to do. According to Sandiford, Bay Land was 'greatly influenced' by its churches and schools, 'all of which placed great emphasis on the value of virtues such as cleanliness, godliness and perseverance'.[13]

Working as many hours as possible because the tiny pension she received for Shamont's death covered only a fraction of the household outgoings, Thelma – known by friends and family as 'Sobey' – would be described by Garry as doing 'such a magnificent job that we all turned out to be happy and successful'.[14] There was certainly no time, or desire, in her life for another man. Besides, Garry believed her mistrust of how a second husband might treat her children was a deterrent to seeking out new love.

In a tight-knit community, there were always neighbours to lend assistance. Garry spent a lot of time in the home of Goulbourne Cumberbatch. Known as 'Dads' and a dedicated teacher of dominoes, he was the first of several men Sobers would come to acknowledge as father figures. Another, Melvyn Brewster, introduced him to first-class cricket by taking him to Kensington Oval during the MCC tour of 1947/48. 'None of us gave our mother any problems and maybe because of that there were always people outside the family to help her look after us,' Sobers remembered.[15] Misdemeanours rarely extended beyond picking fruit off the trees so that they had something to eat without interrupting games of cricket for meals.

The plentiful local produce and warm climate meant that food and clothes were rarely in short supply. The children left for school with a good breakfast inside them, a packed lunch in their bags and the promise of chicken or fish with rice in the evening. And when oldest brother George, a bright boy whose place at Combermere High School had been earned partly through scholarship and partly through his father's wages, left school at 15 to work as a meter reader for the Barbados Electric Company, the household coffers received a welcome boost.

George would eventually follow his father's path by becoming a seaman. Gerry, too, would spend a short time on ships before going to England to play league cricket. Such career decisions were taken over the protests of Thelma, who had seen the sea claim the life of her husband. The importance of the island's merchant seamen in the family's life was evident when, in late 2023, they gifted the Barbados Museum and Historical Society its collection of press clippings. Presumably compiled by Thelma, tucked among the various pages of Test match reports were newspaper stories of the National Union of Seamen's fight to preserve jobs and achieve better working conditions.

Garry, because of lack of funds and academic achievement, would follow Gerry to Bay Street Boys' School; there was no prospect of taking George's path into a higher level of learning. Cecil would also attend Bay Street, while sisters Greta and Elsie went to St Mathias Girls' School. Sport was always of more interest to Garry than studies, although Thelma did remark on his good head for figures. Perhaps that was enhanced by – or can even be attributed to – what became a lifelong passion for horse racing. With Garrison Savannah on his doorstep, and the wide-open course offering plenty of free roadside vantage points on three of its four borders, Garry was an enthusiastic and knowledgeable spectator. 'Even as a little boy I was attracted to the horses,' he said, although it would not be until he arrived in England that racing began to play a large role in his life.[16] He could never have imagined returning to the course in later life as a winning owner – and to be knighted by Queen Elizabeth II.

That he was able to, of course, was down to cricket. Garry reckoned he was three years old when he began playing; not unusual for an island that had the sport at its heart. As renowned Caribbean author Andrea Stuart, niece of West Indies cricket great Sir Clyde Walcott, explained:

> As my Barbadian father [Kenneth] said, every boy on the island played cricket. (Even those who, like my father, were better at tennis.) They played it in people's backyards, on blocked-off roads, and on the beach, where a tennis ball was used and the stumps set in wet sand. And many families, such as my father's, played it every weekend. Cricket's unique place in this complex society was such that if they weren't playing it, they were talking about it, discussing it alongside the latest political crisis or other local gossip. Indeed the game was as intrinsic to the fabric of the community as the sugar that had been so ubiquitously cultivated. So it is perhaps no surprise that a disproportionate number of the cricketers who have represented West Indies were born in Barbados. This small island, of only 166 square miles, must be the most prolific island breeding ground for cricketers in the world.[17]

Any old piece of wood could be fashioned into a bat – coconut tree branches and palings from neighbourhood fences were popular – while balls were often made from rags wrapped around a stone and soaked in tar. Gerry, one year older than

Garry, was a constant playmate, although their sisters might be roped in as additional fielders.

A lot of budding cricketers' early innings were played in a locally popular format where the batter kept one knee grounded behind the popping crease. It encouraged cutting and hooking, while the imperative to bowl underarm led Garry to learn to spin the ball as he delivered it. Tennis ball cricket, on the beach or on grass fields, was a version of the sport that remained widely played among those who had gone on to play a high level of club cricket, and even represented their island.

Often the games were free-for-alls, with as many as 20 or 30 fielders, where those who brought the bat and ball – frequently the Sobers boys – got first knock and batted for as long as they could avoid dismissal. Such was the brothers' dominance that they were often in fear of being given a beating by older boys frustrated at waiting for their turn.

The need to avoid a multitude of catchers saw Garry develop the ability to keep the ball on the ground, rolling his wrists and picking gaps in the field. When playing in the streets, hitting a house on the full meant dismissal, another imperative to perfect his ground strokes. On a broader scale, the prevalence of tennis-ball cricket throughout the Caribbean played a significant role in the development of a generation of batsmen who combined strong back-foot play with the ability to drive a bouncing ball on the up.

In his 1963 biography of Barbadian-born Frank Worrell, Ernest Eytle suggested, 'These forms of cricket sharpen the eye in a way no professional coaching can. What they lack in orthodoxy is compensated for by a passion for hitting the ball hard, getting it away from the fielders ... The subtleties of footwork are unknown, but the zest for hitting and catching the ball grows with each stroke.'[18]

Garry, as history knows, batted and bowled with his left hand. Like many southpaws, he endured attempts to convert him to right-handedness – a smack with a ruler was a popular tactic among teachers – but his mother never went further than encouraging him to use his right hand. He was allowed to stick with whatever felt natural. Besides, there was another manual element to contend with: the fact that he had been born with six fingers on each hand.

The way he described the manner in which he dealt with such an abnormality was typical of him: high on nonchalance and low in detail. 'The first extra finger fell off quite early when I was nine or ten,' he explained. 'I took the second off when I was 14 or 15 and playing serious cricket. The first of the spare fingers came off with the help of a piece of cat gut wrapped around the base and a sharp tug, something like the old fashioned way of removing a child's milk tooth. The other came off with the help of a sharp knife.'[19]

The fortitude it must have taken to perform and endure such self-surgery was never mentioned. Nor was any pain or embarrassment he endured from boys calling him a 'freak' in the meantime.

Perhaps his superiority on the field made him immune to childish cruelty. It was a dominance that Gerry and Garry carried into the formal setting of schools cricket, where they turned Bay Street into a multiple championship-winning team. Gerry was captain, wicketkeeper and star batsman; Garry, despite looking unthreatening because of his small stature and short trousers, the most dangerous bowler. The reputation of the 'Chinese Brothers', as they became known because of their lighter complexions and elongated eyes, spread across the island. At one memorable match, against St Mathias Boys' School, cars lined up along Bayshore Beach's esplanade as spectators watched the boys in action.

When they played against St Giles, they came up against future West Indies opening bowler Wes Hall, who immediately joined the list of admirers. 'Garry was a bowler, a very small man at that time, a left-arm spinner. It was at that time that I really knew he was extraordinary.'[20] Hall added, 'Even in those early days cricketing cognoscenti recognised that Garry was a "superb, loping, natural athlete", who was destined for success … They were aware that he had such natural gifts that he would have succeeded in any game.'[21]

Garry admitted that he and Gerry spent too much time playing sports to be good scholars, but their talent and commitment was recognised and encouraged heartily by Everton Barrow, the boys' sports master, a cricketer at the Empire club.

Outside of school matches, further competition was provided by weekend matches on Bay Pasture – known locally as 'Brisbane' – against groups from rival neighbourhoods. A regular team-mate in these matches was Keith Barker, who went on to play league cricket in England, where he settled permanently. His son, also Keith, signed as a footballer for

Blackburn Rovers before embarking on a successful county career as an all-rounder for Warwickshire and Hampshire.

When Garry wasn't playing cricket, he was happily watching cricketers. He would observe the Wanderers players preparing for their Barbados Cricket Association matches and ended up operating the scoreboard, along with future Hampshire batsman Roy Marshall and brothers Gerry and Cecil. He took the chance to study men such as Worrell and Everton Weekes, who both visited with the Garrison Sports Club, and Walcott, who played for Empire. Of more interest to Garry than the ball speeding to the boundary was noting how the good batsmen moved their feet and picked up their bats; or where the bowlers would put the ball to induce false strokes. In the absence of formal coaching, Garry stored away these images and aimed to put them into practice when playing with his mates.

He would talk cricket, too, often with Wanderers groundsman Briggs Grandison, who arranged for him to bowl in the nets at Denis Atkinson, a West Indian Test player. 'Perhaps it was because I was so small, but I got the impression I was a favourite and there was plenty of encouragement all round,' he remembered.[22] Keen to prepare for facing left-arm Indian spinner Vinoo Mankad in an upcoming series, Atkinson knocked off early from his job as an insurance salesman to face the 12-year-old, placing a shilling* on top of the stumps and allowing the bowler to keep it if he knocked it off. Sobers would describe these sessions as 'the workshop where I first learned my trade'.[23]

---

* The equivalent of 24 cents at a time when Garry would be given four cents per day for lunch.

Garry also had the chance to snag a few real cricket balls when they were too damaged to be of any use to the club. He had suffered a painful blow when he first faced a hard ball – delivered by an adult, Frank 'Pidge' Grant – in a match organised by the Wanderers groundsmen when he was around ten years old.

He had been momentarily forced to reassess his relationship with the sport. But his passion for cricket had returned quickly and now he sought out a local shoemaker to stitch the ragged old balls back together. The repair work created a raised seam that produced prodigious movement and would, Sobers reflected, help prepare him for the moving ball he would face in England.

It was suggested by some that more of Garry's time should be spent helping and supporting his mother, but he was aware enough of his unusual ability to realise that both he and his family might be better served if he dedicated himself to cricket. 'If I became good enough it was the only sport that would allow me to travel and see the world,' he said. 'I would read about cricket in the papers and when the West Indies went to India in 1948 and then to England in 1950 we used to listen in awe to the commentaries on the radio. To a young boy from a humble background this was something magical.'[24]

Which was not to say that other sports didn't capture Garry's attention and deliver different opportunities. Having begun playing for the Notre Dame football club as a left-winger he happily took over in goal, despite his small stature, when the regular goalkeeper was injured. Sobers would recall playing for

Barbados in a 4-1 victory over Guyana at the age of 16 before giving up the sport to concentrate on cricket.[*]

Captain of Notre Dame was Lionel Daniel, a cabinet-maker and joiner a couple of streets from the Sobers home. His workshop became a regular hangout for boys in the district. While lecturing them on the value and importance of money, he would also demonstrate various tools. Gerry and Garry, a frequent visitor between the ages of 11 and 14, quickly picked up the skills of the trade. So much so that, in 1952, Daniel would benefit from their work when he won first prize in the island's Industrial Exhibition with a mahogany wardrobe he had made and the Sobers boys and a friend had polished.

Basketball was another of Garry's favourite sports and he, Gerry and Keith Barker played for the Bay Street Boys' Club, known as the Lakers, winning the local knockout competition in 1951. Sobers, in one of his autobiographies, makes casual reference to representing Barbados at basketball, as well as turning down the opportunity to fill in for the island in a table tennis international in Trinidad because he had not played for two years. Meanwhile, the Sobers boys teamed up in road tennis and were among the best sprinters in the athletics events organised at Bay Pasture. Encouraged by Daniel, Garry regularly competed for sixpence in 100-yard races against a rival, 'Spottie' Clarke.

[*] Details of Sobers's football career and prowess are in short supply. Articles over the years make unsubstantiated claims of him representing Barbados, although there is no mention of whether it was at age-group level or any further information. I found no documented confirmation, while efforts to get the Barbados Football Association to shed further light proved fruitless. There were stories in England in 1960 that Sobers had been invited for a trial by Everton, an opportunity he declined.

While Garry's cricket development was encouraged by those at Wanderers over several years, playing for them in the Barbados Cricket Association, with its roster of wealthy clubs and its Act of Parliament mandate to administrate the local game, was not a serious option. As club cricket on the island had developed over the previous half-century, a strict hierarchy of clubs had evolved. There were exclusively white clubs – although some would allow in wealthy blacks; clubs set up by and for the middle-class cricketers of colour; and, finally, those for which the black lower-classes could play.

Far from creating an environment of apartheid in the sport, the structure was tolerated, even by someone as politically active as the writer CLR James. 'These divisions were not only understood but accepted by players and populations alike,' he explained. 'All these clubs played every Saturday in club competitions and not infrequently a white member of the Legislative Council or president of the Chamber of Commerce would be playing amicably for his club against another, most of whose members were black porters, messengers or other members of the lowest social classes. Cricket was therefore a means of national consolidation. In a society very conscious of class and social differentiation, a heritage of slavery, it provided a common meeting ground of all classes.'[25]

Youngsters from poorer backgrounds tended to end up with the less-well-off clubs in the Barbados Cricket League, founded in 1937. But even young Garry's local Bay Land team in that competition, the Nationals, felt he was too small for a place.

Instead, he ended up playing for Kent, whose ground at Penny Hole was on the opposite south-east corner of the island. Kent's captain, a builder called Garnet Ashby, was a friend of Grandison and had therefore been told about Garry even before he saw him bowl when his team visited Bay Land to play a friendly. Asked to make up the numbers, and playing in shorts, Garry took three wickets, including that of Ashby, who promptly invited him to represent Kent.

First, though, Ashby had to ask Thelma's permission. 'You want to take Garry on the back of a motorcycle to the country to play cricket against big, able men, and on a Sunday?' was her not unreasonable response. 'I don't even know you.'[26] After additional lobbying by Barrow, Grandison and others, an agreement was reached where Garry would stay with Ashby on game weekends.

Leaving school at 14, Garry was given a job as a tally clerk by Goulbourne Cumberbatch, going on to the boats in the docks to make a note of the cargoes. Having made it plain that he had no interest in following his father into the navy, Garry continued to make his mark as a cricketer in 1951* when, as a 15-year-old, he took enough wickets for Kent to earn selection for the BCL's series of City versus Country matches. Named in the Country XI against brother Gerry, the *Barbados Advocate* informed its readers that he was 'a left-hand slow bowler who has been very impressive this season'.

---

* The Barbados league seasons were staged from June to December, with most of the Caribbean's small number of first-class games played between January and April.

He was subsequently picked for the full BCL team to take on the revered BCA at Empire in December. Several West Indies players had used this fixture to move up the island's cricketing hierarchy from League to Association clubs, or even into the Barbados team itself. The match, spread over two weekends, straddled his appearance for the BCL against a Cable and Wireless XI at Boarded Hall, where he took advantage of a soft wicket to take 3 for 10 as the opposition were bowled out for 87.

As well as batting doggedly at number 11 against the BCA, participating in an important last-wicket partnership, Sobers recalled that he 'bowled pretty well, line and length with a little variation', causing considerable trouble for Wilfred Farmer, who played for the Police club and Barbados and was assistant commissioner of the Barbados force. 'Fee', as Farmer was known in sporting circles, had previously seen the youngster playing with a tennis ball and bowling in the nets. 'Talent such as that displayed by the young Sobers is so immediately impressive, so blatantly obvious to anyone with the merest grain of cricketing knowledge,' he remembered, highlighting his 'ability to consistently drive a tennis ball sizzlingly across the turf, to cut with absolute precision, and to execute a series of sophisticated, if traditional, shots'.[27]

Duly smitten, Farmer asked a local fan by the name of Tom Sealy the identity of the youngster. Farmer asked Sealy to invite him for a chat and wasted little time in enquiring whether he was interested in representing the Police. He even had a solution for his target's lack of years and height. 'We'll have to let you try out for the band.'[28]

Farmer had been as impressed by Sobers's demeanour as his performance. 'Here was a boy of promise,' he remembered. 'He was shy, yes, but there was none of the usual shrinking, simpering, tongue-tied, hand-wringing reticence about him. He answered questions and volunteered information frankly and firmly. He bore himself manfully – not by any means mannishly – and met your eyes squarely and directly, with no trace of suspicion or defiance.'[29]

So it was that Police turned up for their BCA Division 1 match against Empire in June 1952 with a recently recruited bugler in the Royal Barbados Police Force Band. Empire's Bank Hall ground was renowned for its pace and, therefore, as a production line for various West Indies quick bowlers, including Griffith. On this day they included 'Foffie' Williams, a former Test paceman who could still bowl at decent speed at the age of 38.

When Williams took the second new ball, Sobers was looking comfortable in his number eight spot and Police had taken their total beyond 200. In his first over, after being slashed for four, Williams offered the young batsman a gesture of slitting his throat before unleashing a bouncer that Sobers failed to pick up. The ball struck his jaw, forcing him to retire hurt with 7 runs on the board. As he sat beyond the boundary, his jaw became stiff and swollen. Police eventually lost the game by ten wickets, Sobers having bowled only three wicketless overs. His band leader, Captain Raison, upon hearing that Sobers would not be able to blow his bugle for a while, correctly reasoned that he had no interest in music and dismissed him from his ensemble.

Farmer had a backup plan. The police force had set up a boys' club based at Bay Street, not far from Sobers's home, and by becoming a member Sobers remained eligible to play for Police's first team as well as playing for the Police Boys' Club.

In the meantime, he was also playing in the BCL for Middlesex. It meant that those reading the *Barbados Advocate* became used to seeing his name pop up in reports of one team or another. He came back from his painful innings for Police by scoring 89 for Middlesex against Mental Hospital before following up a week later with a century as he captained the Police Boys' Club against Chamberlain. There was another all-round performance of note against Mental Hospital – 83 runs and 4 for 19 – and a first-innings hundred for Police on the first day of their BCA match against Lodge School. 'Honours of the day went to Sobers, who top scored with 102 runs in fine style,' said the *Advocate*, whose Sunday edition added, 'His hard hitting and stroke playing was of his best.' He also took nine wickets in the match.

There is even a story, told by Cecil, that Garry played match-winning roles on the same day for two different clubs, Police and Middlesex, in two different competitions, the BCA and BCL, on two different grounds, the YMPC Sports Club in Bridgetown and Bay Pasture. The tale – remarkable if true – has Garry scoring vital runs for Police against YMPC before cycling east to bowl out Belfield for 16. Then it was back on his bike to take some YMPC wickets. Both of his teams were victorious, with Police supposedly unaware of Garry's moonlighting for another team, which they would have prevented. If it all sounds a little far-fetched, then it is testament to the uniqueness of Garry's talent that it can be considered remotely feasible.

The island's cricket spectators would take advantage of the large number of games played in close proximity by venturing from one to another depending on the fortunes of their favourite players. According to Worrell, 'All budding cricketers can catch the eye of the selectors and pressmen, who are themselves numbered among the itinerant spectators.'[30]

Playing for Police allowed a moment that Sobers would consider for his entire life as one of his finest on a cricket field. Lining up against Wanderers at Bay Pasture, in front of his neighbourhood crowd and after bagging a duck in the first innings, he struck an unbeaten 113 on a difficult, damp track in the second to save the match. 'All my friends from the Bay Land were there, seemingly happier even than I was,' he recalled, even though he was playing for the away team. 'I still value that century as highly as many of the others I've been fortunate to make.'[31]

Sandiford and Bertie Callender, writing in 1994, explained that it would not have been simply a question of Sobers being cheered by his mates. Even at that young age he was fostering feelings of local pride. 'Throughout Bay Land there has traditionally been a very strong sense of community. The village lauds its successful products with a considerable degree of intensity.' Success such as that of Sobers, they argued, was seized upon as 'convincing evidence that it is possible for poor youngsters in the district to rise far above their modest origins'.[32]

Sobers would continue to play occasional games for Police into his 40s 'because it was them and Captain Farmer who gave me my opportunity'.[33] And Farmer found that the adult, world-renowned version of Sobers that turned out for his club was not so different to the shy, polite teenager, unaffected by fame and adulation. 'He remains completely unspoiled by it all,' he said in 1973. 'His friends of yesteryear remain his friends today, even though the circle has been much widened by the new acquisitions of a much-travelled, affable and genial personality.'[34]

As well as offering Sobers the chance to meet up with old friends and team-mates, those return trips also provided dream-come-true moments for opponents. One of them was Maurice Foster,* who played for Pickwick in the island's first Knockout Cup final at Kensington Oval. 'I remember the individual shields all displayed on the table,' Foster explained. 'I had been playing about 15 years and with a top score of 49 it had dawned on me I was not likely ever to play for Barbados. But this shield, this trophy, was going to be mine … As I sat putting on my boots someone came up the stairs and I looked up in amazement as Garry Sobers entered. He was back in Barbados and would play for Police against us. I don't remember his bowling, but I do remember his batting as I spent most of the afternoon in the covers returning the ball from the boundary. Well, we lost and I never got my shield. But that day I believe the Lord said something very special to me. "Maurice," he said. "You'll never

---

* Not to be confused with the Jamaican batsman who played alongside Sobers for West Indies.

play cricket for Barbados and you're not even going to get that shield you want so much. But today I have given you something that is worth far more than these. Today you have played against the greatest cricketer in the world.'"[35]

Foster would go on to campaign for a statue of Sobers to be erected in Broad Street in Bridgetown, coming up against a since-overturned government edict not to commission statues of living Barbadians. The figures of Sobers and Wes Hall standing outside Kensington Oval bear handsome testament to that change of policy. Not that Barbadians, especially those from the Bay Land streets that nurtured Sobers, need physical manifestations of what he means to them.

According to Sandiford and Callender, 'Speaking to the inhabitants of Bay Land, one gets the distinct impression that they regard Sir Garfield Sobers as their own pride and joy. It is difficult to convey in words the great awe and affection with which they discuss their favourite son. In their eyes, Sir Garfield is still a Bay Land boy. Garry still sees himself as a product of Bay Street Boys' School, St Paul's Anglican Church and Walcott's Avenue. He is, that is to say, an extremely proud Bay Land boy.'[36]

2

COMING OF AGE

'You're going out a youngster, but you've
got to come back a star.'

Theatre director Julian Marsh, *42nd Street*
(Warner Bros, 1932)

THE TIMES were changing. 'In Barbados in the '40s and early
'50s, a coloured player had to be three times as good as a white
player to play for the island,' Garry Sobers explained. Happily,
he sensed that such issues were dissipating by the time he was
pushing for selection. 'There were several middle-class black
clubs and after the black talent emerged, it was more down to
ability rather than colour.'[1]

His path towards a career in cricket had moved further
forward with his selection, in December 1952, for the annual
Barbados Cricket Association versus Barbados Cricket League
game, to be played over three successive Saturdays at Kensington
Oval. He'd played the year before, of course, but now he found
himself in the powerful BCA team, along with the likes of
Clyde Walcott, Everton Weekes and Conrad Hunte.

The first day found the BCL batsmen struggling on a pitch offering slow turn after recent rain. Sobers, who saw brother Gerry score 70, was able to bowl without the protection of an extra cover, knowing the perils involved in trying to drive. On his way to figures of 3 for 33 off 17 overs, he prompted OS Coppin to suggest in the *Barbados Advocate* that he was turning the ball too much. 'Left-armer Sobers bowled with a rare capacity for spin,' he wrote. 'He is a finger spinner of the old vintage, but he must learn to control his break and adapt himself to the prevailing circumstances. Early in the game, although the wicket was helping him considerably, he was still breaking too much to get a touch.' Sobers – who said of his bowling at that time, 'I rolled the ball more than spinning it'[2] – bowled only six fruitless overs in the second innings of a match that BCA won by six wickets.

Sobers had done enough to earn a place in the trial match for the Barbados team ahead of the 1952/53 first-class season, which would include the first tour of the Caribbean by India. Given the chance to bowl at the first-team batsmen, he kept things tight, took a few wickets and was named in the 12 to face the tourists. He assumed his inclusion was a nod to the promise he had shown and an opportunity to absorb the atmosphere of first-class cricket. Instead, when the West Indies selectors asked Barbados to rest paceman Frank King after he bowled 65 overs in the first Test, Barbados took a chance on their 16-year-old spinner. 'I was one of a number of proud Baylanders at Kensington that day,' recorded Keith Sandiford, 'and we were all in a state of high excitement.'[3]

For the best part of the first two days of the five-day game, Sobers was a spectator, watching Weekes pile up 253. Towards the end of the home team's 154-over innings, Sobers went in at number nine, scoring an unbeaten 7 before skipper John Goddard declared at 606 for 7. 'My personal recollection of that match was bowling and bowling and bowling,' Sobers said, hardly surprising when you look at his workload as Barbados strove to bowl out India twice.[4]

One of India's leading batsmen, Polly Umrigar, was rebuilding their first innings after the fall of three wickets when Goddard turned to Sobers. Telling himself that bowling to Umrigar was less scary than having Weekes and Walcott at the other end, Sobers made an economical start until Umrigar lifted him over midwicket on to the roof of the Kensington Stand. 'It was a bit of a shock but it had the effect of making me even more determined to get him out,' he remembered.[5] He did so when Umrigar had reached 63, bowling him between bat and pad for his first wicket in first-class cricket.

Sobers went on to record 4 for 50 in 22 overs as the Indians were dismissed for 209. His work was just beginning. Over the course of the tourists' second innings, as they fought to 445 for 9 to earn a draw, Sobers bowled 67 overs – 35 of them maidens – a staggering amount for a teenager on debut. Three more wickets came his way for 92 runs, his most dangerous delivery being the one that found the batsman looking for turn that wasn't there. Favouring flight and angles over searching for prodigious spin – which undoubtedly pleased Coppin – not one of the seven wickets Sobers took in the match required the assistance of a fielder. 'I felt so good after that game that I was even half expecting a place in the Test team.'[6]

He was relieved that no such call came his way. 'I didn't want it,' he said. 'I had seen other boys pushed too hard too early in their career.'[7]

* * *

With no formalised, regular inter-island competition until the launch of the Shell Shield in the 1965/66 season, Sobers had to wait until the MCC tourists arrived from England a year later to play another first-class match. Batting at number five and having now grown into a slender near six-footer, he made 46 and 27. He was disappointed, though, to take only one wicket in each innings of a one-wicket victory for MCC, who had just lost the first Test in Kingston, Jamaica.

On the first day, Sobers became unwittingly involved in one of the great controversies of a tour dogged by them. Square leg umpire Harold Walcott – uncle of West Indies batsman Clyde, whom he had once given out lbw for 98 in a Test match – no-balled England's slow left-armer Tony Lock twice in three balls for throwing. The second of them broke the wicket of Sobers. 'Locky let him have his "quickie" which flattened his middle stump,' recalled Jim Laker, who said that Sobers 'had not been halfway through his backlift when the ball fizzed past'.[8]

MCC questioned whether Lock should have been no-balled without prior warning if the umpires were concerned about his quicker ball. The same fate had befallen him in the Jamaica Test match. An angry Lock managed to restrict himself to giving the umpire some dirty looks. MCC captain Len Hutton made sure his bowler did not talk himself into further trouble and switched him to bowl at the other end, only for Cortez Jordan to no-ball him from square leg in the final over of the first day. What made the tourists even more upset was their own suspicion about the manner in which West Indies off-spinner Sonny Ramadhin sent down some of his deliveries.

Sobers was enough of an outsider to the tensions of the Test series to be preoccupied by concerns of his own. He was frustrated by the way in which he'd got himself in a tangle against a Fred Trueman bouncer that did not lift as much as he expected. Belatedly jabbing his bat up towards the ball, he managed to clout himself on the forehead. Feeling foolish, but relieved that Trueman had not had a clear enough view of what happened to give him any verbal stick over it, Sobers made himself a promise that he would never duck another bouncer. 'I always said that the bowler would have to kill me before he made me run or back away.'[9]

The 'unnecessary ill-feeling' that Clyde Walcott felt had been created by the Lock incident was just one element of the controversy that characterised the MCC tour. Others included Hutton banning his men from socialising with the opposition; accusations of poor behaviour by the England players on and off the pitch; more umpiring debates; a preponderance of bouncers; slow scoring rates by the tourists; crowd trouble; squabbling among the islands over selection of the West Indies team – all against the volatile backdrop of Caribbean politics as nations moved towards independence from the United Kingdom.

By the time the series returned to Sabina Park for the fifth Test, West Indies led 2-1. Some days before the match's starting date of 30 March, Sobers was doing what most 17-year-olds on his island enjoyed doing most, playing cricket with his friends. The boys from Bay Land were in action outside the phoneless Sobers home when Ben Hoyos, secretary of the BCA, arrived on the scene.

'We've got a cable from the West Indies Board asking us to advise you to get ready to go to Jamaica,' was the message.[10] Hoyos explained that Alf Valentine, the left-arm spinner who had been one of the architects of West Indies' famous victory in England in 1950, was doubtful for the Test because of a sore spinning finger.

'My heart beat faster and all sorts of things flashed through my mind,' Sobers recalled. 'It wasn't that I was overawed. Even at that early age, I felt confident playing any ball game.'[11] Almost as big a deal to him as his recognition as a cricketer was the prospect of getting on a plane and leaving Barbados for the first time.

Sobers was relieved to find the West Indies players welcoming and keen to practise with him in the nets. When he sat quietly in the changing room after being confirmed in the team they asked if he was nervous. Of course he was. What 17-year-old about to play for his country in only his third game of first-class cricket would not be? At that time only two men had ever played Test cricket at a younger age. 'But I was not going to tell them how I felt.'[12]

Yet Everton Weekes recalled, 'I remember him saying he was more nervous sitting in the dressing room than running around the field because of seeing himself sit next to the name players. We never had to teach him anything. He taught himself. He started making runs, taking wickets and holding catches to overcome that nervousness.'[13]

After skipper Jeff Stollmeyer won the toss and chose to bat, Sobers hoped to enjoy watching from the pavilion and soaking up every lesson he could from being around new team-mates. Yet West Indies were 13 for 4 after 45 minutes. Not long after lunch Sobers was putting on his pads, eventually going out to bat at 110 for 7. West Indies fans were renowned for their island prejudices, but Sobers was overjoyed at the reception he received from a Jamaican crowd who seemed captivated by the story of the youngster thrown in at the deep end. 'I believe the close affinity which I was to have with Sabina Park and the crowd there in future years developed on that first trip,' he said.[14]

Tension accompanied him to the middle. But he knew that not much was expected of him with the bat, despite the match programme describing him as a 'useful batsman' and making no mention of his bowling – an indication of how little was known about him outside Barbados. He also couldn't see how his team had collapsed so badly. Yes, Trevor Bailey was bowling well enough to end with 7 for 34, but the pitch and the light were not troublesome. Having defended resolutely for 15 minutes, Sobers headed for the pavilion when rain enforced an early tea. After the break, he scored his first Test runs off his 16th ball with a four against Laker. He hit one further boundary before being left 14 not out off 32 balls when the West Indies innings ended at 139.

The young debutant was given a rousing welcome back in the dressing room, while *The Daily Telegraph*'s EW Swanton had seen enough to write, 'Sobers had been able to show several wristy left-hander's strokes and to make it clear furthermore that nothing Trueman could send down was too fast to ruffle him.'

England had crawled to 42 without loss in 36 overs when Sobers was given the ball shortly after lunch on the second day. His impact was almost immediate, having makeshift opener Bailey caught by wicketkeeper Cliff McWatt off the first ball of his second over. 'Garry dropped one fractionally short outside my off stump,' Bailey explained. 'I could not resist the square cut, only to discover it was his arm ball, with the result that it was too close and was snapped up behind the wicket.'[15]

Sobers had to wait until his 26th over to strike again, but in the meantime made sure to study the likes of Hutton, Denis Compton, Peter May and Tom Graveney – in the hope of picking up tips for his own batting and to gather information that might be useful whenever he next faced them. Once he had bowled Lock, he quickly removed Johnny Wardle and Laker to finish with 4 for 75. According to Bailey, 'It was a most impressive performance, taking into account the plumb pitch, the small, fast outfield, his youth and his lack of experience.'[16]

Swanton felt Sobers had 'made an excellent impression'. He continued, 'He is a slim young man who runs lightly up to the wicket and the arm almost touches the ear as it comes over … It will be surprising if we do not come to know his name well in the years ahead.'

It was true that Sobers made a mark deeper than that left by the scorers' pens. The very manner in which he moved around the field caught the eye. 'His first ever fielding position in a Test was at short third man,' recorded cricket historian and former Jamaican prime minister Michael Manley. 'In the first over Hutton steered a ball from Frank King in that general direction. Sobers moved to his right, picked up, half pivoted, being a left-hander, and returned the ball like a bullet to the wicketkeeper. The whole thing was done with a feline quality, with that fluidity that is the hallmark of the athlete who goes beyond skill into some other extraordinary realm of unconscious coordination.'[17]

His team 275 in arrears, Sobers found the boundary five times in a 79-minute innings of 26. West Indies managed to make England bat again, but the tourists lost only one wicket in scoring the 72 they needed to draw the series. Skipper Stollmeyer's verdict on Sobers's debut was that 'he acquitted himself with far more credit than most, if not all, of his seniors', calling him a 'more than able substitute for Valentine'.[18]

3

LIVING THE DREAM

'Dream as if you'll live forever. Live as
if you'll die today.'

American actor James Dean

'YOU HAD better get the pads on, lad. You are going to open.'
Denis Atkinson's words hung in the air, the implication sinking
in for an 18-year-old who'd never batted at the top of the order
in his life and had made his Test debut a year earlier as a spin-
bowling number nine.

Australia, who had just racked up 668 runs, had Keith
Miller and Ray Lindwall, one of the great bowling partnerships,
ready to take the new ball against a West Indies team who
had picked only one opening batsman for this fourth Test in
Bridgetown. 'I was being used as a sacrifice,' Garry Sobers
reflected, fully aware that Clyde Walcott, Everton Weekes and
Frank Worrell would not be shunted out of the middle order.[1]

By the time 1955 was entering its third month, James Dean
was about to explode into global consciousness with the release
of the movie *East of Eden*; another rebel, Errol Barrow, was
preparing to launch the Barbados Labour Party and hasten the

path of his nation towards independence; and the Australian cricket team were getting ready for their first series in the West Indies.

In early February, Sobers had scored his maiden first-class century, against British Guiana at Kensington Oval. Having been elevated to number four in the order, he made an unbeaten 104 in the second innings, reaching three figures in 195 minutes with 12 fours.* It was not enough to earn Sobers a place in the following month's first Test in Jamaica, for which he was listed as 12th man amid reports that he was suffering from appendicitis. He had developed sharp stomach pains while in the cinema in Jamaica, but underwent a series of injections in order to delay an operation until the end of the series. Nevertheless, the role of spinning all-rounder went initially to Collie Smith, who had just scored a century for Jamaica against the tourists and was destined to become a major figure in Sobers's life. Smith's hundred in the second innings of the Test, after being moved up the order, justified the selectors' decision, even if it could not turn back a nine-wicket defeat.

Sobers was duly chosen for the second Test and, upon arrival in Port-of-Spain, Trinidad, was assigned to share a room with 21-year-old Smith, the beginning of a firm, if tragically short, friendship. Both were young, aware of their rookie status among two teams containing revered names, and still – at least in the case of Sobers – in the early stages of blossoming socially.

---

* The unreliability of Sobers's memory of detail is evidenced in his 2002 autobiography, where he describes having scored this century prior to his Test debut and while batting at number nine.

Sobers had started smoking a couple of years earlier and quickly advanced to 20 cigarettes per day, believing, like so many teenagers of the time, that it made him appear mature and fashionable. He was rapidly developing a taste for alcohol, too, although whisky was his preferred tipple rather than the rum that was cheap and plentiful in the Caribbean. His taste for Scotch developed further when he began playing in England, and brands such as White Horse and Johnnie Walker Red Label were easily accessible. He had enough awareness, even as an inexperienced drinker, to know that inebriation via whisky carried less of a stigma than being drunk on rum. 'If you drank Scotch all night nobody would take any notice because it was an expensive and sophisticated drink. Get drunk on rum and people would say, "What do you expect? He's a rum drinker,"' he explained.[2]

On their first night in Trinidad, Sobers and Smith made a quiet retirement from the team group and headed to their room. At midnight, there was banging on the door, accompanied by an Australian voice threatening to break it open if he was not allowed in. Opening the door with some trepidation, Sobers was astonished to see Miller and Lindwall in the corridor, determined to join the youngsters for a drink and make them feel part of the Test match scene. Sobers remembered it as a generous gesture on behalf of the duo, one that was repeated on subsequent nights.

After a rain-hit first day, he went out to bat on the second afternoon at a relatively healthy 282 for 4, immediately after Smith's first-ball dismissal. According to Australian writer

Pat Landsberg's account of the tour, 'The Australians crowded round Garfield Sobers in the remaining minutes before tea in the expectation of a wicket through intimidation and psychology. But it didn't work and young Sobers presented a most confident bat to the slings and arrows of the Australian bowlers.'[3]

Sobers maintained his concentration throughout disputes over whether play should continue when rain clouds obscured the mountains beyond the north and west sides of Queen's Park Oval. West Indies skipper Jeff Stollmeyer wrote a note for Sobers, urging him to take advantage of a tiring attack by increasing his scoring rate. Bizarrely, the missive was sent to the field via Lindwall, who, without knowing who it was for, read its contents before passing it to the batsman. Despite being forewarned, Australia could not prevent Sobers executing a flurry of leg-side shots that took him to 43 before rain finally ended the day. The following morning, he fell within three runs of his first Test half-century when he edged Lindwall to the wicketkeeper.

The match ended in a high-scoring draw after Australia reached 600. As further evidence, perhaps, of inter-island prejudice, Sobers as a bowler was accused by the *Trinidad Guardian*'s BR Jones of having 'made a mess of it', despite bowling only three overs for ten runs.

His first-innings runs kept him in the team for the third Test in Georgetown, British Guiana. His pal Smith was not so lucky. One match after scoring a century on his Test debut, he was dropped after being out for a duck in both innings in Port-of-Spain, his place going to Norman Marshall. LD

Roberts, sports editor of the *Jamaican Gleaner*, wrote, 'I regard the omission of Smith as an extraordinary piece of injustice … Here is a youngster who in five innings against the Australians has made two centuries and yet he is passed over for a player who has never faced the Aussies.'

Even the Australians failed to understand the logic. RS (Dick) Whitington told readers of the *Sydney Telegraph*, 'The dropping of Don Bradman in 1928 ranks in cricket history as the most farcical move ever made by selectors. The dropping of Collie Smith suggests that they are envious of the ignominy Australian selectors have borne for 27 years.' And Landsberg concluded, 'The Australians were essentially a team, the West Indies 11 units who never knew where the axe would fall and upon whom.'[4]

Frustrated to be out for 12 and 11, Sobers had the consolation of making a greater contribution with the ball. He took 3 for 20 in 16 overs in the first innings – including the wickets of Ron Archer, stumped, and opposition skipper Ian Johnson, caught, in the same over – and came on first change as Australia made the runs they needed for an eight-wicket victory. According to Landsberg he had 'more than emphasised his worth as a left-handed successor to Valentine'.[5]

When the tour moved on to Barbados, Sobers scored his first half-century against the Australians in the warm-up game before the fourth Test. His disciplined second-innings performance was notable, Landsberg reckoned, because 'he had shown in the first innings how prone he can be to the rising ball, at which he felt it his duty to make some sort of stroke' –

just as he had vowed to himself after his encounter with Fred Trueman. On his second visit to the crease 'he was tempering discretion with recklessness. He had learned his lesson.'[6]

By the time of the Test, Sobers's opportunity to play for West Indies in front of his home crowd for the first time had been overshadowed by another selection row. This one made the dispute over Smith – who was now back in the team – seem like a minor disagreement and went to the heart of arguments about race and prejudice in West Indies cricket.

Stollmeyer, who had missed the first Test, was now out of the series after stepping on the ball and twisting his ankle. His replacement, as it had been earlier, was Atkinson, the Barbados batsman who had enticed the schoolboy Sobers with a shilling for bowling him in the nets. Atkinson, like Stollmeyer and all previous West Indies captains – with the exception of Ron Headley briefly in 1948 – was white. Atkinson had replaced Frank Worrell as vice-captain at the start of the series, much to the annoyance of Stollmeyer, who recalled, 'It was a preposterous decision in any circumstances and was the cause of much of the dissension and bad cricket played by our team in the series.'[7]

The African Welfare League, a Jamaican-based organisation headed by Dr MB Douglas, a dentist in Kingston, staged a demonstration attended by around 2,000 people. A resolution was passed in which it was pointed out that Worrell had been West Indies vice-captain on many occasions, 'a position which should qualify him for the captaincy more than any other event'. It argued that 'the selection of Denis Atkinson could only be on grounds other than Worrell's Test cricket record experience and ability' and called it 'a most flagrant act of discrimination'. The AWL urged the selectors to reconsider their 'senseless decision' and called upon the people of Jamaica to boycott the fifth and final Test in Kingston.

Michael Manley's history of West Indies cricket recorded the episode as an 'insult to Worrell' and believed it 'contributed substantially to Worrell's increasing disconnection from the game locally between 1956 and 1960'. Worrell, he said, would have understood being asked to serve under Walcott or Weekes, 'but Atkinson had no such claim based in cricket'.[8]

This being the West Indies, any racial issues had to be separated from island rivalry. The *Barbados Advocate*, therefore, was somewhat dismissive of the Jamaican protest. 'In every island there are a number of organisations whose pronouncements, if broadcast to the world, would be no credit to the island from which they emanate,' its leader article pronounced, denouncing the AWL as 'either a communist organisation or a communist front'.

The *Advocate* conceded that many West Indians believed – 'probably wrongly' – that the captaincy decision was driven by racial considerations, but added, 'That is a most unfortunate impression to give at this particular stage of West Indian development. West Indians, however, will not be prepared to have a form of mob rule masquerading under a pretence of fighting discrimination.'

Sobers's recollection of the controversy is unilluminating, relating the facts without any hint of his own feelings. 'I couldn't understand it all and thought what a good thing it was that I would never be captain and have to suffer all that turmoil.'[9]

This book will return to the topic in later chapters. For now, of more immediate concern to Sobers was that no batsman had been named to replace Stollmeyer as opener. The reinstated Smith was, like Sobers, a middle-order player. It was not until after lunch on day three, however, that it became an issue, Australia batting until then to rack up 668.

But now, given his instructions by Atkinson, Sobers headed to the middle alongside the Jamaican, John Holt, whose lack of a big score in the series caused him to be greeted by a tasteless banner that read, 'Hang Holt – Save Hylton'. That day in Spanish Town, Jamaica, former West Indies fast bowler Leslie Hylton, aged 50, was being hanged for the murder of his wife.

Sobers knew he was supposed to stick around and take some shine off the ball for the big guns of the middle order. Instead, he approached his task with the spirit of James Dean, batting as though he had big dreams and a short life expectancy for his innings. 'I had nothing to lose and I decided as I walked down the pavilion steps that whenever I saw red I'd throw the bat,' he recalled.[10]

He hit three fours in Miller's first over: a swish to fine leg, an elegant cover drive, and a third that, in the words of Landsberg, 'shot through past point like a typhoon'.[11] Three more followed in Miller's next over, through mid-off, gully and cover. The first ball of Miller's third over was dispatched through a reinforced off-side field – 28 not out, all in boundaries. By this time the crowd of 10,000 were in raptures, cheering wildly as the teenager dismantled the great man. Ron Archer slowed Sobers with a pair of maidens, but Holt batted aggressively against Lindwall before being bowled. The opening partnership of 52 had taken only 40 minutes, during which the batsmen had not changed ends once.

When Sobers finally faced Lindwall, he swung the ball to fine leg for his eighth four. Two more boundaries were taken off Johnson before he tried to hook the same bowler and was caught at short fine leg for 43 off 72 balls. 'It was a frantic innings,' he admitted, 'and, as everybody knew, couldn't last forever.'[12]

Miller recalled, 'For an hour, cricket hell broke loose. This little-known Sobers kept hammering fours at Ray and myself until we were punch-drunk. That one innings set Sobers alight as a batting wizard.'[13]

He had laid down a significant marker, rising to a challenge that might have bowed a young player of lesser temperament and technique. His treatment of the great Miller identified him as a special talent. In one innings he had shifted the cricket public's perception of him as a bowler who could bat to a genuine all-rounder with the potential to be a game-changer. Atkinson, meanwhile, enjoyed the triumph of a double century in a West Indies reply of 510, his only Test century, as the game ended in a draw.

The fifth Test, which went ahead free of any boycott by Jamaican fans, saw Sobers going in at number seven in the first innings, 20-year-old Trinidadian Hammond Furlonge having been drafted in to open. Coming in at 268 for 5, Sobers was left 35 not out after the last four West Indies wickets fell for

16. Replying to 357, Australia piled up 758 for 8, Neil Harvey scoring a double century, and Colin McDonald, Miller, Archer and Benaud all reaching three figures.

Sobers moved up to number five in the second innings, hitting Richie Benaud for three fours in an over before skying a sweep and being dropped by Archer. Landsberg would record that Sobers 'had been flashing away briskly outside the off stump and sweeping most indiscreetly' until he 'calmed down to a considerable degree and was content to play as the situation demanded – that of caution and the preservation of his wicket'.[14]

After 142 minutes, he reached his first half-century in Test cricket and was eventually out for 64, caught at fine leg off Lindwall. 'Sobers had batted with splendid concentration for 181 minutes, even if it had started off at a reckless rate,' Landsberg concluded. 'He had tempered his game to the demands of the side, yet never forgot to punish the loose ball with all the power that his frail form can command.'[15]

Despite Walcott's second hundred of the game, West Indies slid to a defeat that left Australia 3-0 winners in a series to which Sobers contributed 231 runs at an average of 38.50 and six wickets at 35.50. Miller had been sufficiently impressed to present Sobers with one of his bats at the end of the tour.

Weekes, meanwhile, was keen for Sobers to continue his cricketing education as part of an invitational touring team he had been asked to lead, even though doctors were advising that he should rest after having his appendix removed. 'I had the pleasure of taking a team to Bermuda, of which Garry was a member,' recalled Weekes. 'From those early days I was able to recognise something different about his approach to things generally. Some people say genius – I probably agree with them but, then again, how does one recognise genius when one does not know what to look for?'[16]

Already Sobers's favourite of the three Ws to watch, Weekes had endeared himself to the wide-eyed youngster on their first meeting, pretending to mishear his name and calling him 'Soapbox'. 'We got on pretty well,' Sobers remembered with affection. 'Everton was interested in my career, saying he would do all he could to help me, and did I need any equipment? I heard later how he said, "This boy has a great prospect in cricket." It would have heartened me more to have heard it at the time. But I never forgot his kindness and his help.'[17]

* * *

Christmas 1955 was a very different experience for Sobers, spent en route for New Zealand on the luxurious – for its time – cruise liner SS *Southern Cross*. Still in its first year of service, the ship, built in Belfast and launched by Queen Elizabeth II, boasted air-conditioned cabins, all with hot and cold running water. The inside cabins, where Sobers and most of his West Indies team-mates were housed, featured circular lights that came on gradually in the morning, giving its occupants the same sensation of sunrise that those in the more expensive outer cabins experienced. As if the very act of leaving the Caribbean wasn't enough for a 19-year-old on his first tour.

Departing Trinidad on 22 December, the 15-strong West Indies party, led by the white duo of captain Atkinson and player-manager John Goddard, would not arrive at their destination in Wellington until 16 January. Stopping off for a game in Fiji,* the players had to make use of the ship's 5,000 square-feet sports deck to maintain fitness.

With neither Walcott nor Worrell making the trip, Sobers batted first wicket down in three of the four Tests, opening in the other. He did little, though, to contribute to his team's 3-1 series win, making a top score of 27 and taking only two wickets as an occasional bowler. Sobers, who was never to enjoy great success in New Zealand, felt the wickets were under-prepared. Weekes was the chief run-scorer for the tourists, making a century in each of their victories, before the home team hit back in the final match, their first Test victory.

Sobers, along with three team-mates, flew home in time to put in a confidence-boosting performance for a West Indies XI against an EW Swanton XI, captained by Colin Cowdrey, in a five-day unofficial 'Test' in Trinidad, taking three wickets in each innings and scoring 71 in his only knock. It was not his most fluent innings, but he took heart from the manner in which he dealt with the pace of Frank Tyson, hero of England's Ashes victory in Australia a year earlier. Taking the advice of Weekes, he played Tyson with virtually no back-lift.

It couldn't completely erase his fear that events in New Zealand, which he called 'an eye-opener', had left his Test place open to question. With no home matches in the 1956/57 season, West Indies' next engagement was the tour of England

---

* West Indies lost after being bowled out for 63.

that summer, the trip that Sobers craved more than any other. Listening to the BBC World Service radio transmissions of Test matches as a boy had allowed him to fantasise about stroking the ball around lush green outfields, his deeds described by the likes of Swanton, John Arlott and Rex Alston, whose words had created romantic images of English cricket.

He knew he had to impress in a trial match at Port-of-Spain at the end of January, a five-day contest which had no first-class status but which would play a large part in determining the make-up of the 17-strong tour party.* Batting at number three for Weekes's team against Walcott's, he scored 129 and learned something of the manner in which such trials could be manipulated. Under the instructions of his skipper, he went easy on fellow Barbadian Wes Hall in order to ensure he made the tour, while being harsher on the more experienced Frank Mason, who hailed from St Vincent. Sobers's runs ensured that his next innings would be three months hence in Eastbourne.

* * *

Back under the leadership of Goddard, the West Indies squad embarked on their 12-day voyage from Kingston to Southampton on the SS *Golfito*, a passenger-carrying banana boat, whose first-class quarters were beyond the budget of the West Indies Cricket Board of Control. Sobers remembered that his colleagues spent much of their time during a rough

---

* In the end, three players made the tour despite not playing in the trial matches: Gerry Alexander, Nyron Asgarali and Andy Ganteaume.

passage in their tiny cabins being seasick, although he claimed that his discovery of port and brandy immunised him against such misfortune.

His first impression of England on arrival in late April was disbelief that it could be so cold even when the sun was out. On visiting Lord's for the tourists' welcome reception he was left wondering why the square and the outfield appeared to be the same hue of green. When he failed to hold a slip catch off Hall in the opening game against the EW Swanton XI he realised what a challenge fielding would be with numb fingers.

But in little more than two hours on a windy first afternoon on the south coast, Sobers drove his way to an unbeaten 110, riding his luck when he played the ball against his stumps on 14 without dislodging the bails. Swanton's colleague on *The Daily Telegraph*, Michael Melford, described him as 'a batsman of great potential and natural ability, immensely improved since he played his first Test'.

It marked the beginning of a summer in which Sobers made steady progress as an international player rather than taking giant strides towards the greatness he would ultimately reach, although he didn't always need to play to make an impression. Sobers was rested for West Indies' early-tour game against Essex, but his mere presence on the ground impressed future England all-rounder Barry Knight. 'The first thing that struck me about Garry was how he moved,' he recalled. 'He just looked like an athlete. He moved and walked like a panther.'[18]

Playing in all five Tests, of which West Indies lost three and drew two, Sobers averaged 32, scoring fifties at Edgbaston and Lord's and a couple of forties. They were consistent contributions, if not game-changing, and more than respectable for a 20-year-old with no experience of the alien conditions. With the ball, he managed only five expensive wickets.

Observing his half-century in the first Test, Bill Bowes, in his report for *The Cricketer* said, that Sobers 'convinced me he is going to be another great player. He has lots of time for his strokes.' At the end of the series, Bowes noted, 'Sobers showed ability to punch from his back foot. Tall, almost [Frank] Woolley-like at times, he stroked the ball with power.'

The turning point of the series came in that Edgbaston Test, after England found themselves 288 behind on first innings. Captain Peter May (285 not out) and Colin Cowdrey (154) shared a stand of 411 as England totalled 583 for 4 and then almost snatched victory by having West Indies 72 for 7 at the end of the fifth day. Significantly, talismanic West Indian off-spinner Sonny Ramadhin, who had taken seven wickets in the first innings, was blunted by the English duo, largely through their tactic of playing him with their pads. He bowled 98 overs for only two wickets.

By this stage of his career, Sobers, who bowled 30 wicketless overs in this innings, had been experimenting with a faster style of bowling in the nets. At one point, Goddard was urged by team-mates to take the new ball and give it to Sobers, but his first experience of bowling quickly in a Test match would have to wait. Sobers called the Englishmen's pragmatic approach to tackling Ramadhin 'one of the most depressing sights I have seen in Test cricket. The game is meant to be played with the bat, not the pads.'[19] Ramadhin, whose clever control of his wrist had made him so difficult for the English batsmen in 1950 – bamboozling them with off-breaks and leg-breaks with seemingly the same action – took only five more wickets in the series. Meanwhile, the big three of the batting line-up, Weekes, Walcott and Worrell, all achieved only roughly half their batting averages of 1950, with the latter the only one to score a century.

In total, Sobers scored more than 2,000 runs in all tour matches, averaging more than 43 in first-class cricket.[*] His four first-class hundreds included a maiden Lord's century against MCC – hitting 18 boundaries in an unbeaten 101 – and his first career double century a week later, an unbeaten 219 against Nottinghamshire at Trent Bridge, the place he would later call home.

His ability to drive the ball in conditions offering lateral movement to the bowlers was particularly noteworthy. In his review of the tour, author Bruce Harris called Sobers 'very much a cricketer of the future', concluding, 'He may well become the leading left-handed batsman in the world. Grace of movement and fluency of execution are stamped all over him.'[20]

In the final Test at The Oval, after England made 412, Sobers scored 39 and 42 in West Indies' paltry totals of 89 and 86, spinners Tony Lock and Jim Laker combining for 16 wickets on a crumbling wicket that Weekes described as

---

[*] West Indies played 38 matches in total during four and a half months in England, Sobers appearing in 32 of them. The tourists remained unbeaten in first-class games outside of the Test matches.

a 'beach'. Sobers was said by Harris to be 'by temperament not a young man of the steady and stolid sort',[21] but Sobers himself explained, 'I proved to myself then that I could play in difficult conditions, that I could put my nut down, graft and concentrate.'[22]

According to Tony Cozier, Sobers demonstrated 'the skill only vouchsafed to those of extraordinary talent',[23] while England batsman Tom Graveney was prompted to predict, in highlighting the crop of young West Indian players, that Sobers 'will turn out the best of the lot'.[24]

4

RECORD BREAKER

'From the little spark may burst a mighty flame.'

Italian poet Dante

THE TEST career of Garry Sobers had, by the early months of 1958, been a series of little sparks; flashes of brilliance that illuminated short periods of play in his 14 matches. A mighty flame was about to ignite at Kingston's Sabina Park.

The Caribbean was at a crossroads, on and off the field. The New Year saw the inauguration of the West Indies Federation, where the major islands came together as one with the intention of creating a single political entity that would go on to achieve independence from the United Kingdom. Historian Michael Manley called it 'an enterprise as ill-fated as the 1957 tour of England'.[1] In some ways, though, it was the perfect reflection of cricket in the region, given that internal conflict over its governance and functionality caused it to collapse after three years.

Meanwhile, the West Indies team was evolving from that of the 1950s into one that would illuminate much of the next decade; the mantle passing from Weekes and Walcott,

Ramadhin and Valentine to Sobers and Kanhai, Gibbs and Hall. One man, above all others, would be responsible for the successful transition.

'In 1958, wider historical omens apart, the West Indies did far more than entertain Pakistan on their first visit to the islands. West Indians witnessed the coming of age of the game's third superstar,' Manley recorded. 'In the 19th century one man towers absolutely, WG Grace; between the wars, Don Bradman is the colossus. After the war, Garfield St Aubrun Sobers completes the triumvirate.'

Sobers welcomed the Pakistan tourists at Bridgetown by scoring an unbeaten 183 for Barbados, before being out for a duck in the second innings. A week later he began the Test series with 52 in a big West Indies total that featured an innings of 197 by Everton Weekes. Facing a first-innings deficit of 473, Pakistan were saved by a prodigious effort of concentration and technique by opener Hanif Mohammad, who played the longest innings in the history of first-class cricket. For hour after hour he remained at the crease, eventually scoring 337 in 970 minutes. His marathon ensured that even in a six-day Test the home team were unable to force a victory. Hanif also had some fun during the formalities of the West Indies' 11-over second innings, bowling both right- and left-handed.

In the second Test in Port-of-Spain, Sobers scored 52 and 80 in a 120-run victory. More little sparks. He had now made six half-centuries in 16 Test matches. On one hand, Sobers welcomed being regarded as a frontline batsman and the expectations that came with it. But he felt somewhat resentful towards those critics who held against him the fact that he had not yet made three figures. They had forgotten, he believed, that he had been picked originally as a spinner and had played several matches down the order.

He was in no doubt that a century was close. He was too confident a 21-year-old to have developed any kind of mental barrier and was already wise enough to know that the manner of his batting was maturing. He knew he could be impetuous and acknowledged that his desire to continue playing shots and taking chances had prevented him capitalising on some good starts. 'As you gain experience you start to realise the value of your innings for the team and you start to improve your concentration,' he said.[2] Yet the perception of others was nagging at him. 'I was becoming a little anxious about it,' he admitted. 'There were those who were wondering if I really would fulfil my potential as a batsman at Test level.'[3]

In the third Test in Jamaica, the Pakistan first innings ended on the second day at 328 all out. The tourists' attack was quickly depleted by injury to Mahmood Hussain, who was able to bowl only the first five balls of the West Indies reply before breaking down. Conrad Hunte, who marked his Test debut with 142 in the first Test, and Rohan Kanhai had put on 87 before Sobers came to the crease at the fall of Kanhai's wicket. 'Not my best position,' he remembered of the number three slot, 'but on such a good wicket and with so many good players in the side you wanted to get in as early as possible. I felt I was batting better in that series than at any time in my career.'[4] Sobers was

20 not out at stumps, Hunte having reached a century in the final over of the day.

The third day, a Friday, began with the team being presented to the Governor of Jamaica, Sir Kenneth Blackburne, Sobers the first in line to be introduced by captain Gerry Alexander. The clouds rising from behind the Blue Mountains at the north end of Sabina Park and the breeze that fluttered the flags on the pavilion were not enough to deter Sobers from walking out sweater-less and with sleeves rolled up.

Around him, the stands were packed to overflowing – to the point of danger, some might have said. In the cheaper seats, spectators bunched together, their almost uniform wearing of white shirts giving the impression of a sightscreen spreading around the arena. The members' enclosures featured splashes of colour; its occupants dressed as though ready in advance for their Sunday church services.

Yet the spectators were not restricted to the designated seats. Legs dangled from the front of the second tier of the popular stands; bodies filled the trees like flocks of birds; others balanced atop the sightscreens; and, most precariously, the roofs of the stands were invisible under the additional layer of observers who had clambered on to them via a neighbouring building.

Two years later, during England's visit, several people would be injured, including one who suffered a broken leg, when a section of roofing collapsed under the weight of interlopers. Noting that the official capacity of 15,000 'looks more than the ground can safely hold', EW Swanton observed,

'The atmosphere of Test matches in these islands is quite tense enough without such additional hazards as this, and it is impossible in this case not to condemn both the ground authority and the police ... Every facility was strained to bursting point and beyond.'[5]

On the field, Pakistan's attack was further depleted by the non-appearance of spinner Nasim-ul-Ghani, who had fractured his right thumb while fielding the previous day. The visitors now had only two fit frontline bowlers, meaning skipper Abdul Kardar would be forced to ignore doctors' orders not to bowl his slow left-armers because of a fractured finger. The stage was set perfectly for Sobers to achieve his elusive milestone.

Revelling in the fastest wicket he'd encountered, he moved into the 40s with three consecutive fours off Khan Mohammad. By lunch he was on 76 and his tenth boundary, scored off Kardar, saw him reach 97, one stroke from his century. He was happy to get there one run at a time, eventually reaching 100 in 191 balls with a single off Kardar. 'I was concentrating so hard I remember little about it,' he explained. 'The shot, the bowler or the reaction of the crowd. I felt a sense of great relief; a vast obstacle in my career had been removed.'[6]

Taking a deep breath, he settled himself by playing out a maiden and then, his burden lifted, launched into attack. He raced to 150 with a burst of run-a-ball scoring that included a further eight fours. At 144 he had reached 1,000 runs in Test cricket. He went to tea on 170, not far behind Hunte's 196.

With his partner passing 200 soon after the interval, Sobers now had his own double century in his sights, proceeding with more circumspection. It was not until he was ten runs away that he found the boundary again. On 199 he faced Khan, reaching his landmark with a five. Once again he celebrated his achievement with a flurry of fours. When play closed, West Indies were 507 for 1, with Hunte (243) and Sobers (230) having become the fourth pair to bat unbeaten throughout an entire day of Test cricket.

For once, Sobers was unsettled by the talk of potential records. Len Hutton's highest score in Test cricket, 364 for England against Australia at The Oval in 1938, was conceivably within range of either batsman, which gave him a restless night. Not that he was fretting about the spectre of dismissal. 'I felt I could bat on and on and that no one could get me out.'[7] Nor did he arrive at the ground feeling tired. Excitement and adrenalin pumped life into his limbs.

The Hunte–Sobers partnership ended early on day four at 533 when Hunte was dismissed for 260, thrown out by substitute fielder Aijaz Burt when he tried to push Khan for a quick single. The duo had put on 446, a West Indies record for any wicket and only five short of the then-record for the second wicket in Test cricket, set by Donald Bradman and Bill Ponsford against England. In fact, it was a piece of misinformation that contributed to the partnership's termination, Hunte having believed that one run would tie the record. Sobers could also have been run out when new batsman Weekes played Khan through midwicket and sent back his partner when he set off for a run. Substitute Waqar Hussain's throw to the wrong end meant Pakistan's only chance of dismissing Sobers had gone.

Soon after, he took a single off Khan to reach 250 for the first time in his career.

It was only when Weekes was caught at slip shortly after lunch, bringing Clyde Walcott to the wicket, that Sobers became fully awake to the possibility of a record. At 602 for 3, he assumed that skipper Alexander must be contemplating the termination of the innings, but Walcott greeted him with, 'Don't worry. Settle down. Take it easy. The runs will come and I will give you as much strike as I can.'[8]

Sobers insisted in later years that a declaration would not have disturbed him. Even before the record was the target of a score of 300. Fours became sparsely dotted amid the singles and occasional twos that kept his score ticking towards that mark. The boundary he scored off Mahmood to go to 299 was only his third in his previous 52 runs. Two deliveries later, he became his country's first triple centurion. He gave up trying to put the record out of his head; instead, he attempted to convince himself he was new to the crease and needed to score 65 to win the match.

His delight at passing another landmark had once again taken away any physical tiredness and, following the pattern he'd established after reaching 100 and 200, he was sufficiently tension-free to go back on the attack, smashing Khan for four boundaries in two overs. At tea, taken at 730 for 3, he was on 336, Hutton's mark only 28 in the distance.

Now he was back to picking up his runs in ones and twos, Hanif running in from the outfield to shake his hand when he went past his 337 of the first Test. 'It was an unblemished innings, full of delightful strokes, though we who were on the end of it could perhaps be excused for not sharing in the delight,' Hanif recalled. 'Only once did it seem possible there was a chance when he played a ball which took the outside of his bat, and went towards the slips, where Fazal was supposed to have been fielding. He, however, was standing somewhere near third man, tired after having completed a long bowling spell and was nowhere near.'[9]

The landmark of 350 was relevant to Sobers only as a stopping-off point towards the record that everyone was willing him to achieve. 'The noise from the spectators was incredible,' Sobers noted of a stadium that Swanton observed was traditionally more reserved in its behaviour and less appreciative and knowledgeable than those in Bridgetown and Port-of-Spain.[10] In Barbados, there was barely a transistor radio not tuned in to events in Kingston.

When he had reached 363, Pakistan offered a second over of the innings to Hanif, the man Sobers had always imagined would be the one to beat Hutton's record. After Walcott scored a single off the second ball, Hanif changed from right-handed bowler to left. In Sobers's usual retelling of the moment, he was informed by the umpire of the change and responded, 'He can bowl with both hands if he likes.'

Sobers stroked the second ball he received down the ground to long-off and comfortably took the run that tied the record as the crowd erupted. While the cheers intensified, Sobers took the opportunity to clear his head, watching as Walcott took his own score to 88 by launching Hanif into the stands.

New over, Fazal Mahmood running in to bowl. Wide. Then a dot ball. Then Sobers pushed into the covers, Walcott called for the run and Sobers's dash to the bowler's end gave him the highest score in the 81-year history of Test cricket. According to Manley, he had 'redeemed all the pledges that had been implicit since the first morning against Hutton's side four years earlier'.[11]

Sobers accurately recalled that 'Sabina Park was in a state of bedlam'.[12] While those on the roofs and sightscreens fought to maintain their balance as they cavorted with joy, hundreds at ground level raced to the square to pat their new hero on the back, or merely to be in the vicinity of greatness. 'It might have been quite a shock to some people,' Weekes suggested, 'but to some of us who were very close to him we realised at that stage he had the ability to do what he did.'[13]

By the time the crowd had dispersed – and Alexander had confirmed his team's declaration – Pakistan skipper Kardar was canny enough to complain that the pitch had been damaged by the stampede and required overnight repairs.

'Pandemonium broke out,' the *Barbados Advocate* noted. Reflecting the ever-present island rivalry, it continued sniffily, 'The unprecedented display of enthusiastic but bad behaviour by a section of the record crowd of 20,000 that watched the day's play brought an abrupt ending 55 minutes before the scheduled close in an atmosphere of wild scenes and confusion that marred the glamour, brilliance and history-making achievement of the gifted left-hander.'

Sobers ended the day feeling guilty that his chanceless 575-ball, 614-minute innings, which included 38 fours and a five, might have jeopardised his team's chances of forcing victory by costing them bowling time. 'That is one of the reasons why I have always scored my runs quickly,' he would explain. 'I can never remember making runs just for the sake of making runs.'[14]

Yet with two days remaining, he hardly needed to worry about a few lost minutes and West Indies duly dismissed Pakistan for 288 early on the sixth and final day, taking a 2-0 lead in the series.

Sobers's life had changed irrevocably. 'From that moment on I was instantly recognised throughout the Caribbean and the cricketing world,' he said.[15] When he returned home, the proud Barbados Cricket Association arranged for him to be driven through the streets to take the cheers of his people. There was no immediate impact on his bank balance, however. He had to be content with the basic match fee of 150 British West Indies dollars – not much more than £30 at that time – which offered good value for the West Indies Cricket Board of Control.

The series moved on to Georgetown, where Sobers opened the batting and scored 125 in just over four hours, sharing a second-wicket partnership of 269 with Walcott. He batted at three in the second innings, taking guard with 125 of the 317 required to win already scored. There was still enough opportunity for him to rattle off his third consecutive century, hitting an unbeaten 109 off 130 balls as the target was reached for the loss of two wickets.

The run of three-figure scores came to an end in Pakistan's consolation victory in the final Test in Port-of-Spain, but by the time the series ended his overall Test batting average had been raised to 53.43. It would never again dip below 52 and, in fact, would spend most of the next 15 years climbing higher. Almost unnoticed under his pile of runs was the fact that Sobers managed only four wickets in the series at an average of 94.3. But, having totalled 824 runs at an average of 137.3, no one cared too much about his bowling.

As the series ended in the Caribbean, a new record was all the rage across the sea in the United States, reaching number one on Billboard's most-played chart and staying there for four weeks, selling more than a million copies and earning its performer, Laurie London, a gold disc. It was a reworking of an old African-American spiritual, but it reflected perfectly the new status of Garry Sobers: 'He's Got the Whole World in His Hands'.

5

GIANT AMONG MEN

'He shall be our ally against our enemies.'

Lilliput's sixth rule for the 'Man-Mountain', *Gulliver's Travels* (Jonathan Swift, 1726)

JOHN LOWE couldn't believe his luck. As a member of the committee at Radcliffe Cricket Club, founder members of the Central Lancashire League, he had taken a gamble late in 1956 when he approached Garry Sobers to become the club's professional. Sobers was happy to accept the deal, seeing it as an opportunity to follow a path previously taken by Frank Worrell and a chance to earn decent money from his sport.

Sobers recalled his Radcliffe salary being £500, although other sources have estimated his contract at £800. Clubs never made those figures public and annual financial statements typically included a line for 'wages', which lumped groundsman, barman and any other staff costs in with payments to the club professional.

Lowe felt that investment in Sobers was money well spent, even though he was then an unproven quantity at Test level. But Radcliffe would have to wait until the summer of 1958 to see him appear at their home at the Racecourse, the beating heart of a town that had once boasted a cotton mill and paper mill but was being swallowed up by modernity and nearby Manchester. 'If you wanted to watch sport you had your local football teams like Bury or [Bolton] Wanderers, or you watched the cricket,' former chairman John Heaton, who also played alongside Sobers, told Tanya Aldred decades later. 'There wasn't a right lot else to do.'[1]

Sobers's arrival was delayed by his selection for the 1957 West Indies tour of England. Fortunately for a nervous Lowe, a committed chain-smoker at the best of times, Sobers came through the series unscathed, his fitness intact and his reputation enhanced. And then came his world record against Pakistan. Suddenly, Radcliffe had bagged themselves the biggest draw in the world game.

The 1958 season in league cricket began with what *Manchester Evening News* writer John Kay called, 'the accent on highly-paid overseas professionals and a couldn't-care-less attitude about the support at the gates'.[2] Sobers and other young West Indies internationals Collie Smith (Burnley), Roy Gilchrist (Middleton) and Conrad Hunte (Enfield) might be what Kay called 'magnets for the crowds', but new forms of income, such as football pools, sponsorship and bingo nights, meant the clubs were no longer reliant solely on spectators' money or membership fees – or the jumble sales and whist drives that provided a back-up to rainy days of lost revenue.

Formed in the same year as the Lancashire League, 1892, the Central Lancashire League covered a wider area, ranging from Stockport, south-east of Manchester, to Walsden, these days part of West Yorkshire, taking in various cotton towns and semi-rural districts in between. Clubs had always employed professionals – often a batsman and a bowler – although the tasks for which they were paid were, ostensibly, to prepare the ground and provide coaching. As clubs began engaging others to mow the square and the professionals' primary function became to score runs and take wickets, more overseas players were engaged, particularly from Australia and the Caribbean, where playing cricket was a strictly amateur pastime.

Historically, Central Lancashire League teams were unable to match the wages of the rival organisation. Aussie fast bowler Ray Lindwall, for example, was thought to have earned £1,000 for a season with Nelson in 1950. Even so, a professional in either league could still expect to earn more than many county players would receive for playing every day.* And by the late 1950s, teams were prepared to dig deeper than ever to get their men. As Australian all-rounder Cec Pepper, playing for Oldham, was able to state on the eve of the season, 'Never in the history of the Central Lancashire League have clubs paid so much to so few.'[3]

There were those who felt that league cricket had come to depend too strongly on which team had the better professional, a view that even Worrell expressed. Kay had written in *The Cricketer* several years earlier, 'To see Worrell hit a century

---

* Famously, Sydney 'SF' Barnes, one of England's finest bowlers of the early 20th century, had barely played first-class cricket because of the greater rewards on offer in the leagues.

is undoubtedly good sport for a Saturday afternoon cricket public that wants nothing more than the spectacular. If they are content to feast their eyes upon the ability of one man and ignore the other members of the side League cricket has much to offer them. A century by Worrell gained at the expense of some aspiring young bowler who has youth, enthusiasm and a desire to make progress at the game has its drawbacks.'[4]

Now, ten years after Worrell scored a league-record 1,501 runs in his first season with Radcliffe, Kay predicted that 'Sobers will appeal to the technical experts rather than the "anything goes" brigade of spectators who like to see their runs go up in fours and sixes.'[5] But Sobers was shrewd enough to realise what was needed to maximise his earnings.

His basic contract had to cover his living expenses, and without the collections that were taken at the grounds when the professional achieved 50 runs or five wickets he knew he would struggle to survive. He understood that the more dashing his play, the more generous would be his supporters. He had even been advised by Worrell not to give away his wicket 'until I heard that last penny drop in the box', knowing that the collections were likely to cease when the beneficiary was dismissed.[6]

He was also aware of opportunities to generate additional income by guesting in midweek matches in other competitions, something he could do more freely as a Central Lancashire League professional than if he had signed for the more restrictive Lancashire League. He would even cross the Pennines on occasions to play in Yorkshire, where a good performance could earn £50 from the collection tin, and would team up with other overseas professionals to play Sunday exhibition games around the country for a share of the gate.

None of which would count for much if he was unable to deliver on the field. Yet any concerns on that score were eradicated in his debut league game. Playing at home to Milnrow, who included Australian spinner JW McMahon, he raced to an unbeaten 127 and took 8 for 26. Observers would recall several balls struck by Sobers joining the discarded prams and tyres in the area of stagnant water that sat between the back of the pavilion and the neighbouring housing estate. 'It did not take long to realise that we had acquired the services of an exceptional talent,' recalled team-mate Robert Hamilton.[7]

Pepper predicted, 'That century in his first innings for Radcliffe by young Sobers ought to pull the spectators in at the Racecourse.'[8] Indeed it did. Crowds in excess of 4,000, paying a shilling apiece, would regularly squeeze through the ground's six turnstiles.

A couple of weeks later, it was Worrell's turn to forecast, 'If conditions are good Garfield Sobers will break every batting record in the league this season. I know that a player has got to become acclimated to the atmosphere, responsibility and wickets of league cricket, and this normally takes a year or two, but … Sobers is a good enthusiastic player who has the advantage of being a left-hander.'[9]

In the end, rain restricted Sobers to 1,252 runs and 88 wickets for a disappointing Radcliffe side. But he established a pattern of prodigious feats that would continue throughout his five seasons at the club, by the end of which he had scored 5,708 runs at an average of 64.96 and taken 532 wickets at 11.58. The modern day club's pavilion is full of photographic reminders of one of the most exciting periods in its history, as well as boasting a function room called the Garfield Sobers Lounge.

In 1959 he struck eight centuries in amassing 1,454 runs at 90.88 and took 86 wickets at a cost of 13.08 apiece. In both 1960 and 1961 he achieved the double of 1,000 runs (1,113 and 1,008 respectively) and 100 wickets (101 and 144). In the second of those seasons, Sobers bagged 20 five-wicket hauls as Radcliffe won the league and the prestigious Wood Cup, a two-innings competition contested on weekday evenings. Only in his final season of 1962, hampered by a knee injury, did he fail to score 1,000 runs (901), though he still managed 118 wickets.

Some of his performances acquired the status of legend. Like the 186 he scored against Ashton in 1959 in only two hours, including 25 fours and six sixes; or a 13-minute 50 at Rochdale; and the first over of a match at Middleton in which he bowled three opponents. Then there is the oft-repeated tale of a home game when he was bowling from the tennis-court end and a tailender, crowded by close fielders, had the temerity to swing his bowling high in the direction of the sightscreen. 'Leave it to me,' yelled Sobers, turning to race towards the boundary to catch the ball as it dropped from the sky a few yards from the rope. That version came from a former Radcliffe colleague talking to the *Bury Times* in 2006, yet other accounts, including Kay's book, *Cricket in the Leagues*, record the event – or perhaps an identical one – having taken place in later years when Sobers was playing for Staffordshire side Norton against Crewe LMR.

The details seem less important than the images that are conjured up by the telling of such tales. Like the one about Sobers, taking time away from Radcliffe in his first season, marking a guest appearance for the Pakistan Eaglets touring team against Leicestershire's second XI by scoring 145 in 115 minutes, hitting a six and 26 fours in a team total of 213 and clubbing amateur seam bowler Don Goodson for eight consecutive fours before being caught on the boundary going for a ninth.

Meanwhile, Sobers served as motivation for others. In 1960, Basil D'Oliveira, who had arrived at Middleton from South Africa to escape the restrictions of apartheid and would eventually play for England, was the leading batsman in the Central Lancashire League. 'Averages have never bothered me apart from that season, when I was determined to top Sobers,' he remembered. 'Although he was like a god to me, I was determined to try to beat him in the averages. I aimed for Sobers, which was ridiculous, considering he was such a great all-rounder and I was a novice. I kept looking for his performances every week in the local paper ... but I found out later from the Radcliffe lads that Garry did the same for me.'[10]

Sobers did more than rack up remarkable statistics and rake in cash from collections. He developed his craft. 'The wickets were not good and an average bowler could run up, put the ball on the spot and more often than not something would happen,' he said. 'My cricket started to improve, especially my batting as I learned to play each ball on its merit.'[11]

He also took the opportunity to experiment with new methods of bowling: wrist-spin and the fast swing that would become such an important part of his armoury. The lower quality of the batsmen allowed him to try new things without fear of harsh punishment. 'The more ways I bowled the more chance I had of taking those magic five wickets and receiving a much-needed collection from the crowd,' he explained.[12]

Team-mate Hamilton recalled, 'Sobers could bowl fast, medium and slow. I suppose it was similar to having 13 players in a team and, as a result, he was often asked to bowl at one end for most of an innings.'[13] Heaton often found himself at slip to Sobers. 'He'd start off with his quick stuff then he'd switch to his left-arm orthodox, then his googlies,' he explained. 'I couldn't read him; that's probably why I dropped more than I caught. He could catch anything, he was so quick, you knew you were playing with someone world-class.'[14]

Having found Londoners somewhat distant during his 1957 visit, Sobers was happy in his Lancashire life, whether it was carrying his team on the field, playing football on training nights, or making friends with the locals. 'He was just one of the lads, there was no ego about him,' remembered Heaton, adding, 'He was an attractive man so lots of ladies flocked around him. He was a very, very popular member of the team and the town.'[15]

Warned about gangs of 'Teddy Boys' who might loiter late at night in search of trouble, he was engaging enough to persuade them to drink with him at the Boar's Head, where he initially lodged before moving into digs with a landlady, Mrs Mathers, who had previously looked after Worrell. He never experienced, or certainly never noticed, any prejudice caused by the colour of his skin. Besides, he discovered enough families of West Indian extraction who were only too happy to invite him to their homes for a meal. And, he explained, 'I enjoyed the social scene of the pubs and clubs in England even though they often wanted to know what a professional sportsman was doing out so late.'[16]

Significantly, it was during this period that Sobers began to bet on the horses more frequently. Visiting a bookmaker's shop in Manchester, where he could listen to the races on the radio, was a way of killing his vast amount of spare time. It was also an easier environment in which to bet than the racecourse, where he ended up spending so much time talking to friends – particularly among the jockeys – that he rarely had time to study the form and make a calculated selection. Not that making money was the prime objective of his pastime. He lacked the patience of the professional gambler to sit for days waiting for the right race on which to gamble. He wanted the thrill of following the fortunes of his chosen horse – and if it won, so much the better. 'Eventually I looked forward to having a bet every day and at times spent more than I could afford, betting when I knew I had some money coming in to cover the losses. I suspect that I became a little addicted.'[17]

Australian Bill Alley, a league professional for a decade before playing for Somerset and going on to become a Test umpire, suggested, 'Sometimes I thought Sobers loved the horses more than he did his cricket.'[18] Which meant he was occasionally grateful for friends who would not let him get in too deep. Cec Pepper's brother, Keith, recalled, 'When Garry

Sobers was first playing in the leagues Cecil would pay off his gambling debts.'[19]

* * *

By the time Sobers arrived at his second home in league cricket, his new team knew exactly who they were signing: the world's premier cricketer. His five-year stint at Radcliffe had ended with his commitment to the 1963 West Indies tour of England, which had been a triumph for Sobers and his team. For the summers of 1964, 1965 and 1967 he plied his trade at Norton in the North Staffordshire and South Cheshire League.

Norton were one of the 12 founding members of the league, which began in 1963 as a breakaway from the Staffordshire and District League. One of the eight clubs based in and around Stoke-on-Trent, Norton's fortunes were guided by chairman Tommy Talbot, a big name in plumbing and decorating in the area who had previously successfully recruited Worrell and Jim Laker. He was also the benefactor of the knockout cup that bore his name and which was played between the league's teams over 25 or 20 overs on Sundays or weekday evenings.

Sobers signed a five-year deal worth £50 a week to play at a National Coal Board-owned ground that could accommodate 2,750 spectators in three-tiered seating and whose pavilion looked across the square to the imposing and ever-growing pyramid of Ford Green Colliery's spoil tip. Talbot was not only ambitious and generous in his offer to Sobers but wise in the ways of bending league rules. While professionals were free to live anywhere – Sobers choosing a flat in Manchester –

amateurs were required to live within ten miles of the ground. Sobers's brother Gerry played as a wicketkeeper-batsman for Norton and to disguise the reality of him sharing his brother's apartment, Talbot registered his address as that of his own office in High Lane, Burslem. Meanwhile, Gerry and fast bowler Dave Wilson were officially employed by Talbot's plumbing business.

Sobers's arrival in the chilly Potteries, fresh from playing for an EW Swanton XI in Kuala Lumpur, was enough to attract news cameras, to whom he said he was happy to leave the sunshine for 'a class of cricket that has done a lot for me'. And he was destined to do a lot for Norton, winning three league championships in three seasons.

In a competition where runs were generally harder to come by than in the Central Lancashire League, Sobers finished the 1964 campaign with only 549 at 49.9. His highest score was 81. Yet he was unstoppable with the ball. As Norton entered the final three matches on top of the table, he took 6 for 38 against Porthill Park and 9 for 41 against Nantwich. The two wins ensured that the title was clinched in the final game when rain brought an early end against Knypersley. Sobers had taken 97 wickets at 8.4, with the nearest rival 30 wickets behind him – a competition record that stood until 2002.

Wisden noted, 'Sobers stood out as the ideal league cricketer in that he regards the game not just as a medium for obtaining personal records in batting and bowling but as a match to be won in the shortest possible time and at the sacrifice of personal performance if necessary.'[20]

His bowling efforts included eight wickets against Leek; 5-47 after scoring 59 against Chell; another five wickets, plus 62 runs, against Porthill Park; a fierce ten-over spell that included six maidens as Norton defended 67 to beat Bagnall End and reach the semi-finals of the Talbot Cup; and 6 for 67 and a half-century against Crewe. Team-mate Dave Brock recalled, 'He would always ask who the opposition's best player was then step it up a level.'[21]

Sobers was frequently content, having taken a bagful of wickets, to let his team-mates score the bulk of the runs, sometimes to the disappointment of expectant crowds. 'I've done my job now you do yours,' was his message to team-mates. 'He did what he wanted,' Brock told author Scott Oliver. 'The captain couldn't control him and neither could Tommy Talbot. He would often disappear at tea and go for a tot of brandy in the secretary's office.'[22]

Such an approach illustrated Sobers's lack of ego rather than any tendency towards arrogance or laziness. 'He was very down to earth,' said another colleague, Frank Reynolds. 'He didn't put himself above others.' Reynolds continued, 'As a batsman Garry went out to enjoy his game, certainly compared to Frank Worrell, who played a steady grafting game and got his head down. Garry was a flair player and went in to play shots and entertain. He took chances.'[23]

But Sobers could only afford to drop down the order once he knew that the collection tin had been around to reward his bowling. 'Garry always needed money,' remembered Vince Lindo, a Jamaican playing for local rivals Sneyd. 'He once gave me £100 to put on a horse, which was two weeks' cricket wages for him. I'd never been in a bookies before. I told Garry, "You can't put £100 on a horse," and he said, "Don't you tell me what to do with my money."'[24]

A couple of years later, journalist Gary Newbon was a young reporter working for a local news agency at West Indies' match against Cambridge University early in the 1966 tour. 'I had a message to say the legendary groundsman Cyril Coote wanted to see me in the pavilion straight away,' he recalled. From there he was taken to the West Indies dressing room on the top floor, where Sobers greeted him with, 'Do you know where the nearest betting shop is, kid?' Newbon continued, 'Sobers then pulled a roll of tenners out of his pocket and peeled off £100 for me to place on an odds-on shot that was running in the evening meeting at the now-defunct Alexandra Park. I was on £8 a week before deductions, so I thought this must be a racing certainty so I put my £5 on. Lesson learned: the selection was unplaced and is probably still running!'[25]

Former Glamorgan batsman Roger Davis tells another cash-related story. 'Notts had played Oxford University just before us and Garry had had his wallet pinched from his blazer after hanging it up in the dressing room. Apparently there was about £1,100 in there that he had won the night before. That was two years' salary for me. I am thinking, "Bloody hell. He is heavy into his gambling."'[26]

Sobers, who would always find young fans waiting at the ground eager to help him carry his equipment, again experienced no difficulties related to his colour in his new home, even though former West Indies fast bowler Roy Gilchrist had not long since been banned from the Staffordshire District League for striking a spectator who called him a 'black bastard'.

The 1965 season, which Sobers began a month late because of West Indies commitments, saw him take 76 wickets at an average of 8.04, although his batting was modest. The league campaign hinged on the final game, in which Norton were bowled out for 134 by Knypersley. Sobers then took wickets with the first three and final two deliveries of his second over to reduce the opposition to 7 for 5. Bowling spin in fading light later in the innings, he ran his figures to 9 for 41 as the title was clinched. Norton had already lifted the Talbot Cup, Sobers having taken 5 for 31 to defend 90 in the final against holders Longton.

Another trophy came Sobers's way in the Inter-League President's Cup, in which he was able to team up with Hall, one of four professionals allowed to play for each team. The NSSCL faced the Yorkshire Cricket Council in the final in front of 4,500 at Great Chell. Sobers took 5 for 10 as the Yorkshire side finished 20 runs short of a small target.

After another triumphant march around England with West Indies in 1966, Sobers was back at Norton in 1967, scoring his only century for the club against Longton, who had won the league in his absence. He then wrapped up victory with a spell of 8 for 41. Norton duly marched to another championship, unbeaten with 13 wins and nine draws. Sobers racked up 95 wickets. In three seasons, he had totalled 268 league wickets at a miserly 8.63.

Talbot, accused of buying his club's success, was forced to argue in the *Stoke Sentinel* that the presence of Sobers was positive for the league and ensured that other clubs benefited by pulling in their biggest crowds. But it was not going to be an issue any longer. By the time Norton began their 1968 season, the landscape of English cricket had shifted again and Sobers had more lucrative opportunities to pursue.

6

LIFE AFTER DEATH: PLAYING FOR COLLIE

'To lose a friend is the greatest loss of all.'

Syrian writer Pubilius Syrus

GARRY SOBERS learnt a lot in 1959. On the field, he expanded his game by working out how to score runs in an unfamiliar environment, and then he discovered the lengths that some rivals would go to in order to stifle his talent. Yet the most profound lesson, one he would carry with him into matches like a piece of equipment, was the weight of grief. Too young to fully experience the pain of losing his father when he was a child, the death of his great friend, Collie Smith – and the circumstances of his passing – cut deeply and painfully, leaving him to learn how to bear the scars as his career progressed down what was supposed to have been a shared path.

Even before West Indies arrived in India for their 1958/59 tour, Sobers had had his eyes opened to the reality of being a Caribbean cricketer trying to earn a living from his sport. In July, three months after the party to visit India and Pakistan had been named, the West Indies Cricket Board of Control announced that Sobers – along with three others who played professionally in England, Conrad Hunte, Sonny Ramadhin and Collie Smith – would not be travelling after all because of a dispute over payment.

Looking back some years later, Sobers was worldly enough to recognise the hypocrisy of those in positions of power. They would happily accept the money that ticket sales injected into the sport but felt tainted by handing any of it to professionals to play for their country when, previously, there had been enough men of independent means to wear the maroon caps. At the time, though, he simply wanted to travel and play cricket. Rather than jeopardising his place in the team, he accepted the 'very small' amount being offered.

There had already been intrigue over the touring party, West Indies having taken the historic step of naming Frank Worrell as its first black captain. The WICBC's selectors, though, had been too busy congratulating themselves on taking such a progressive step to check whether Worrell was available for the five-month excursion. He wasn't. His studies towards a degree in economics at Manchester University took precedence. Worrell had already declined the opportunity to captain against Pakistan the previous year for similar reasons and now his university wrote to the WICBC to advise them that breaking his studies would 'seriously endanger and might even jeopardise his university career'.[1]

His subsequent withdrawal, coming on the heels of Clyde Walcott and Everton Weekes announcing their retirements from Test cricket, meant that West Indies would be taking the field without any of the Three Ws for the first time since the Second World War. Gerry Alexander resumed captaincy duties, while two men, batsman John Holt and bowler Wes Hall, were required to replace Worrell as a player. India, meanwhile, would pick 24 players and four different captains in the course of five Test matches.

Sobers opened his tour with a century and a 90 in the warm-up games, but developed back and stomach pains, possibly linked to the spinal injections and subsequent surgery from his bout of appendicitis several years earlier. He was well enough to score an unbeaten 142 in the drawn first Test in Bombay's* Brabourne Stadium, hitting eight fours and a six, but it was far from a painless process in temperatures that rose to 110 degrees. At one point his back went into spasm and he slumped at the crease. When he left the field he was taken to Beach Candy Hospital, where a doctor prepared to administer a pain-killing injection with a syringe that Sobers joked was like a cricket stump. When the contraption touched a nerve, his screams could be heard around the hospital.

Outside of health issues, Sobers was loving his first experience in the invigorating environment of cricket-mad India. But there was an obvious deficiency in the social side of the tour, prohibition having been imposed in many states since independence in 1947. As visitors, the West Indies players were given coupons to acquire limited amounts of alcohol but in the

---

* Now Mumbai.

main they were reliant on invitations to private parties if they wanted the kind of drinking session to which Sobers had become accustomed. Meanwhile, there were limited opportunities to fraternise with the opposite sex, given the local moralities of the time. He learned to accept that 'the social side was secondary; I was happy to concentrate on the cricket'.[2]

There was, however, an opportunity for a night out during the second Test in Kanpur after he and seam bowler Eric Atkinson, younger brother of former Test captain Denis, met a group who boasted that they had access to a supply of whisky. They invited the players to meet them after the second day's play. Sobers and Atkinson returned to the team hotel around 2 a.m. and, seeing no one else, assumed their escapade had been undetected. Later that day, India's first innings concluded at 222 all out, identical to West Indies' total, and Sobers soon found himself batting after openers Holt and Hunte were dismissed without a run on the board. A little under four hours later, Sobers reached another century, having hit 15 fours, and was still unbeaten on 136 at stumps.

Tour manager Berkeley Gaskin was waiting for him when he returned to the dressing room. 'It's a good thing you got those runs,' Gaskin told him. 'I saw you come in late.'[3] Gaskin would not be the last manager to discover that Sobers's late-night antics rarely impacted on his productivity.

Sobers narrowly missed out on a double century the next day when he was run out for 198, made in 340 minutes and including 28 fours. 'He played with such ease and authority that old men chanted his name,' said Tony Cozier. 'And when he left ... the young maidens adorned his youthful shoulders with garlands of roses.[4]

His efforts helped to set up a 203-run West Indies victory and represented his fifth century in five Tests. He ended 1958 with an aggregate of 1,193 Test runs at an average of 132.56 and, for good measure, he'd gone into the third Test in Calcutta[*] on the back of 161 not out against Indian Universities.

While Hall had done the damage in Kanpur, with six wickets in the first innings and five in the second, Sobers had made his own significant breakthrough, dismissing both India's opening batsmen lbw in the first innings.. They were his first successes after four wicketless Test matches, by which time his career bowling average had risen above 52, the highest it would ever be.

When Sobers got the opportunity to bat in Calcutta, at number six, he began the new year by scoring 106 not out. On this occasion he was the support act to Rohan Kanhai's 256 as West Indies won by an innings and 336 runs.

He contributed little with the bat in a 295-run victory in the fourth Test in Madras[**], but his 4 for 26 in India's first innings was his best return so far in Test cricket and the first time he had taken four wickets since his debut.

An undistinguished performance with bat and ball in a drawn fifth Test in Delhi was the prelude to a disappointing series in Pakistan – a 'trip from hell', as he described it.[5] His 72 in the third and final Test was his only half-century in a 2-1

---

*   Now Kolkata.

**   Now Chennai.

series defeat that gave him an indication of how far some teams would go to neutralise his considerable threat.

In the ten-wicket defeat in the first Test in Karachi, Sobers was aghast to be given out twice lbw, having been convinced that the ball was missing leg stump in the first innings and had struck the inside of his bat in the second. He began packing his bags on his return to the dressing room and announced that he was going home. It seemed apparent to him – and was confirmed by the loose tongues of Pakistan players – that the umpires would give him no opportunity to add to the pile of runs he had scored against them in the Caribbean. He explained to Gaskin that he worried about the morals of the sport. 'It was the worst umpiring I ever came across in my career,' he reckoned.[6]

He was persuaded not to leave the tour, but his mood darkened further in the second Test in Dhaka,[*] another Pakistan victory, when he was given out lbw again on 29, even though he believed that the ball was missing leg. He made sure to keep his pads out of the way as he scored 45 in the second innings, and made his half-century as West Indies gained a consolation win by an innings in Lahore.

* * *

Sobers's 1959 season for Radcliffe ended with a memorable encounter with the most controversial member of the West Indies touring team. Roy Gilchrist, the Jamaican fast bowler,

---

*   Now in Bangladesh.

had been banished before the end of the Indian leg of the tour after defying Alexander by bowling bouncers and beamers at North Zone tailender Swaranjit Singh. Having already clashed with his captain several times on tour and been left out of the second Test, Gilchrist was ordered home. Aged 24, he would never play for West Indies again.

On the first Saturday in September, Gilchrist's club, Middleton, faced Radcliffe in the final match of the Central Lancashire League season. Gilchrist got into an argument with Radcliffe captain Bill Moore and even waved a stump in his face before Sobers, batting with Moore, helped the umpire separate the combatants. Sobers scored 101 before Gilchrist bowled him.

Gilchrist was due to join Sobers that night for a drive to London for a charity game the following day, along with West Indies team-mates Tom Dewdney, opening bowler at Darwen, and Collie Smith, the professional at Burnley. When Gilchrist had still not turned up an hour after the appointed time, the trio set off. At least the traffic would be lighter now. Smith took first turn behind the wheel, followed by Dewdney. When Sobers settled into the driver's seat, Dewdney sat next to him, while Smith stretched out to sleep in the back.

The exact details of those few hours have always remained a blur in Sobers's memory. The one abiding image is 'the blinding blaze of headlights' that 'come like a curtain across my mind'.[7]

It was around 4.45 a.m. – on the A34 Manchester to Birmingham road, on a notorious bend about a mile north of Stone, in Staffordshire – when Sobers's car collided with a cattle truck, said to weigh ten tonnes. 'Before that moment I remember nothing,' he said when he discussed the specifics of the incident for the first time seven years later. 'Not where we are, or where we have been or where we are going. Afterwards, the doctors and police say this is very common in people who have had a bad crash. But I am tortured by not knowing.'[8]

As Sobers regained his senses, feeling as though he was looking down on events as an outsider, he saw Smith on a stretcher, seemingly unhurt but 'crying terribly'. He attempted to comfort Dewdney, who was 'walking around talking wild'. At this point one of Sobers's accounts had Dewdney telling him, 'Don't worry about me. Look after the Big Fellow' – referring to one of the diminutive Smith's ironic nicknames. In a later retelling, Sobers said that it was Smith who told him to 'look after the big boy', meaning Dewdney.

All three were taken to North Staffordshire Infirmary, in Stoke-on-Trent, where Sobers and Dewdney were treated for head and face lacerations and severe bruising. Sobers had also damaged nerves in his left wrist and a finger. Smith was found to have a spinal injury, and was described as 'critically ill'. The seriousness of his condition was originally withheld from Sobers, who, believing his great friend to be relatively unhurt, kept asking, 'Can I see Collie?' He explained, 'I learn through rumours that Collie has his spinal cord broken and he is unconscious.'[9]

The next day's newspaper reports suggested that Sobers's car had failed to take the bend properly, being completely wrecked after it crashed into the truck driven by Andrew Saunders of Cumberland, who was unhurt. Among the first visitors to the hospital was Frank Worrell. He was allowed to see only Sobers and Dewdney and told reporters, 'I gather the outlook is not very promising for Smith.'

Three days after the accident, O'Neil Gordon 'Collie' Smith died, aged 26, from a fracture of the spine and contusion on the brain.

'The Mighty Mouse is gone from me, and I am so lonely inside me I don't know how I can live without him,' said Sobers. 'Nothing makes sense. One moment the world and all of life is yours. The next moment it is all gone from you.'[10]

Two days later, the inquest, led by the Stoke city coroner, was adjourned until Sobers and Dewdney were released from hospital and well enough to offer evidence. In the meantime, Sobers learnt that a notice of intended prosecution had been served on him, although a police spokesman said that it was a formality intended to meet required timelines. It was quickly resolved that no criminal charges would be brought, although Sobers could still have to answer to a traffic offence.

Released from hospital, Sobers felt 'as if I walk through another door in life. Everything seems different to me.'[11] And once he had given evidence at the inquest in early October, it became clear how close things had been to taking an even more drastic turn, with the loss of his liberty or even his life.

'I approached a bend at about 30 miles per hour,' he told the court. 'I saw no light approaching so I thought it was safe to go round the bend. Then suddenly, as I was approaching the bend, I saw two bright lights which shone straight in my eyes. My reaction was to pull away from the lights and that is all I remember. To my knowledge I was never on the off-side of the road.'

Saunders, driver of the truck, said he had seen a car approaching at a very fast speed near the centre of the road. 'The car then seemed to leave its left-hand side of the road and go to the off-side. I put on my brakes and the truck had almost stopped when the car collided with it.' The driver's speed on the brake pedal might well have saved the lives of Sobers and Dewdney.

Coroner FG Hails made it clear in his remarks to the jury that he did not trust Sobers's version of events. 'Sobers has not explained how he undoubtedly came to collide with this truck on his off-side of the road, or how, having regard to the course of the bend, he could have been dazzled by approaching headlights. There is no evidence against either driver, however, which could justify a manslaughter verdict. Suspicion there may be, but suspicion is not enough.'

Instead of anything more serious, Sobers received a summons for careless driving. After a couple of adjournments and having pleaded not guilty, he was fined £10, banned from driving for a month and ordered to pay £16 17s in costs. Prosecuting, EWB Whitehead said Sobers had failed to take a corner properly, although Sobers argued that being blinded by headlights had caused him to lose his sense of direction. In passing sentence, chairman of magistrates CC Bullock told him, 'We are bearing in mind it has been a disastrous episode for you.'

The details of the incident, and particularly the coroner's apparent scepticism about the appropriateness of Sobers's driving, add a jarring element to a story related years later by Indian Test star Sunil Gavaskar. Having hosted some Indian players at his Barbados home while they were touring early in 1976, Sobers took them back to their hotel through the narrow streets in his Jaguar. 'The way … he was driving, we thought we'd be lucky if the four of us in his car reached the hotel alive,' said Gavaskar. 'It was [Erapalli] Prasanna who asked him why he drove so fast and how did he know there was no other car coming from the opposite side when he was taking a sharp curve. Garry replied, "It's my nose, man. I can smell a car if it's coming the other way."'[12]

Preparing for the upcoming 1959/60 season, Sobers could not escape the darkness that enveloped him after the traumatic episode. Before returning to the Caribbean he worked with Dr Bertie Clarke, a former West Indies leg-spinner, and at Middlesex's indoor nets with renowned coach Alf Gover and Jamaican bowler Stanley Goodrich to get himself back in physical shape. 'Garry asked the bowlers to bowl short of a length on his middle and leg stump so that he could practise his "flip" shot,' Gover recalled. 'To do this he balanced on his left leg as he swung the bat left-handed and pulled the right leg across himself, giving the bat room to swing freely at the ball. The shot required perfect timing. The normal left-hander would be satisfied with a defensive push, but Garry, one of the all-time greats, would invariably crack it to the leg-side boundary.'[13]

But his gains in fitness and the growing confidence that his body would allow him to continue playing his favourite shots meant nothing to Sobers, who had lost more than an on-field buddy. Three years older than Sobers, Smith had been a confidant and advisor. He was the room-mate who could keep Sobers talking all night as they consoled each other in failure, celebrated success and dreamed about the future. He was the friend with whom meaningful communication could be passed without any words, with a mere look or gesture.

There was no professional support to help him through his grief and his guilt, although the WICBC sent a telegram to Worrell asking him to help Sobers deal with events. 'It is now up to all of us to do our bit to help this youngster to overcome the terrible shock and aftermath,' said Board director Lindsay Grant.[14]

But mostly Sobers found his help in a bottle. 'When I return to the West Indies I begin drinking. I mean really drinking – and not just social drinks. Looking back, I see the foolishness.' The effects of alcohol might not have been obvious on the field or training ground but Sobers knew that those close to him were aware of it and thought badly of him. But he knew no other way.

Depressed and afraid of being unable to sleep or having bad dreams, he lived by night even more than usual. 'I wasn't going to jump under a bus, commit suicide or anything like that, but in my own way it was as if I was trying to destroy myself,' he explained.[15] The more brandy and Scotch he consumed, the less he felt the effects. The demons inside him were becoming more powerful. He could drink from one day to the next without sleep.

Trevor Bailey would write, 'He was determined to crowd into his own life as much pleasure as possible for, after all, it was only fate that had decreed he should live and Collie should die. Money became merely something to spend. He gambled more heavily and never contemplated the future because it so easily might never come. Also, for the first time, he began to drink heavily. Until then he had been just a social drinker; now he became an expert performer, who could dispose of a bottle of Scotch or brandy in a session without any trouble.'[16]

In the end, it was the imminent return to Test cricket in the series against England early in 1960 that broke the cycle of self-destruction. If he couldn't shake the ghost of his friend by drinking then he would take him on to the field. 'I realised that I would be letting my country down if I disappeared into the mists of an alcoholic haze. It suddenly struck me forcibly that I no longer had to play for Garfield Sobers. I had to do two men's jobs.'[17]

The drinking didn't cease overnight, but he had found a way to control it.

7

MASTERING HIS ART

'Maturity is the ability to postpone gratification.'

Psychoanalyst Sigmund Freud

THE MCC tourists of 1959/60 arrived in the Caribbean with the dual ambition of beating the home side and fully restoring cordial relations between cricketing nations after the rancorous 1953/54 series. The first goal was achieved via victory in the one Test to produce a definite result; the second accomplished in spite of a riot in Trinidad.

A year on from failing to justify their status as favourites in the latest Ashes series in Australia, England were considered underdogs. An innings of 154 by Garry Sobers helped Barbados beat them by ten wickets ahead of the first Test, a result that strengthened the opinion of those predicting a home win. In his chronicle of the series, EW Swanton said that Sobers's performance had been 'like slaughter', adding that 'the class and the sheer power of [his] batsmanship were a revelation' to those opponents who had not previously experienced it first-hand.[1]

For Sobers himself, it was proof that the recent tragedy of Collie Smith, far from eroding his skills, might even have bolstered them. 'In all my innings,' he said in later years, 'I played with him inside me, trying perhaps to give him the innings that death denied him. Such power I felt flowing into the strokes, such exhilaration, such purpose, that I was two men in one.'[2]

Despite his success over the previous 12 months, the absence of global television coverage of Test cricket meant that most English players had not yet seen Sobers at his brilliant best. And cricket followers around the world, including those at home, would not be entirely convinced of his credentials until he scored significant runs against the established powerhouses of the sport. Runs against Pakistan and India were nice enough, but England and Australia were the opponents who really mattered.

The home fans had to wait to see their hero with bat in hand in the opening Test as England racked up the first big total of the series at Kensington Oval. Ken Barrington and Ted Dexter both reached three figures before the innings closed at 482. Sobers failed to take a wicket in his 21 overs but was by now confident enough to bowl his wrist-spin in Test matches, mixing the stock delivery that turned away from the left-hander with the googly that span away from a right-hander's outside edge. The latter was the only delivery that gave the elegant Dexter any problems during his unbeaten 136.

It was with the bat, though, that Sobers was establishing his reputation and England must have endured disturbed sleep when he ended the third day on 21 not out. English writer Alan Ross was taken more by Sobers's equipment than his strokeplay in this first phase of his innings. 'Sobers, for all his scarlet bat-handle and extravagance of his power, had small opportunity to wield either,' he wrote.[3]

Sobers had been joined at the crease by Worrell at 4.50 p.m. on Friday, with the score 102 for 3. The senior batsman warned Sobers to keep his head down. The duo were not to be separated until 11.40 a.m. on Tuesday, the sixth and final day, by which time they had put on 399, still the highest partnership for West Indies against England.

A hot and breezy fourth morning saw Sobers making sedate progress in support of Worrell, who had not played first-class cricket since 1957 because of his studies. On 40, Sobers was dropped by Fred Trueman at midwicket off the bowling of off-spinner David Allen. 'Sobers every so often pulled and cut with the savagery of one who sees a sudden way out of captivity,' said Ross, who described him as 'contained but ruthless'.[4]

After five hours and 20 minutes at the crease, an accelerating Sobers was first to his century, shortly before rain halted play with Worrell 91 not out in a score of 279 for 3. The sight of Sobers raising his bat to mark the first of an eventual ten Test centuries against England prompted reminiscence from Swanton. 'One remembers him so well, coming in with his strange gangling walk as a lad of 17 against England at Kingston six years ago. He was a player of unmistakeable class then: now he is the finished article, an experienced, balanced, fully organised cricketer … Sometimes in England we have seen Sobers somewhat headstrong. Not so now, and he is much the more formidable.'[5]

If Sobers felt refreshed after a rest day it was not evident as tight English bowling and athletic fielding resulted in slow progress. Only 34 runs were scored in 90 minutes before lunch and Worrell took an hour to get the nine he needed for his century. Sobers could have been dismissed by Ray Illingworth when he offered a difficult chance to Colin Cowdrey at mid-on and an air of relief went round the ground when he swept Barrington twice for four. Not that the Bridgetown crowd – who filled the stands and watched from sofas and deckchairs on self-constructed viewing positions on roofs outside the ground – were likely to show any disapproval of their own man. As Swanton recorded, 'There are no more hospitable folk than the Barbadians, nor any with a deeper pride in their island and in its cricket achievements.'[6]

On a benign pitch – shaved of any grass – and with wickets in hand, there might have been an opportunity for West Indies to push towards a declaration, but such a course was neglected. Sobers's successive fours off Alan Moss took the partnership past 300 and kept him on course for a double century. 'Sobers and Worrell remained content to cruise gently along,' Ross complained. 'It had all the inevitability of a long sea voyage and about the same element of drama.'[7]

For the third consecutive day, Sobers (216) and Worrell (177) took their team to stumps. The pair had established an evening routine that took advantage of being able to leave the team headquarters at the Marine Hotel and head for their homes. Worrell would go and have dinner with family and friends, sometimes taking Sobers with him. If they had dined separately, they would wait for each other at the hotel and, even if it was already the early hours of the morning, head to the bar, often until around 5 a.m.

Sobers had his marathon innings halted on the final morning when Trueman pitched on middle stump and the ball stayed low to bowl him for 226. He had batted for 647 minutes and struck 24 fours. The rest of the day was an exercise in futility and frustration, Gerry Alexander feeling compelled to declare with Worrell, who it was claimed had ignored orders to get a move on, stuck on 197 not out. Worrell admitted he had been given plenty of time to reach 200 and Sobers dismissed the conspiracy theory that Worrell had batted deliberately slowly in order to deny Alexander the chance of a victory that might further delay his own ascendancy to the captaincy. 'I spoke to Frank about that match many times and he told me he was so tired that if Gerry had let him bat for another hour he wouldn't have scored the three he needed,' he explained.[8]

West Indies' 563 for 8 had taken just short of 240 overs, and England responded by scoring only 71 runs off the final 42 overs of a match Ross called 'as demoralising and painful as the water torture'.[9]

For those lucky enough to be in attendance, Sobers and Wes Hall provided greater entertainment in an intra-squad game ahead of the second Test in Port-of-Spain. Writer CLR James was among them, noting how Hall took it easy when bowling at Sonny Ramadhin for risk of injuring him. 'But when he bowled at Sobers he made up for the restraint,' James recalled. 'He ran to the wicket and delivered as fast as he could, obviously determined not to forego the pleasure of sending Sobers's wicket flying. Sobers returned in kind. I have never seen a fast bowler hit back so hard. It was not a forward push, it was not a drive; it was a hit. Sobers lifted his bat right back and did not lift the ball. He hit one or two of these balls to the on boundary, almost straight drives. Hall did not fancy it and bowled faster. Sobers hit him harder.' This was a carefree manner of batting that Sobers had yet to demonstrate under the weight of responsibility in a real match. James saw it as an example of what he might bring to his game if he could bring himself to unleash 'the panther' inside him.[10]

By the time the second Test ended with the England victory that decided the series, few people were discussing big hits and fast bowling. Not after a crowd riot that prompted Swanton to say that he'd 'never had a sadder tale to tell'.[11]

When West Indies replied to England's first-innings 382, Sobers was out third ball, driving at a wide delivery from Trueman and being caught in the slips by Ken Barrington via a parry by skipper Peter May. Later that day, the third of the match, the home side slid to 98 for 8 when Charran Singh was run out by Dexter's throw. The batsman apparently had no dispute with umpire Lee Kow's decision, but boos turned into a deluge of bottles – some already broken – causing May to usher his fielders to the safety of the square and then to lead them from the field behind police officers when it became clear that a large number of spectators intended to join them in the middle. They left an outbreak of fist fights behind them, with police eventually turning a fire hose on the mob.

According to Swanton, 'It is perhaps a fair assumption that the disturbance, among the few who actually provoked it, was compounded of a mixture of sun and rum, sheer disappointment, and sheer evil mischief.'[12] The glass in the Radio Trinidad commentary point was smashed and it was only the arrival of mounted police that halted the violence, which left 30 people requiring a hospital visit and 60 more needing treatment at the ground. Trinidad prime minister Eric Williams fired off a telegram to Lord's, expressing 'deepest regrets and apologies'.

MCC were happy enough, though, when West Indies were all out for 112 on the fourth morning. The tourists batted again, leaving the home team having to survive ten hours to force a draw. They fell well short, losing by 256 runs, Sobers lbw to Trueman for 31.

* * *

Sobers had every reason to feel trepidation as the series arrived in Kingston, Jamaica for the third Test at Sabina Park, the home ground of Collie Smith. More than ever, he felt the burden of Smith's unfulfilled potential weighing heavily upon him and feared the fans' response. He need not have worried. The Kingston crowd had cheered the skinny Barbadian kid on his Test debut and marvelled at his world-record Test innings. Now they were prepared to forgive him and mourn with him.

'While it was so melancholic that you could feel the sadness in the atmosphere, there was not a scrap of animosity towards me from anyone, not even his family,' he remembered. 'All the people at that famous ground made me feel at home and welcome.'[13]

He was not about to let them down. After Hall had taken seven wickets to dismiss England for 277, Sobers was 17 not out at stumps and began the third day with a burst of fours off Trueman, including a push through midwicket and two cuts over and through the slips. Another triple assault followed, including drives either side of the wicket and a turn off the legs. This was a far more fluent Sobers than Barbados had witnessed. Two square cuts off Allen took him to his fifty and he reached lunch on 70 as May settled for giving the strike to struggling opener Easton McMorris, who scored only nine all morning.

The action slowed after lunch. McMorris retired a few minutes after a ball from Brian Statham had struck him under the heart and caused him to spit blood. When Sobers reached his century by swinging Dexter to the rope, his second 50 runs had taken twice as long as the first. Accelerating again after tea, Sobers had advanced to 142 by stumps, with 'batting of smoothness, power and utmost certainty', according to Ross.[14]

Sobers was out early the next day for 147, in 371 minutes with 21 fours, lbw again to Trueman. He was cheered from the field in a manner that Smith would have recognised and approved of. His departure precipitated a collapse from 299 for 2 to 353 all out and West Indies ended up needing 230 to win in just over four hours on the final day. Sobers's run-out on 19 and the loss of Kanhai for 57 ended the chase.

Sobers compiled another hundred in the fourth Test, a game condemned to a draw by Georgetown's intermittent rain and a painfully slow run-rate. Having almost been caught when he swung wildly before he'd scored a run, Sobers made 109 of the 192 runs that were scored by West Indies on an attritional fourth day. Initially driving with certainty against Trueman and later being tied up by Illingworth, he took 317 minutes to reach three figures. His first 50 runs had taken three and a half hours.

In the evening session, Sobers drove Allen on to the metal roof of the press box, the ball rolling into a canal behind the stand and being spirited away by an opportunistic youngster. 'It was Sobers's day,' said Ross, 'though a hundred is an insignificant landmark to him. He merely shifts the gum from one side of his mouth to the other, and on he goes.'[15] Following the pattern of the previous match, Sobers was 142 overnight and dismissed early the following morning for 145.

Earlier in the match, Sobers, bowling in his cap – as was his habit at the time – was erratic but picked up three wickets via a couple of long hops and a well-placed googly that found Barrington's edge. He gained another victim on a meaningless final day.

A draw in Port-of-Spain, which assured England a series win, saw Sobers take three first-innings wickets as he extracted bounce and turn from a dry wicket. He got one to pop off a length to dismiss centurion Cowdrey – skipper for the last two Tests after May returned home following an abdominal operation. With more rain interrupting West Indies' reply and Cowdrey happy to set defensive fields, Sobers again proceeded in staccato fashion. Ross observed, 'His inability to pace an innings and to impose his own tempo remained odd in one so variously gifted.'[16]

He was out for 92, before taking two more wickets in an England second innings that was declared on the sixth day. Sobers made an unbeaten 49 to lift his record for the series to 709 runs at 101.28. It was appropriate that he should be at the crease at the conclusion of the series for, as Ross pointed out, 'Sobers, baby-faced and gum chewing, seemed in one's mind's eye to have been batting non-stop right through the series.'[17]

His time in the middle had not always been the joyous experience that his batting in Test matches over the next decade or so would frequently be. *Wisden* described Sobers as 'perhaps a little vulnerable when starting his innings' and added, 'Sobers, once allowed to settle, was completely in control and the Englishmen seemed resigned to big innings from him. They managed to prevent him scoring very quickly but rarely looked like getting him out.'[18]

Swanton even suggested 'it would have been even better for his team if someone with his wide range of strokes had made rather fewer runs at a greater speed', although he concluded, 'It is wonderful to think that his maturing powers should be available to the West Indies for another ten years at least. He is only 23 – by no means too late to bring his off-break and googly bowling almost up to the quality of his batting and fielding.

'Sobers is a dangerous bowler when he "drops it" but of course slow left-arm off-break and googly bowling is essentially an extravagant form of attack. Sobers's approach and method, and his loose-limbed, casual air, remind one a lot of Denis

Compton … The promise is there. He could easily become a consistently dangerous change bowler.'[19]

Returning to his batting, the struggle Sobers faced to score at a higher rate was reflective of a series that, while acclaimed in England for the touring team's victory, was dogged by negative tactics and slow over-rates. 'Time-wasting had been seen occasionally before, but never to such a concentrated or planned extent,' *Wisden* noted. 'England must take the biggest share of responsibility.' Having unexpectedly won the second Test, the tourists' only ambition was to avoid defeat in the remaining matches. 'By partly negative cricket and at times overdone time-wasting they succeeded.'[20] According to West Indies captain Alexander, 'Cricket had really descended into a war of attrition and a tug of war.'[21]

Such damage to the Test game was at the forefront of discussion when West Indies prepared for their next action: the 1960/61 tour of Australia, where memories of a dull Ashes series two years earlier were still fresh. Ian Meckiff, who would be taking the new ball against West Indies, described England's 106 runs in a day at Brisbane as 'one of the worst days of all-time'* and recalled, 'A lot of people said cricket was literally going to be dead.'[22]

Yet it turned out to be one of the most thrilling series ever played. The new West Indies captain, in himself a historic appointment, made sure that confidence in the sport was restored.

---

* It was during England's second innings, which saw Trevor Bailey score 68 in 458 minutes.

8

ON THE RISE DOWN UNDER

*'Perfection is not attainable, but if we chase
perfection we can catch excellence.'*

American football coach Vince Lombardi

DEBATE ABOUT the identity of the man who would captain
West Indies on their 1960/61 tour of Australia began during
the home series against England, accelerated by reports that the
West Indies Cricket Board of Control would make its choice at
the conclusion of the MCC tour. To some there was no need for
deliberation or delay: Frank Worrell, not the white incumbent
Gerry Alexander, was the only man for the role.

According to CLR James, the WICBC was thinking 'in
terms of 30 or 40 years ago' by even considering Alexander,
a white wicketkeeper-batsman who had played 20 Tests
without a century by the end of the series against England.
'Their main point (and I have seen it in writing) is that the
captaincy was offered to Worrell twice and, having appointed
Alexander, they are sticking to him,' he wrote in Trinidad's
The Nation in early March ahead of the fourth Test. 'It is
pathetic to see how they miss the point. The question is: what

right has Alexander to be captain of a side on which Frank Worrell is playing?'

James, who saw it as his duty to campaign for a black captain of West Indies, argued that failure to appoint Worrell would be 'a declaration of war and defiance of the opinions and attitudes and expectations of the cricketers and the cricketing public the world over'. The England tourists sensed that the desire for such an outcome was not confined to press and public, but was shared by the home team's players. 'They did not seem keen to be ordered about by Gerry,' suggested Ray Illingworth. 'One felt all the time they were just waiting for someone like Frank Worrell to take over.'[1] A black player, in other words.

Worrell was born in 1924 in the same St Michael parish of Barbados that produced Garry Sobers just over a decade later. With his mother having moved to New York and his father spending most of his time at sea, he was left in the care of his grandmother. High academic achievement at Roebuck Street Boys' School, along with the money sent home by his parents, saw him gain a place at Combermere School, where he established his reputation as one of the island's best young all-rounders.

His involvement with the Barbados senior team was relatively brief, however, following his decision to move to Jamaica in 1947 to work for the Social Welfare Department, not long before his Test debut. He had been led to seek a new home by his discomfort with the strict racial hierarchy and social conditions of Barbados, an island described as 'the world's first slave society' by historian Hilary Beckles, who explained, 'This island is unique, not only for its beauty, but this is where the greatest experiment in human terror in the modern era was first put in place.'[2] Issues of colour and class were inescapable, whereas, according to its former prime minister Michael Manley, 'By the 1950s Jamaica had become a far more open society, with greater social mobility and less precise contours of racial prejudice.'[3]

By the time the Australia tour was looming, Worrell had scored more than 3,000 Test runs, including nine centuries, and had no peer as the statesman of West Indies cricket. Yet players such as Learie Constantine and George Headley had been overlooked for captaincy in the past despite similar claims. 'To put it plainly,' argued Constantine, 'if two men went for a job or were considered for a Test team, and one was black and the other brown skinned, superior ability in the black man would not get him the job or the place. No, not once in one thousand times.'[4]

When Headley was offered the opportunity to lead against England in 1948 it was for two matches only – in Barbados and Jamaica – as part of a curious job share with the white duo, Jeff Stollmeyer and John Goddard. 'These appointments marked the start of a decade of muddle, hubris and humbug by the Board of Control,' said Simon Lister in his biography of Worrell. 'For social reasons it was inconceivable to appoint Headley alone. Instead, loyalty to the deeply entrenched mores and customs of colonial conservatism prevailed.'[5]

Worrell understood only too well that his skin colour and his history of protest against the WICBC's parsimony were given more prominence than his playing record, the esteem in which he was held by his team-mates and his deep understanding of the game. His anger at being overlooked was grounded in injustice, not – as Manley pointed out – 'attributed to some singular egotism'. According to the same writer, 'To have denied him the captaincy in the twilight of his career would have meant his final assassination as a cricketer.'[6]

His claims had by now achieved overwhelming levels of support, notwithstanding English writer Alan Ross calling James 'a malicious xenophobe' and an 'irresponsible agitator'.[7] Conrad Hunte, who would eventually become Worrell's vice-captain, said, 'The timing was perfect. That campaign electrified the people of this country [Barbados], Trinidad and the whole of the Caribbean. The selectors had nowhere to go except make him captain. He was the perfect choice.'[8]

WICBC committee member and former captain Stollmeyer, who was present at the meeting at which Worrell was chosen as captain, revealed that Alexander made the decision easier by stating that he didn't want the job. '[He] had confessed to me that he was suffering from "Worrellitis",' Stollmeyer said.[9]

Even years after such events, Sobers, characteristically, preferred to protect his own views on Worrell's right to the captaincy and any thoughts on whether he felt an injustice had been committed by making him wait. Such debate was beyond his realm of comfort. He preferred simply to praise Worrell's leadership, calling him 'the best captain I played under'. His tribute continued, 'He was able to motivate people and he knew the game. He was able to do things in such a diplomatic way that if you had enough sense you would understand what he was trying to put over. He was never harsh with anybody. He was flexible and would listen.'[10]

Another crucial achievement of Worrell's captaincy would be his ability to make his players act like a team rather than individuals. Writer and professor Maurice St Pierre highlighted the challenge that presented, and the reason why only a black captain could have overcome it. 'The position of the West Indian cricketer was like the man in the ghetto,' he wrote in his 1973 social history of the region's cricket. 'He is so accustomed to grovelling for an existence that when he gets a chance to get out, he climbs on top of his brother's shoulders in his haste to leave the ghetto. Such a situation cannot fail to breed individualism and to abort any sense of team spirit. It is very clearly up to the captain to infuse whatever *esprit de corps* is possible. This was not always possible where the captain was usually white and in many instances a less competent cricketer, not worthy of a position on the team, much less as a leader.'[11]

* * *

Sobers opened his first tour under the new captain by scoring 119 against Western Australia in Perth, an innings that inspired colourful prose. In his book about the tour, Australian writer AG 'Johnnie' Moyes, a former first-class cricketer, called Sobers's batting in a post-lunch session 'sheer joy and certainly the effort of a master player'. He went on:

> His driving was prodigious, as when he lifted one
> from the fast bowler, Hoare ... clean over mid-off and

then crushed a few more to the boundary. His cutting was textbook stuff, feet in perfect position and the bat coming down on top of the ball, while his shots through midwicket were superb, his feet moving into position so quickly and wrists and timing doing the rest. This portion of his innings provided some of the most gorgeous batting seen for years and Sobers in that period certainly wore the purple robes as one of the kings of the batting art. Such stroke play and such amazing power combined gave many people a new conception of what batsmanship could be.[12]

Yet Sobers was out of form by the time the first Test in Brisbane arrived several weeks later. At least he had taken 5 for 63 in the most recent state game against Queensland. No less an expert than Sir Donald Bradman assured him that the runs would come when it mattered and, as Sobers proved throughout his career, imperfect preparation was rarely an impediment to great feats.

He certainly didn't give the appearance of being stressed as the Test approached. According to opponent Lindsay Kline, 'Before the first day of the series there were five or six West Indian players and five or six Australian players in Garry Sobers's room playing calypso records. I have never seen that happen before.'[13]

Worrell won the toss at The Gabba and saw his team lose openers Cammie Smith and Hunte with 42 on the board, sending Sobers, capless and rolled-up sleeves, striding eagerly to the middle. He tucked Alan Davidson, the left-handed taker of both wickets, off his legs for four to get off the mark, but Davidson was soon celebrating the removal of Kanhai to leave West Indies 65 for 3. The scene was set for one of Sobers's greatest innings. 'He came in when we needed somebody to do something extraordinary,' said Hunte. 'Garry was one of those men who rises to the occasion.'[14]

Sobers moved into the 40s in only 51 balls and then launched into an assault on the leg-spin of Aussie captain Richie Benaud, striking him to the boundary three times in the space of four balls. The first time he did it, Sobers stepped out to meet Benaud with an off-drive, expecting a googly, but he held back at the last moment and simply thrashed the ball back past the startled bowler. Benaud withdrew his hand from an attempt to stop the ball and, instead, used it to applaud the stroke. The third boundary in the sequence, laying back to cut, brought Sobers his half-century in only 57 minutes.

Benaud, who had bowled Sobers for a duck in the recent tour match against New South Wales, had not been fooled into thinking he wielded any great power over him. 'Someone wrote that morning that I had the wood on Sobers,' he remembered, 'and that was very unnerving.'[15] He added, 'He played an innings which I put into the top bracket of anything I have seen, an explosive exhibition of strokeplay and power.'[16]

Worrell had foreseen the importance of Sobers being able to combat Benaud. He had told Australian broadcaster Alan McGilvray, 'Benaud doesn't bother me but it bothers me the effect he has on my team.' McGilvray explained, 'He wanted a left-handed and right-handed combination to beat Benaud. He insisted he must get on top and Garry must help him. [Benaud] took only one wicket for 160* in the match.'[17]

Sobers had sensed from his first few balls that his form had returned and was determined to take the attack to the bowlers. 'The pitch was a beauty and I was seeing the ball as big as a breadfruit,' he said. 'In no time it seemed I reached 50 and I couldn't remember having played better.'[18]

Walcott was happy to manoeuvre himself to the non-striker's end as Sobers rocked back to swing Ken Mackay with an extravagant arc of the bat through square leg for four, before forcing him through off with an elegant flourish. At lunch, Sobers was on 69 out of 130 for 3 after what Australian TV commentator Norman May called 'one of the most entertaining mornings in modern cricket history'.

It was exactly the type of cricket that Benaud and Worrell had been promising. 'To still play with the exhilaration that they had, despite losing wickets, signified the whole series,' Davidson recalled. 'Sobers got his fifty in just under the hour and to me that was the finest innings ever played in Test cricket because he didn't just beat us. It's all very well to play shots and beat the field, but Garry in that innings bisected the field so beautifully ... it didn't matter what we bowled to him, he hit it for four.'[19]

Among the qualities that made Sobers so dangerous on the true wickets in Australia was the manner in which he could wreck a bowler's length. If a seamer tried to bowl the standard

---

*   1 for 172 in 55 overs.

containing delivery, a little short of a good length and around off stump, he had the speed of eye, feet and hands to jump into his preferred position on the back foot and hammer the ball through the covers. And as his career developed, aided by his experience on the green wickets of England, his front-foot driving became ever more lethal, meaning there was rarely any profit in a seamer deciding to pitch the ball a little fuller to negate that favourite shot.

According to Davidson, 'His whole defence was attack. His stroke range was so phenomenal. He could hook, he could pull, he had an array of shots which normal batsmen don't have.'[20]

There was more to come for a crowd that grew bigger as the day progressed. At times Sobers swung with such vigour that the effort lifted him off his feet. The 100 partnership with Worrell was achieved in 90 minutes and a fierce drive off Benaud, followed by an extravagant cut and another straight hit took Sobers close to his hundred. On 95, he punched Benaud past mid-off for his 15th four, then smoothly stroked a single to reach his landmark in only 115 balls and 125 minutes. Against left-arm wrist-spinner Lindsay Kline, he remained on one knee to watch his powerful sweep race to the boundary, an extravagant shot that met with disapproval from his captain. According to Mackay, Worrell 'stalked down the wicket and called testily, "Enough of that. This is a Test match. Settle down."'[21] Sobers responded by clipping Meckiff off his legs through midwicket.

In the *Sydney Daily Telegraph*, Phil Tressider said Sobers 'gave Australia's Test bowlers their most humiliating thrashing in decades', while writer and BBC Caribbean Service broadcaster Ernest Eytle recorded, 'Sobers thrashed the bowling in an innings that became the innings of all time.'[22] Even Mackay confessed, 'One cannot "hate" an opponent the way one should in Test cricket when one sees an innings like this.'[23]

'I spent nine hours at first slip,' recalled Bobby Simpson, 'and occasionally he would be trying to square cut or hit shots off the back foot. Richie's toppie [top-spinner], which was a great delivery, used to slide on very quick and I used to be terrified that if he got a nick I was going to get cut in half. But he never did. He just kept smashing it. It was probably the best innings I have ever seen played.'[24]

It was impossible for any Australian opponent to fail to be impressed. 'He was devastating,' said Norman O'Neill, who had never seen a better innings. 'He hit all the bowlers with such tremendous power that our fieldsmen had no chance of stopping his boundaries.'[25]

Moyes concluded, 'Sobers in his first-innings century reached heights of real grandeur. His batting was full of character and he displayed an art that must surely rank him among the immortals.'[26]

When Sobers tamely spooned an easy catch off Meckiff on 132 it brought to an end an innings that – at just under three hours – might not have been anywhere near the longest or largest of Sobers's career but would continue to be considered one of his finest. Had events later in the match not made their own mark in the sport's history, it might have been more widely remembered. 'When Garry scored 254 in Melbourne [in 1972]

I went down and congratulated him,' said McGilvray. 'He said Don Bradman said it was the best ever played. I said, "Well, Don knows a lot about cricket but I wouldn't say it was better than the one you played in Brisbane," and he agreed. That was in my opinion, and in his, his greatest innings.'[27]

West Indies were all out on the second day for 453 and Australia embarked on their reply of 505, Sobers picking up a pair of wickets. He had come on first change to bowl his swinging medium-pacers, delivered with a single sweep of his left-arm, which trailed behind him as he approached the crease; no trigger wind-up or whirling of arms in the style of, for example, team-mate Hall.

Meckiff observed, 'He could take the new ball and swing it in the air both ways and cut it off the wicket with deadly accuracy. His pace off the wicket was far greater than was apparent from a spectator's point of view [and] it often caught batsmen napping.'

In his second innings, Sobers was bowled for 14 by Davidson's inswinging yorker. 'Garry always early in the innings was looking for the ball on the leg side and was prone to hit across it a bit,' the bowler explained. 'I thought I would give him a quick yorker that will move a little bit away from him, which it did, and he hit slightly across the line.'[28]

Meckiff continued, 'A flaw we found in his batting was that early in his innings he nearly always gave us an opportunity to get him out because he played with his bat a long way away from his pads. This proved to be his undoing on quite a few occasions. Davo is quick to find any weakness in a batsman's technique.'[29]

Davidson's six wickets left Australia needing 233 to win in 300 minutes. They fell to 7 for 2 when Sobers took a diving one-handed catch at gully to remove Neil Harvey. The effort dislocated a finger in his right hand, which was quickly put back into place by wicketkeeper Alexander, whose medical experience was as a qualified vet.[*]

Taking tea at 109 for 6, not out batsman Davidson remembered it being typical of the teams' positive approach that Australia were determined to go for the win. With ten minutes remaining, no further wickets had fallen and the home side needed only seven runs. But then Davidson was run out by Joe Solomon's direct hit from midwicket and the final eight-ball over began with five needed and three wickets still to fall. 'Get stuck in,' Worrell urged. 'Bowl tight and field tight.' A single off the first ball was followed by the dismissal of Benaud, caught behind as he swung at Hall's bouncer, which Worrell had ordered him not to bowl. 'What would have happened if he had got a top edge and it had gone for six?' he asked. Hall shrugged at the admonishment.

Two more runs came off the next three balls, meaning four were needed from three balls. It became three off two when Hall, who had earlier risked overthrows with a wild heave at the stumps, failed to hold an easy catch to remove Wally Grout. In his excitement, the bowler had almost run over the better-placed Kanhai as the ball popped up on the leg side. 'I was under it, waiting for it, and from nowhere there was a black arm over my face,' Kanhai recalled.[30]

---

[*] After his cricket career, he became Jamaica's Chief Veterinary Officer.

Turmoil and chaos were everywhere, including in the scorebox. 'The scoreboard operators, I am sure, didn't know what the score was and had stopped operating,' said Colin McDonald.[31] Meckiff smacked the sixth ball into the deep and two runs were taken to tie the scores, only for Grout to be run out as he tried to complete a third. The Australian camp would later complain – only partly in jest – that the ball would have gone for four had the outfield been cut in the morning by groundsmen who claimed to have run out of time.

Before he could bowl the seventh ball of the over, Hall was reminded by Worrell, 'Wes, if you bowl a no-ball you know you will never be able to go back to the West Indies.'[32] Meanwhile, Sobers stood at leg slip, thinking, 'Don't let this ball come to me.'[33] Hall made sure to deliver well short of the popping crease and Kline deflected the ball to square leg. Meckiff charged from the non-striker's end but was short of his ground when Solomon threw down the stumps. Test cricket, in its 498th match, had seen its first tie. 'I don't think I would have hit the stumps under those circumstances,' Sobers confessed.[34]

In the confusion on the field, some had lost track of whether they had won or lost. Meckiff was still choking out, 'Fancy getting beaten like that,' when the players were all back in the pavilion.[35] The teams got together to let the moment sink in and would not leave the ground for several hours. 'The scene in our dressing room afterwards was quite amazing,' Harvey recalled. 'All the West Indians came in and players, officials, pressmen and umpires stood around slapping each other on the back in a frenzy of excitement.'[36] But when Bradman suggested to Benaud that 'this is the greatest thing that has ever happened to the game of cricket', the Australian captain, having seen his team throw away a winning position, replied tersely, 'It's not at the moment.'[37]

It was asking too much, of course, for the remainder of the series to match the drama of Brisbane, but it came mighty close as both teams maintained their commitment to positive play. A sign of the tourists' popularity would be the boos directed at Benaud after Australia successfully appealed for Solomon's wicket when his cap fell on the stumps during the second Test.

Another feature of the series was the camaraderie between the two teams, something in which the gregarious Sobers revelled. After post-play gatherings in the dressing rooms, players from both teams would often go out together, frequently attending the same parties. Worrell's policy of treating his players like grown men who didn't require the constraint of curfews enhanced the happy and relaxed atmosphere. His one rule was that no one should be caught in bars or clubs in the early hours of the morning, preferring them to do their drinking and staying up late in the confines of the hotel, away from prying eyes and accusing fingers. Sobers, a man who could find enjoyment anywhere as long as there was no ticking clock, believed the respect that Worrell engendered from such an approach helped performances, underpinned by the players' fear that such privileges would be withdrawn if they underperformed.

The second Test saw Australia achieve a seven-wicket victory inside four days at Melbourne, where Sobers fell for

9 and 0, before West Indies levelled the series with a 222-run win at Sydney. Sobers hit an unbeaten 152 on the first day, overcoming a scratchy start to reach his century off only 149 balls. By the time he was out for 168, having hit 25 fours and a six, the memories of his more artisan and sedate performances against England a year earlier had been well and truly banished.

In particular, the shot with which he scored his maximum would remain in the memory of the bowler, Meckiff, who thought he had beaten the batsman on the front foot with a slower ball, only to see Sobers hit it as high as possible – more in the hope of making any catch a difficult one – before watching it sail over long-on. 'An exceptional shot,' was the description by Harvey, who added, 'It's the only time I have ever seen it done, something like that.'[38] Moyes described the innings as 'magnificent batting by a master technician who was setting the field alight with the brilliance of his stroke play'.[39]

In the second innings, Alexander's one and only Test century left the home side needing 464 to win. Sobers, opening the bowling after Worrell had taken the new ball with Hall in the first innings, removed opener Simpson, and Lance Gibbs took five wickets as Australia got little more than halfway to their target.

West Indies then seemed certain to take the lead in the series when they had Australia nine wickets down in their second innings at Adelaide with more than an hour and a half remaining and a winning total far in the distance. Sobers had taken three wickets and Gibbs had achieved a hat-trick as Australia got within 27 runs of West Indies' first-innings 393, before Kanhai – nimble on his feet but quick to lose his balance while sweeping – scored his second century of the match in a declared total of 432 for 6.

Much had been made in the press of a rivalry between Kanhai and Sobers, highlighting Kanhai's apparent desire to score more than the man he had grown up alongside in Test cricket. While insisting there was no animosity between the two, Sobers admitted that Worrell had been forced to address the dynamic and had 'sorted it out in his usual perceptive and diplomatic manner'. Worrell had joked that batting at number three brought the best out of Kanhai because, without knowing what Sobers might achieve further down the order, he would do his damnedest to score as many as possible.[40]

'My rivalry with Sobey might have been there initially,' Kanhai admitted years later, 'but then Frank Worrell talked to us about how we were both bulwarks of the batting.'[41] The relationship between Sobers and Kanhai would remain the subject of debate throughout international careers that ran virtually parallel, with the Guyanese man ending up as Sobers's last Test captain. 'I think there was a rivalry between the pair,' observed Davidson, although he added, 'also admiration.'[42]

Sobers took two wickets – reaching 50 in Test cricket – as Australia looked to save the game. When last man Kline came to the crease, the Australian cause seemed lost. Sobers was bowling wrist-spin from one end and standing under the batsman's nose at silly mid-off at the other. Left-hander Mackay pushed forward at Worrell and Sobers snapped up the ball. The

West Indies players barely bothered to appeal as they turned towards the pavilion. Yet umpire Col Egar was adamant that Mackay's defensive shot had jammed into the ground. Looking incredulous under the upturned brim of his floppy sun hat, Sobers tossed the ball back to the bowler's end and his team-mates made no attempt to hide their disapproval. Worrell was required to step forward to calm his players and remind them that there was still plenty of time.

There was almost an hour remaining when the new ball was taken. West Indies hurried through the overs to bowl as many as possible, although some suggested a little more thought and precision might have been more profitable. Mackay and Kline, with the whole of the fielding team clustered around, held firm to save the game.

It meant that the series would be decided in the fifth match in Melbourne, where 90,000-plus attended the second day's play and the other four days averaged more than 45,000, which added up to a Test record at the time Sobers made 64 in his team's total of 292, followed by his first five-wicket haul in Test cricket in Australia's reply of 356. He removed both openers, Simpson and McDonald, after they had put on 146 and helped to restrict the home team's total after they'd stood at 309 for 5. Sobers had begun the innings bowling wrist-spin, but with Worrell unable to bowl on day three Moyes reported, 'Sobers, bowling fast-medium, kept one end going from start of play until the innings finished just before ten minutes to three – except for one over which Hall bowled – and his 5 for 120 off 44 overs was a splendid piece of sustained hostility.' Sobers's workload had been increased by the absence of Valentine, off the field with swollen fingers caused by playing the bongo drums.

When Australia began their second innings late on the fourth day, they needed 258 to win. Benaud sent out Simpson with the instruction to 'take Hall apart'. Simpson responded by scoring 18 off Hall's first over and nine more in his second. 'That was very important in the context of the way the game was going,' Benaud explained.[43]

Having been easing towards victory at 236 for 5, Australia lost two more wickets. But they needed only four to win when Grout cut Valentine behind the wicket and ran two, only for wicketkeeper Alexander to point at the fallen bail. 'He got an inside edge and it went on to the stumps … the bail fell forward,' claimed Alexander, who was thought by some to have inadvertently dislodged the bail himself, perhaps by stepping on a crack that made the stump move.[44]

Sobers accepted that if umpire Egar had made a wrong call it was an honest mistake and wondered if Grout had sportingly balanced the books when he swung carelessly at the next ball he faced from Valentine and skied a catch. A two-wicket victory was completed a few balls later, making Australia 2-1 series winners and the inaugural holders of the Frank Worrell Trophy, the prize having been named to honour the touring captain, who had done so much to endear himself and his team to the public.

After being introduced by Bradman to hand over the trophy to Benaud in front of the MCG fans, Worrell had to delay his turn at the microphone while the crowd completed a rendition of 'For He's a Jolly Good Fellow'. Manley noted, 'It is fair to say that Frank Worrell … struck a blow for cricket and simultaneously redeemed all the pledges that seemed inherent in his great predecessors, Headley and Constantine. You would have to be black, and from a colonial background, to understand fully what this meant to the West Indies.'[45]

Yet Worrell had clearly come to mean a lot to the people of Australia, too. Benaud's comment that he 'will remain in the hearts of cricket lovers in this country for many a long day' was endorsed two days later when more than 50,000 lined the Melbourne streets to cheer the West Indies team as they were paraded in open-top Triumph Heralds while confetti and streamers fell around them.

'I was there trying to fight my way through to the Town Hall,' Meckiff remembered. 'I had a lump in my throat – I couldn't help it as I looked at my friends from the West Indies, who were clearly overwhelmed and didn't bother to stop the tears streaming down their faces.'[46]

Sobers described the well-wishers as 'a wonderful bunch of people who appreciated what a group of cricketers from another country came and did.'[47] Which was all somewhat ironic given that this was a time when the 'White Australian Policy' was restricting the opportunities for people of colour in the country. Officially known as the Immigration Restriction Act 1901, the policy aimed to restrict non-white immigrants to Australia – who could work or study for a maximum of five years but not settle permanently – and allowed for the deportation of migrants considered 'undesirable'.

Sobers, who recalled receiving one racist remark during all the years he played in Australia – making the offender pay by scoring a century – would never have dreamt of raising such contentious issues during cocktail-party small talk. Yet team-mate Hall, a future politician, was unafraid to challenge the cricket-loving prime minister, Sir Robert Menzies, with, 'I really don't understand your White Australian Policy. My brother, who is better educated and a nicer guy, you won't have, but you will have me because I play cricket.'[48]

It was a contradiction highlighted by the Dean of Melbourne, Dr Barton Babbage. 'It is a sobering and humbling thought that the West Indians, whom Australia welcomes as cricketers, would not be welcome as citizens,' he said as the tour concluded. 'Their skin is the wrong colour. They may play with us but they may not stay with us. It may be that the game of cricket will pave the way for more generous national policies. If only we could cultivate the spirit of cricket in all our dealings, one with the other. It is not far from the spirit of Christ.'

9

SHIELD OF STRENGTH

'Haul away, you rollin' king! Heave
away, haul away!
Oh hear me sing! We're bound for South Australia.'

'South Australia', traditional sea shanty

GARRY SOBERS had left a mighty impression on the
Australian cricketing public. At his best, Johnnie Moyes
suggested, Sobers was 'probably the finest player in contemporary
cricket', someone who had 'a touch of genius'. But there was
an air of the mercurial about his play, which could make him
appear 'careless' and not as reliable as Rohan Kanhai. 'He failed
far too often for one of his ability,' Moyes concluded.[1]

Yet that could not dampen Sir Donald Bradman's desire
to see him playing for South Australia. He raised the subject
several times during the West Indies' tour. Finally, when Sobers
was back in England for the 1961 summer, he informed him
that he had secured for him a job in Adelaide that would allow
him to play grade cricket and for the state in the Sheffield
Shield – there being no 'professional' cricketers in Australia at
that time.

Sobers would work in a public relations capacity for Victoria Cars Services, where his boss, Gordon Winkley, was thrilled to have a superstar on the payroll and a famous partner on the golf course. According to Sobers, Winkley would be responsible for 'encouraging and opening up my golf play', adding, 'Pity I didn't take it up earlier in life.'[2]

Sobers would be paid A£500* by Victoria Cars for the summer, which was effectively his salary for turning out for Prospect District Cricket Club, where Winkley was a vice-president. 'We won the premiership this season without Sobers,' crowed club secretary Mel McInnes. 'Just imagine what we will do with him next season.' A further A£500, in essence to cover his appearances for South Australia, would be forthcoming from the local newspaper, *The Advertiser*, in return for a ghostwritten weekly column and his participation in *Advertiser*-branded coaching clinics.

In the meantime, the South Australia Cricket Association had made sure, by writing to immigration minister Sir Alexander Downer, that there would be no infraction of the White Australia Policy if Sobers was to be employed for several months a year for three years. Downer, a South Australian, gave them the reassurance they sought and also contacted the London-based immigration office to ensure there would be no obstacles when Sobers travelled.

What followed was three summers of high achievement and high jinks, summarised by author Michael Sexton thus:

---

* The Australian pound was replaced by the Australian dollar as the nation's currency when decimalisation was introduced in 1966.

'He charged past midnight, wore out barmen, gambled, chased skirts and lit every scene with the sunshine of possibility that beamed out of him.'[3]

Lodging in his first Australian season with another club vice-president, Len Sandford, Sobers reported for duty late in 1961 at Prospect Oval, in one of Adelaide's northern suburbs. He surprised team-mates by being the first to show for training and proceeded to bamboozle them in the nets with his variety of bowling. 'He could have bowled right-handed to me and I would have struggled,' said Bob Gilbourne.[4]

Club captain John Ducker, the back-up wicketkeeper for South Australia, deferred to Sobers in asking where he would like to bat – number four, so that he could assess what type of innings was needed – but never found the superstar threatening to undermine his authority.

Sobers's first game for his club was against Kensington, the team Prospect had beaten in the previous year's Grade A grand final. Matches were spread over two consecutive Saturdays, with more than 1,000 spectators watching Sobers take three wickets on the first day. An even bigger, more excited crowd turned up to watch him bat the following week, only to see him prod indecisively at his first ball and send a return catch to bowler Ken Horsnell. 'O, Mr Sobers!' read the advertising placards for the next day's *Sunday Mail*. There was at least time left in the match for Sobers to claim 6 for 13 when Kensington batted again.

The following week, he faced University's left-arm spinner David Sincock and was bowled first ball by a delivery that turned so much Sobers needed the umpire to point out that his wicket was broken. In the second innings, he holed out off a Sincock long hop for 1. Again, he compensated by taking eight wickets in the match.

Sobers was one of three West Indies players in Australia that summer. In his Sheffield Shield debut for South Australia he finished on the losing team after a brilliant second-innings century by Kanhai for Western Australia, and he lost his second match against Wes Hall and Queensland. South Australia would end up winning only three and losing five of their eight matches.

Wickets proved easier to come by than runs and by the time Sobers played his seventh and final Sheffield Shield game of the season, against New South Wales at the Adelaide Oval, he had only a couple of half-centuries to his name. South Australia captain Les Favell suggested he had struggled with the gap in quality between club and Shield cricket. Sobers was out for 2 as his team surrendered a first-innings lead of 59. But the big innings fans had been waiting for arrived at last when South Australia batted again. Ending the second day unbeaten on 38, Sobers set about the bowling the next day to reach 251. However NSW captain Richie Benaud organised his bowlers, Sobers dismantled them, the most memorable shot coming off an Alan Davidson bouncer with the new ball that he swatted over mid-on for six.

According to Ian McLachlan in the field, 'He leant back with a perfectly straight bat and, with all that amazing flexibility you used to see with Tiger Woods on the golf course, he hit a six which landed just five yards short of the right-hand part of the bar. I measured it one day and it was about 135 yards off the back foot with those light bats.'[5]

Barry Gibbs, a future executive manager of the SACA, was in the crowd, marvelling at how anyone could play such a shot with 'little more than a flourish'. He said, 'Watching Garry Sobers play at the Adelaide Oval was a wonderful privilege for the many thousands who were able to do so. It took cricket watching to a new plane.'[6]

One day later, Sobers completed South Australia's victory – the only defeat of their opponents' season – by taking 6 for 72, the best figures of his first-class career at the time. With West Indies due to begin a Test series against India three days later, the game signalled the end of Sobers's first state cricket campaign, which he completed with 573 runs at 44.08 and 35 wickets at 22.09. His six matches for Prospect had produced only 98 runs, with a top score of 58, but an impressive 51 wickets at 12.80. It was all a mere warm-up for what was to come over the next two seasons.

In the meantime, Sobers's early departure, for which he forfeited A£125 of his season's salary, left a slot open for 18-year-old leg-spinning all-rounder Ian Chappell. Grandson of former Australian captain Vic Richardson, Chappell had come to the attention of the state selectors largely via an innings of 67 for Glenelg against Prospect's Sobers-led attack a couple of months earlier, following it up with his first grade century in his next match. 'I was picked for South Australia not for the amount of runs I scored but for who I got them against,' Chappell suggested.[7]

* * *

Over the next two Australian summers, Sobers achieved something no cricketer had ever. Twice. He scored 1,000 first-class runs and took 50 wickets in the same season.

But first the diligence of the SACA resolved a medical issue that might have posed a real threat to his longevity as a cricketer. For about five years he had noticed a steadily worsening pain and stiffness in his left knee. Yet, much like Ben Stokes six decades or so later, his hectic schedule meant he could never quite find the time to get it fixed.

To protect their investment, the SACA arranged – insisted, in fact – for Sobers to see an orthopaedic surgeon, Sir Reginald Watson-Jones, in London at the completion of his 1962 English season, which he cut short in order to receive treatment. Sobers was told that his knee resembled that of a man twice his age and an operation was needed to relieve compression under the kneecap. The SACA paid for the procedure, including rehabilitation costs, and suggested that Sobers returned to Australia for the new season on a cruise ship, allowing him to undertake regular exercise, rather than being bent double in an aeroplane. 'I have never worked so hard as I did on that boat,' he said, determined to reward the SACA for its investment.[8]

With England touring for an Ashes series in 1962/63, the Sheffield Shield ran the risk of being overlooked, but Sobers did his best to keep it to the forefront, helping South Australia move up from the previous season's third place to second. He made a disastrous start with the bat, out for 1 and 0 against Victoria, but again posted career-best bowling figures with 6 for 41 in the first innings. Then he ran into the MCC party for the first of two meetings during their tour, run out by Brian Statham one short of a century in the second innings after making 42 in the first. England bowler Barry Knight said it was 'the first time I thought I was watching an exceptional cricketer'. He continued, 'What stood out to me was that Garry could do whatever he liked on a good batting wicket; he scored at will. Those two innings were works of art. They could have been framed and hung next to the Mona Lisa.'[9]

When the teams clashed once more over Christmas, Sobers was again denied three figures, making 89 and 75 not out. MCC seamer David Larter remembered, 'In this game I had bowled a pretty good over and tried a yorker for my last ball. This was whipped through midwicket before anyone moved and my abiding memory is this flashing toothy smile and a growl of, "Well bowled."'[10] In between the two MCC matches, he scored back-to-back centuries against Western Australia and New South Wales.

In the return against Western Australia in Perth, Sobers was at his most lethal with the ball, ripping out the top of the order on his way to another six-wicket haul to seal victory. And in the penultimate match of the season, against Queensland in Brisbane, he made his great friend, Hall, pay for dropping him early in an innings of 196. Furious at his blunder, Hall pitched faster and shorter, watching the ball fly to greater distances behind square leg, before one shot cleared the midwicket fence to take Sobers into the 90s. 'No other batsman had ever done that to me,' he recalled. 'Even the great hookers ... always hit it backward of square.'[11]

That night, over dinner, Hall asked Sobers how he'd managed to react quickly enough to play the shot. 'His explanation taught me a sobering lesson,' Hall recounted. 'He said if my hand was forward of vertical at the point of release, he knew it would be a short ball and he would be ready on the back foot to hit me out the ground.' Such episodes left Hall to draw only one conclusion. 'I don't believe there is anybody in the world who understands cricket like Sobers.'[12]

By the end of the season, Sobers had racked up 1,006 runs for his state team, averaging 62.87, and had taken 51 wickets at the cost of 26.56 apiece. And he'd enjoyed himself to the full. Living in a hotel, his regular late-night companions were Prospect team-mate 'Clacker' Clarke and South Australian bowler Neil Hawke, who marvelled at his powers of recovery and his ability to sleep off a late night in the dressing room until it was time to take the field.

Sobers rarely felt the need to know what had been going on before his turn at the crease. 'I wouldn't know, because I'd be sleeping,' he once explained. 'That was the time for sleeping for me. I'd never watch. Somebody would wake me when it was time to go in. On the cricket field you have to have a concentration that you can rely on to take you beyond the average man. You cannot waste those levels of concentration. It has to be fresh and ready when you need it.'[13]

The goodwill trips South Australia made to country locations for exhibition games were welcomed by Sobers as an opportunity to experience even more of what this wonderful country had to offer. After a night out in Crystal Brook, Sobers napped his way through the early stages of the match against the Rocky River Association before going in at number eight and smashing a quick hundred.

It was his love of gambling that raised eyebrows among team-mates as he readily parted with his wages in all kinds of betting activity, from slot machines to casinos and racetracks. Hawke said that 'gambling comes to him as naturally as playing cricket, and he will back a trotter as readily as hit a four'.[14] Barry Jarman told Sexton about the time Sobers gave him A£400 he'd won on a horse to look after, instructing him not to let him have any of it. When Sobers later began pestering him for the money, Jarman was forced to escape by taxi to their shared hotel room where he placed it under Sobers's pillow.

* * *

Sobers returned for his third season with South Australia as champion of the world, his performances in England on the victorious 1963 West Indies tour having cemented his status as the sport's premier exponent.

An early encounter with the Test visitors to the country, South Africa, held a special meaning. Knowing he would never, in the days of apartheid, have the opportunity to wear his West Indies colours against them, he asked skipper Favell if he could bat in his maroon international cap. Receiving the permission he sought, he turned up the peak so that he looked like a jockey and strode out to hit 155 in 286 minutes, including 18 fours. He had achieved his mission of making sure the South Africans got a good long look at the West Indies' headwear.

Chappell, who batted a couple of places below Sobers and made an unbeaten half-century himself, recalled, 'It was mostly a magnificent experience batting down the other end to Garry. The only problem was he was such a hard hitter of the ball and straight driver you had to really be on your toes at the other end because he hit a lot of balls hard straight down the pitch. You had to make sure you were quickly back in your crease so you didn't get run out off the bowler's hand or get collected with one.'

It was Sobers who had suggested over a beer that Chappell, after being bowled behind his legs by Australian Test bowler Ian Meckiff, switch to a leg-stump guard. 'What I will never forget is that here was this guy who was the greatest cricketer in the world and he was treating me as an equal. For an 18, 19, 20-year-old kid just the opportunity of batting down the other end to him would have been enough, but for him to treat me as an equal always meant a lot to me as a human being.'[15]

Chappell also remembered the match, in December 1962, when he scored his maiden first-class century in the first innings against New South Wales, but was struggling in the second when Benaud bowled round the wicket into the bowlers' footmarks as South Australia chased 202 to win. Batting at the other end, Sobers put his arm round his partner in mid-pitch and assured him, 'Don't worry, son. It will be over soon.' Chappell assumed he was being dismissive of his chances of survival. Instead, Sobers took control of the situation, hitting fours at both ends, stealing singles at the end of overs and finishing 107 not out to steer his team home without the loss of any more wickets.[16]

By the end of the 1963/64 Sheffield Shield season, Sobers had scored five hundreds, led the competition with 973 runs and helped South Australia win their first title for 11 years. In all first-class games, his 1,128 runs were scored at an average of 80.57 and his 51 wickets were taken at 28.25. He had finally been productive with the bat for Prospect, scoring 175 in his final match and averaging 79.50 to help secure them another Grade A premiership.

His highest first-class score was achieved in Perth, after some heavy losses at the track the night before. Glamorgan batsman Alan Jones, who was spending the season with Western Australia, chatted with Sobers at the close of the first day, which was New Year's Day. 'In those days the opposition came into our dressing room to have a drink,' he explained. 'I asked Garry where he was going that evening and he said, "I am going across the road to the trots."* He was quite a big gambler in those days. I said that our boys were going across, too.' Jones didn't run into Sobers at the races but passed him the next morning as they went to and from the nets. 'It was very rare that Garry had a net,' he added.

'How did you go last night?' Jones enquired.

'Alan, I had a terrible night,' came the reply. 'I lost A£150. But it is OK, I am going to make it back today.'

---

* Gloucester Park trotting track, which sits adjacent to the WACA ground.

Jones continued, 'I had no idea what he meant. Anyway, when he came in to bat he just took us apart. He got 195 and Barry Jarman also got a hundred. That evening he came into the dressing room again and I said, "Garry, you said to me this morning you were going to make up your A£150 today. What did you mean?" He said, "Every run I get over 50 for South Australia, they give me a pound." So he was a fiver short!'[17]

As well as the need to refill his wallet, Sobers had also been fired up by a radio commentator's suggestion at lunch that he was struggling against leg-spinner Terry Jenner. 'We made sure Garry knew about this and when he went back after lunch he was after someone's blood,' Favell remembered.[18] Sobers's response was to blast 23 fours and a six in his 223-minute innings. 'He was such a joy to watch,' said Jones. 'He had this lovely follow-through and sometimes the bat would come through so quickly you could hear it whoosh through the air. It was incredible. His timing and footwork were so good and he made the game look so easy. David Gower was a brilliant timer of the ball but Garry was the tops.'[19]

With the ball, Sobers was used by Favell as a three-setting bowling machine. His swing bowling had developed to the point where he was regularly taking the new ball. Jones, one of his seven victims in that Perth contest, argued, 'His best bowling was his quick stuff, no doubt about that. The odd bouncer he bowled was just as quick as Wes Hall and he could swing the ball back into you or push it across. He bowled such a good line and length that he made you play at him all the time.'[20]

His skipper remained keen to employ both of his slow variations as well. Frequently, after an opening spell, Sobers would hear Favell call, 'Right, new bowler. Sobers from the other end bowling orthodox slow left-arm,' and a few overs later, 'Sobers from the other end, bowling wrist-spin.'

Chappell remembered one game in which Sobers, fielding at leg slip, stepped forward to replace the bails on the stumps before the match official reached the crease. 'Ah,' said wicketkeeper Jarman. 'You've done everything else in this game – now you want to umpire.'[21]

As someone who was keen to be involved all day and who felt the responsibility of being paid to perform, Sobers was quite happy when Favell asked him for 'just a few overs'. Not to mention that he was now effectively being paid by the wicket, having moved to an incentive-based salary of A£40 per week, plus additional cash for runs and A£5 per wicket in either state or grade cricket.

Again, his paymasters were varied, including *The Advertiser*, Coca-Cola and John Martin's department store, for whom he undertook appearances and public relations duties. He also had use of a car.

By the business end of the season, with South Australia looking to maintain top spot in the Sheffield Shield, it was as a new-ball bowler that Sobers was at his most effective, developing a happy knack of removing the leading opposition batsmen in single figures. It was a trait highlighted by CLR James in his essay for the book, *The Greatest All-Rounders*. 'It is impossible to find within recent years another fast bowler who in big cricket so regularly dismissed for little or nothing the opening batsmen on the other side,' he wrote.[22]

In the penultimate game against New South Wales, the first three wickets fell to Sobers – each man out for a duck – as he returned figures of 6 for 81. Despite a Sobers first-innings century, South Australia went down by six runs with two minutes remaining, meaning they needed to beat Victoria in their final match to maintain a chance of being champions.

Favell called a team meeting on the eve of the match, but his decision to stage it at the South Terrace apartment in which Sobers was now living meant that the host treated it more like a party. He had staged what he called 'whoop-ups' at regular intervals during the season and now he handed out beers and casually assured his captain – frustrated that no one was taking the meeting seriously – that he'd score a century and take five wickets.

Sobers began delivering on his promise by taking two Victoria wickets with only ten on the board and finishing with three wickets and three catches as the visitors were bowled out for 101. Having scored 124 in a South Australia total of 480, he then took six second-innings wickets to seal victory. This time, he reduced the opposition to 22 for 3 by removing Test men Bill Lawry, Ian Redpath and Bob Cowper inside his first 21 deliveries. The front page of *The Advertiser* pictured Favell and Sobers striding side by side in triumph from the field.

'We were a very happy team in South Australia and I am proud that they considered me mainly responsible for their winning the Sheffield Shield in the 1963/64 season,' he said.

'Winning with South Australia and the Prospect club was my way of saying thank you for your generosity to me, for your unlimited kindness, your trust and above all your warm and sincere friendship.'[23]

Sobers left Adelaide with many memories of good times. He'd even found himself making tabloid headlines for a romantic link with local television presenter Glenys O'Brien. More importantly, he felt that his Sheffield Shield experience had added to his arsenal as a player. He said a few years later, 'English league cricket is grand to play, but in Australia their league cricket is often of higher standard than county cricket. And I think there are no other games played against any other part of the world as hard as Australia's Sheffield Shield cricket.'[24]

10

WORRELL'S FINAL TRIUMPH

'Man's greatness consists in his ability to do, and
the proper application of his powers to things
needed to be done.'

African-American reformer Frederick Douglass

THE WEST Indies tourists, led again by Frank Worrell, travelled to England in the spring of 1963 by either boat or plane, according to their previous commitments. As had been the case in Australia a few years earlier, their arrival couldn't come soon enough.

'The game was on its beam ends when West Indies arrived,' said the *Daily Mail*'s Ian Wooldridge in his account of the summer. 'A poor series against Pakistan [in 1962] followed by a grim finish in the winter campaign in Australia had left a mood of cynicism and despair. We looked to Worrell to work a miracle.' Referring to the vessel that carried the bulk of the West Indies party, he added, 'If the good ship *Golfito* had been bringing back receipt for the last instalment of the national debt it could hardly have been awaited more eagerly.'[1]

Caribbean-based writer JS 'Jack' Barker had no doubt that the tourists, along with the large number of supporters they would attract from Britain's West Indian immigrant community, would deliver a summer of high spectacle. 'On the field or off it, player or spectator, the West Indian is there to enjoy himself,' he said. 'He has only contempt for the death before dishonour approach of the rest of the world.'[2]

Since the epic 1960/61 series in Australia, which they lost narrowly, West Indies had played only one series, overwhelming India 5-0 in the early months of 1962. Sobers had amazed onlookers by arriving in Port-of-Spain for the first Test looking remarkably fresh barely three days after finishing his Sheffield Shield season in Australia. In the meantime he had flown from Adelaide to Sydney and then, via various refuelling stops, to New York, where he had raced around the airport to find an airline heading to Trinidad. Forced to stand in the field when India won the toss a few hours later, Sobers's performance prompted Tony Cozier to write in the *Barbados Daily News*, 'With the ball moving around, it was inevitable that something would happen and soon, defying medical theory about jet-lag, he was casually collecting slip catches off Contractor and Umrigar.'

Sobers averaged more than 70 with the bat and picked up 23 wickets, the most he had taken in a single series. In the second Test, played in Kingston, he continued to fulfil his pledge to Collie Smith by treating the Jamaican crowd to another century, 153 in 320 minutes with 11 fours and four sixes. The fifth and final Test was also at Sabina Park and once again Sobers delivered, scoring a century in his fourth consecutive match at the ground and taking five wickets for the first time in a home Test match.

The West Indies selectors named the squad to tour England seven months in advance, their hands forced by the imperative of giving amateur players, who comprised the majority of the party, an opportunity to get their affairs in order ahead of a six-month trip. It also allowed time for the professionals to negotiate their contracts.

In the case of Sobers, that was no straightforward matter; not when the £800 basic pay he was offered, plus a daily expense allowance, meant he could earn more by signing up for another year of league cricket, for which he would be required to work a lot less. According to Wes Hall, 'the £800 was less generous than it appeared' because some players had to give up Australian earnings by departing early from their Sheffield Shield teams.[3]

In Australia when he received his offer, Sobers spoke with Sir Donald Bradman, who agreed that he was being treated unfairly and was deserving of more. Yet Bradman urged him to see the tour as 'perhaps the beginning of something else for you'.[4] Richie Benaud echoed those views when he ran into Sobers. And when Worrell wrote to him stressing the importance of representing his country, Sobers sent a telegram to a relieved West Indies Cricket Board of Control accepting their terms.

With only one century in the eight first-class games he played before the first Test,[*] Sobers began earning his wages in the first innings when the series began at Old Trafford,

---

[*] Sobers ended up playing in 24 of the 30 first-class matches on the tour.

making 64 in a West Indies total of 501 for 6, anchored by Conrad Hunte's 182. The highlights of Sobers's knock were a hooked six off Brian Statham and a straight drive beyond the rope against off-spinner David Allen. According to Wooldridge he was 'bending like a longbow' as he hit the ball just wide of the sightscreen.[5] He picked up two wickets in each innings as West Indies won by ten wickets, Lance Gibbs having taken 11 wickets in the match.

Sobers found himself at the centre of controversy in the one game the tourists played ahead of the second Test at Lord's, a six-wicket win against Sussex. Cricket's no-ball law had long been a matter of contention and, until this summer, had required a bowler to land his back foot safely behind the bowling crease, regardless of where his front foot ended up. Canny fast bowlers had perfected the art of 'dragging' their back foot after landing it in safe territory, which meant their front foot might be several feet down the pitch when they delivered the ball. A new rule was being trialled in county cricket ahead of wider adoption, requiring part of the front foot to be behind the popping crease. It was agreed that the experimental rule would not be applied to West Indies' matches, yet umpire Fred Price began calling Sobers repeatedly for 'dragging' on the second day at Hove.

Sobers demonstrated his frustration by running up and going through his action without bowling the ball, forcing Price, who had again called 'no-ball', to yell over to the scorers to cancel his decision. The West Indies players were furious and, without the calming influence of Worrell, resting while Alf Valentine led the team, they complained loudly. Price responded by firing off a letter to MCC complaining about them. Sobers, having been given out lbw for 99 in the first innings, finished the match by smashing two successive sixes.

There was drama of a far more palatable nature in the second Test, a match that was instantly ranked alongside the tied Test at Brisbane for excitement. Barker felt bold enough to call it 'the greatest, most electrifying Test match ever seen in England'.[6]

Under grey skies on a challenging Lord's pitch, Sobers was promoted to number three, with the purpose of setting about Derek Shackleton, the 38-year-old England had brought back after more than 11 years to replace Statham. He managed only two scoring shots in his first half-hour at the crease, before hooking and slashing Shackleton for fours. He also enjoyed the introduction of Brian Close's medium-pacers before edging Allen on 42.

West Indies were dismissed for 301, to which England replied with 297, an innings that included a sparkling 70 by Dexter, one of the most famous short innings in Lord's history. In little more than an hour, the England skipper lifted his team from 10 for 2 to a score of 102 before Sobers turned a ball inside his defensive shot and trapped him lbw. 'The faster they bowled the more savagely he cut and drove and pulled them,' Wooldridge said of a 75-ball innings that included ten fours.

That West Indies achieved a small first-innings lead was due largely to Charlie Griffith, who removed England's openers and took five wickets. Born in Barbados a couple of years after Sobers, Griffith was to be the tour's controversial figure. It had been his short ball in a tour match at Kensington Oval that had struck Indian captain Nari Contractor on the back of the skull, causing a blood clot that ended his career and almost took his life. Worrell had been among those who volunteered to give blood to help save him.

Griffith would take 119 first-class wickets on his first England tour, including 32 in the Tests. But he was dogged by accusations of throwing, especially when he bowled a bouncer or yorker, even though he was not no-balled in a Test match. Sobers felt Griffith – whose habit of collapsing his front leg at the point of delivery and sometimes shortening his arm swing gave him a more jerky, angular action than partner Hall – was 'unfairly persecuted'[7]. Griffith became withdrawn and gave outsiders the impression of surliness, which was not his usual demeanour.

At Lord's, once West Indies had been bowled out for 229 in their second innings, Griffith and Hall, bowling from the Pavilion End with no sightscreen behind him, delivered 70 of the 91 overs in a nail-biting run chase over a rain-hit final two days. England, having not scored 200 to win a home Test since 1902, required 234, a distant-looking target at 31 for 3. Then Cowdrey was struck above the right wrist by a rising ball from Hall, departing with a fractured forearm.

The start of the final day was delayed until 2.20 p.m. and, after Ken Barrington was out for his second half-century of the game, England required 104 in 150 minutes with four wickets down. It was Close's turn to play an innings of 70 that, while it could hardly have been different in nature to Dexter's of the same score, would live alongside it in Lord's lore. Taking the majority of the deliveries from Hall, who charged in unchanged all day, Close avoided putting his bat in the way of dangerously flying short balls by letting them thump into his torso. 'He took Hall's thunder on thigh, hip, chest and shoulder,' Barker recorded. 'His judgement was unfailing.'[8]

At the close of play, Close would show off his right side, with its patchwork of circular welts and bruises, to press photographers – and would reprise his performance, albeit for far fewer runs, against Michael Holding, Wayne Daniel and Andy Roberts at Old Trafford 13 years later.

With 20 minutes remaining, England needed 15, West Indies three wickets. The BBC interrupted its scheduled programmes to remain at Lord's. At Wimbledon, English reporters turned their backs on what was happening on the tennis courts to crowd around the television in the press room. Wooldridge recalled, 'In my own office, the *Daily Mail*, the production of the paper came to a standstill. More than 100 men had stood on chairs and desks and window ledges to get a glimpse of the tiny televised figures playing out the last act of the drama. Within two minutes of its end I was receiving telephoned orders from my editor, Michael Randall, to describe the last over, ball by ball, thrill by thrill, for the front page.'[9]

Towards the end of his innings, Close began walking down the wicket to Hall and Griffith. The first time he did it to Hall, the bowler pulled up without delivering and seemed to rick his back. Close smiled. But when he did it again against

Griffith, a feathered touch down the leg side was taken by Deryck Murray.

England began the final over needing eight. During the previous over, Brian Johnston had told BBC's viewers, 'Not many people can have seen a better Test than this ever.' Shackleton and Allen took singles off the second and third balls, but when Shackleton was late seeing Allen running down the wicket after the fourth, Worrell won the race to the stumps at the non-striker's end. Cowdrey came out, to a hero's reception, with his left arm in plaster – an act that looked more dramatic than it was, given that there was no imperative for him to face a delivery. Allen dropped a dead bat on the final two balls and the match was drawn.

It was considerably less tense at Edgbaston, where England levelled the series with a 217-run win, in spite of what Wooldridge called 'a remarkable demonstration of how it was that West Indies were virtually going into the Tests as a 13-man team'. Of course, he was alluding to Sobers, who, as a seamer, was 'about to exploit English conditions as though he had been born to them'.[10]

After several days of rain produced a soft, green wicket, England found Sobers swinging and cutting the ball with devastating effect. 'His lithe and supple style enabled him to bowl without stress and to move the ball with deceptive cunning,' wrote The Times' correspondent John Woodcock. He bowled Dexter with a quick ball and dismissed Barrington with a seamer that took the inside edge before hitting his stumps. Another delivery swerved back in to deceive Micky Stewart, who was lbw after playing no shot. In the *Daily Mirror*, Brian Chapman reckoned he had 'moved the ball a colossal footage across and away from the bat', while Barker would call his spell on the first day '20 overs and nearly three hours of intelligent, controlled hostility'.[11] Sobers completed a five-wicket haul on the second day by getting Jim Parks to edge behind and winning an lbw decision against Close.

England's 216 was enough to earn them a first-innings lead of 30. Then the home team declared on 278 before shooting out West Indies for 91. Sobers was one of only three wickets not to fall to a rampant Trueman, caught slashing wearily at Shackleton. 'Sobers, charity suggests, had been doing too much bowling for his batting's good,' Barker opined.[12]

Three more games against the counties failed to relocate Sobers's broadest bat. In fact, he spent most of the third, against Middlesex, on the balcony of the Lord's pavilion with his arm in a sling after a whitlow on a finger on his right hand turned septic. An automatic selection for West Indies for almost a decade, he appeared likely to miss the fourth Test at Headingley.

Wooldridge's assertion that Sobers's finger 'claimed as many column inches in the newspapers as news of a small matter in Moscow where a few men were seeking to save us all from being poisoned by nuclear fallout'[13] might have been a little overstated but it reflected the status of Sobers and was exactly what all West Indies fans dreaded. CLR James had even concluded a letter to Sobers earlier in the tour by writing, 'I wish you all the luck in the world and particularly to take as much care of yourself off the field as on it. You do a lot on it, as much as any cricketer I have ever seen, and I am mortally afraid that you may not be yourself by August and September.'[14] James's worst fears looked like being realised a week or so early.

Doctors advised Sobers to sit out the Test, but lack of form and the criticism that came with it from some quarters hardened his resolve. When Worrell told him, 'I want you to play,' there was no way he was going to miss the match. 'There were precious few precedents of Test sides gambling on invalids and winning,' said Wooldridge. 'Nevertheless, deep down there must have been the suspicion that no precept applied to Sobers any longer.'[15]

On the morning of the match – with the front pages reporting an historic treaty between the USA, Soviet Union and the United Kingdom to restrict nuclear tests to underground – Sobers had his finger lanced and heavily bandaged and was given another dose of antibiotics. When West Indies lost their third wicket on 71 not long before lunch, he placed his hand carefully inside his batting glove and headed to the middle. He recalled 'searing pain' the first time he hit the ball. He gritted his teeth and struck consecutive sizzling fours through the off side.

He was not interested in histrionics, no public show of coping with the agony he was undoubtedly suffering. Even when the fastest of all England's bowlers, Trueman, unleashed a bouncer he hooked him for four and allowed himself no more than resting his right hand across his chest. After a period of playing second fiddle to Kanhai, he greeted Fred Titmus by striking his second and third balls to the boundary.

Reaching his fifty gave him the impetus for another flurry of fours.

He and Kanhai brought up their 100 partnership in just under two hours and his partner looked set for a century until Tony Lock was finally thrown the ball in the 83rd over, bowling Kanhai with the first ball of his second over. The stand of 143 was the duo's highest in their eight years together in Test cricket.

Sobers soldiered on 'in his most determined, responsible mood', according to EW Swanton in *The Daily Telegraph*, seeing off the new ball and punctuating singles with the occasional four as he moved towards three figures. It was the kind of performance that would have Wooldridge summarising Sobers's series by writing, 'To be the greatest anything is a burden of frightening responsibility but the title rested lightly on Sobers's shoulders.'[16]

When, on 98, he cut Lock through the covers, the ovation began even before the ball reached the rope. 'Yorkshiremen have honoured very few invaders in such a way, but Sobers deserved it,' Wooldridge observed.[17]

Next ball, he connected sweetly with a straight drive, only to see Lock, the man whose brilliant fielding had caught him at slip and run him out in a Test on the same ground six years earlier, dive to his left to pull off a brilliant one-handed dismissal. 'Why does he always pick on me?' Sobers asked happily when back in the dressing room.[18]

Chapman offered a typical tabloid take on events in the next day's *Daily Mirror*. 'It stands out as the greatest "doping" coup of all time. Not on Epsom Downs but Headingley Test ground. Those antibiotics pumped into Garry Sobers did their stuff so well that the gamble came off, the long-shot miracle happened.'

West Indies batted again with a lead of 223 after Griffith's six wickets had skittled England for 174. Sobers knocked up 52 in 80 minutes, hitting six fours, as the home side were set 453 to win. Just as Hall was removing his sweater to bowl, Sobers was thrown the new ball. He took out Stewart's off stump with the last ball of his first over and later removed Barrington and Brian Bolus when bowling his wrist-spin. England were all out for 231 and West Indies headed to The Oval for the fifth Test with a 2-1 lead. But that was almost a month away. There were six more first-class games to play before then.

In one of them, Sobers scored a hundred against Yorkshire, but the game against Surrey at The Oval provided him with one of his less pleasant memories of the tour. This was 1963, a time of continued racial unrest in some parts of the country while the Caribbean diaspora looked to achieve improved living conditions and employment opportunities through revised Race Relations Acts. Sobers recalled the team receiving anonymous letters from those urging them to 'get back in the trees' and delivering various insults.

When things crept on to the field, Sobers found it more difficult to laugh off. Without ever naming names he recalled Surrey fans and players becoming abusive at tense moments in the match. He was shocked by some of the on-field language and said Worrell had not taken it well. 'It left us feeling very disappointed and bitter,' he said. 'Some of the people who were saying things, we never thought of in that context.'[19]

It had been against the same opposition six years earlier that Worrell remembered he and Clyde Walcott having to put up with similar treatment. 'We were abused when the players were changing ends,' he said, describing the language used as 'violent'. It was why he said he would 'never regard [Surrey] as a good cricket team'.[20]

Back at The Oval for the series finale, Sobers, moving the ball both ways, picked up the wickets of openers Bolus and John Edrich after they had shared a half-century stand, although he lacked his usual accuracy with his slower bowling. He was then run out on 26 as West Indies found themselves trailing by 29 on first innings.

Day three saw an ironman effort from Sobers, who bowled his medium-pacers from 12.45 to 6 p.m. with a break of only four overs. But for dropped catches, he could have picked up more than the three wickets he recorded via edges by Bolus and Dexter and another lbw against a sweeping Close. England were dismissed for 223. Not one of their batsmen had made a century in the series, the first time that had happened to them in a five-Test contest. Sobers's work for the series was done, Hunte's unbeaten century seeing West Indies to an eight-wicket win that secured the *Wisden* Trophy, put up for the first time by cricket's 'bible' to celebrate its century in print.

More than 25,000 attended the final day – two-thirds estimated to be West Indies fans, mostly in their dark, slim-fitting suits and narrow ties. Thousands charged good-naturedly across the field to gather in front of the pavilion for the presentation. This was their triumph as much as Worrell's, given the contribution they had made to the summer. Almost half a million spectators had produced gate receipts of £200,000, not to mention the vibrant backdrop they lent to the matches. 'Their players and supporters enriched the game with their exuberant cricket on the field and their infectious enthusiasm and incessant banter in the background,' said *Wisden* editor Norman Preston.[21]

Such had been the tourists' performance that the Imperial Cricket Conference* agreed in mid-tour to revise its future plans, which did not have West Indies scheduled for a return to England until 1971. They ended up touring twice more in the 1960s.

Sobers ended the series within two wickets of becoming the first player to score 4,000 runs and take 100 wickets in Test cricket. *Wisden* named him as one of its Five Cricketers of the Year in its 1964 publication, along with team-mates Griffith, Hunte and Kanhai. Calling him the 'key man in the series', his citation concluded, 'Sobers is essentially a cricketer for the big occasion. The tougher the struggle the more he enjoys it.' Its tour summary said, 'In almost every game he played he contributed some outstanding performance. He left his imprint on every field he played, taking wickets at a vital time, making runs quickly when necessary and swallowing up 29 catches, mostly in the slips. His form in the last month of the tour

---

* Renamed the International Cricket Conference in 1965 and the International Cricket Council in 1987.

qualified him as the outstanding performer and all-rounder in present-day cricket.'[22]

England had not even seen the best of him yet.

Wooldridge marvelled at the energy of a man who had not had more than a six-week rest from cricket in the past six years. 'Going stale did not occur to him,' he wrote.[23] Sobers, meanwhile, agreed that Worrell's instructions to reduce drastically the amount of card games played during breaks in play had helped maintain sharpness, the skipper having studied medical reports that said such close-up eye activity could temporarily impair the vision required on the field.

Yet the days of following Worrell's instructions and examples were at an end. Bound for a career in Jamaican politics, where he became a senator, the skipper had already announced that the England tour would mark the end of his 15-year career in Test cricket. Few men had done more for their sport, which Worrell was departing as a hero, not just in the Caribbean islands, but in Australia and England, where his engaging, enterprising captaincy had illuminated successive tours. His side, Preston suggested, 'stand unrivalled for the manner in which they play the game', adding, 'Worrell led his men with dignity and tenacity. A sound tactician, he imbued his talented team with confidence and when a difficulty arose he soon poured oil on troubled water.'[24]

The Lord Mayor of London, Sir Ralph Perring, invited the tourists to Mansion House and argued that 'a gale of change has blown through the hallowed halls of cricket'. Even Buckingham Palace and Downing Street were lining up to pay tribute, with

Worrell given a knighthood in the New Year's Honours List several months later.

'It was fortunate that a man with the qualities of Frank Worrell should have been the first black [West Indies] captain, for it was a crucial examination,' said Tony Cozier. 'Had he been a failure, it would have been a grave trauma. Instead, he made it such a success that the reputation of West Indies cricket never stood so high as under him.'[25]

It would be a daunting task for whoever was to follow in his footsteps.

11

SONGS OF PRAISE

'Who's the greatest cricketer on Earth or Mars?
Anyone can tell you, it's the great Sir
Garfield Sobers.'

'Sir Garfield Sobers' (Mighty Sparrow, 1966)

THERE ARE certain sports stars who reach the top of their professions via hard work and discipline; figures such as Geoffrey Boycott or Kevin Keegan, who make you believe that perhaps you could have done that if only you'd had the same drive, determination and opportunity. Then there are those who have a genius so unworldly that their feats are clearly unattainable. They appear to have been sent from an unknown universe into a place in our heads and hearts. We can feel and be moved by their actions, but we can't possibly dream of emulation.

Often those performers – and Garry Sobers was one, of course – are either instinctive talents or simply figured things out for themselves as they went along. It was especially true in his era. 'I was completely self-taught,' Sobers explained. 'I watched and listened, took in what I thought would benefit me and rejected the rest.'[1] It is why so many of the most successful sports people didn't succeed as coaches and managers; why those forced to work harder and accept guidance have been better placed to develop the careers of others. And it is why those such as Sobers often struggle to articulate the source of their artistry.

He put his name to numerous books that have between them produced hundreds of thousands of words about his career. None contain the secret of his success. Nor should they be expected to. It was undefinable. The coaching manual, *Gary Sobers' Way of Cricket*, published in Australia in 1985, gives few clues. It is a book of bog-standard advice on technique to which Sobers has apparently allowed his name to be attached, containing little in the way of personalisation. It is certainly not the kind of publication with which Sobers would ever have consulted, while the rigid, square-on backward defensive stoke that he is photographed playing on the front cover is not one too many people would have associated with him.

His 1965 instructional, *Cricket, Advance!*, begins with the statement, 'I don't believe in too much coaching,' and the chapter on batting begins by stressing the importance of 'position and balance', and an order to 'watch the ball, watch the ball'. Sobers is more interested in examining ways of getting mentally prepared to play a significant innings than he is in talking about technicalities, although a series of photographs offer MCC-style coaching guidelines and there is text advising on the best location for the feet and head when playing certain shots. The words could be by anyone.[2]

His last autobiography, in 2002, teases you with a chapter called 'On Batting', but he reels off lists of grounds where he scored the most runs, bowlers against whom he took more care, and batsmen he most admired. The thrust of any strategic element is: play safe early on and go for your shots when your eye is in.

Therefore, in trying to explain how, by 1963, Sobers had become the world's greatest all-rounder – and how he retained that status for the best part of a further decade – one relies on the testimony of others to support the occasional glimpses of insight he offers.

He was assured enough in his batting to believe that, in most cases, only he could bring his downfall. 'I would weigh everything up, decide the most likely way I was going to get out – and eliminate it,' he explained. Allied to the elimination of incorrect shot selection was the certainty of being in a position to avoid being bowled. 'Once you cover the stumps and the ball is outside your body, there is no way it can hit the woodwork,' he said. 'The only way you can be out is by making a mistake.'[3]

Such faith in his own ability manifested itself, according to Tony Cozier, in his every movement. 'His eyesight, his reflexes, his coordination had to be exceptional but, to me, there was nothing as fascinating about Sobers as his self-confidence. I never saw him tense before a big match, never worried about the conditions or his own form. Quite the contrary, he appeared to take all cricket as he took his boyhood games in the Bay Land.'[4]

* * *

As a batsman, Sobers felt his preference for faster wickets, where the ball was coming on to the bat, explained the fact that he never scored big runs on the slower tracks of New Zealand, although mastery of similar conditions in England was quickly achieved, especially through his stint in league cricket. 'It taught me to watch the seam bowler off the wicket, not just from the hand but right up to the last split second,' he said, making it far more likely that lack of success in New Zealand was a statistical quirk rather than a deficiency in his game.[5]

No one can succeed with the bat without sound footwork, yet the fact that Sobers was uncoached meant that he developed a simple, minimalist method that allowed him to make late decisions rather than plunging his right leg down the track – the method that batsmen of the time were typically expected to adopt against the swinging ball, especially in England. With his great eye and the speed of his hands, a subtle shift of balance was all he needed to get into position for his shots.

England's Barry Knight observed, 'A remarkable feature about Garry's batting was his concentration, and how he watched the ball out of the bowler's hand and on to the bat. If he saw the ball move off the seam he had the quickness of mind and the reflexes to move his hands or adjust his shot at the last moment and play his best shot. A curiosity of Garry's batting was that he never adjusted or moved his feet. He believed it was his hands that followed the ball and not the feet.'[6]

Former Leicestershire man Jack Birkenshaw, an opponent at county and international level, backed that up by describing a particular photograph. 'It is Lillee bowling to Garfield, and the ball is halfway down the wicket,' he explained. 'Lillee is bowling up in the 80s or 90s [mph] and Garfield has not moved an inch; he has not picked his bat up, or gone back and across as the modern players would. He just stood there and the ball was halfway down the pitch before he started to move. That shows how unbelievably late he could play. He was prepared to wait until the ball is delivered and seeing where he thought it was going to land before committing himself. His eye must have been terrific to get so quickly into position.'[7]

Pat Pocock, another England off-spinner, cited another example of how late Sobers could determine his strokes. 'I would bowl a ball and hold it back and he would get there a bit early. The ball hadn't arrived and he would say, "Well bowled," and then hit it for four. But he played in an orthodox way. Some people you bowled to made you think you had to do something different because whatever you bowled he was going to give it a whack. But Garry would most certainly play the ball on its merit.'[8]

Indian off-spinner Erapalli Prasanna explained, 'The strangest thing about his batting was that he never stepped out to flighted spin. This intrigued me whenever I bowled to him. There was a scarcely perceptible transfer of body weight, either on to the front foot or the back foot according to his reading of the length, when he played a shot through a gap in the field. He could play every shot in the book, plus a few of his own. But his on-side play was spectacular. His wrists came into play at the last minute and his flick – almost like a tennis southpaw's forehand cross-court drive – left the fieldsmen standing.'[9]

Derek Underwood, who would become the last man to dismiss Sobers in Test cricket, conceded, 'When Garry was on form I don't think there was any bowler who could hope to keep him quiet. He had every stroke and was equally strong off front and back foot. He seemed to pick up the line of the ball so early and be in position to play his shot before anybody else.'[10]

Sobers's preference was to remain on the back foot, believing it gave him more time to adjust to any movement and protect the edge of his bat. He said in the early 1970s:

> The way I strike the ball could be called my unconscious style. But I'm very aware of getting the basics right. I think I pick up the flight of the ball quicker than most players. To me the most important thing in batting is moving my feet immediately to get behind the line of the ball. Playing forward or back isn't really important to me, particularly against pace bowling. I tend to follow the swing or play at the ball more than most English players, who tend to get locked into one set stroke. For instance I could start playing at the ball as it's on the way, intending to hit it straight back past the bowler. If it moves away from me in the air I'll adjust in mid-stroke to hit it through the covers or even cut it if it really swings a lot.[11]

That ability meant that the delivery that traditionally caused most problems for left-handers – just short of a length on off stump and slanting towards the slips – could be a rich source of runs. If the bowler pulled back his length a little, then Sobers was a fierce cutter and puller; if the ball was pitched further up to a good length, he could lean forward and drive on the up.

If that sounds easy, then even his preparation for batting was a statement of how simply the game came to him. Nets had little worth in his view. Turning up in time to get changed was usually enough. He had no need of a thigh-pad, while the lightness of the Slazenger bats he favoured meant that he owed little of his power to his equipment. Despite that, it is the ferocity of his shots that comes up repeatedly in his contemporaries' memories.

Sunil Gavaskar recalled, 'The speed with which the ball went to the boundary showed what superb timing he had and that one does not always need a bat with a lot of meat in it to hit the ball as powerfully as one wants to.'[12]

Lancashire's David Lloyd added, 'Garry hit the ball harder than anybody. We had an off-spinner called John Savage, who came to us from Leicestershire. When he was bowling at Garry, I remember he drove the ball so hard it just knocked me back in the covers. It pushed me further and further back. He was drilling the ball.'[13]

It was why former England all-rounder Peter Walker said, 'Fielding in the covers to Sobers, one always stood 20 feet deeper than for other mortals.'[14] And why another England man, Basil D'Oliveira, admitted, 'I used to dread fielding in the slips to Garry because he followed the correct doctrine that if you are going to flash at the ball, flash hard. You could never stand too far away in the slips for my liking when Garry batted.'[15]

Roger Davis, one of Glamorgan's specialist close fielders while Sobers was in county cricket, remembered, 'He was the one guy I would not go short leg to. He whipped the ball very late and very hard and kept very still until the last minute, so you couldn't pick his movement.'[16]

Neville Cardus, inevitably, found a romantic way of articulating the source of Sobers's strength. 'To describe [his] method I would use the term lyrical,' he wrote. 'His immense power is concealed, or lightened, to the spectator's eye, by a rhythm which has in it as little obvious propulsion as a movement of music by Mozart (who could be as dramatically strong as Wagner!). A drive through the covers by Sobers sometimes appears to be quite lazy, until we see an off-side fieldsman nursing bruised palms, or hear the impact of ball striking fence.'[17]

Sobers's power did not always need to be heard rather than seen, however. There were many occasions when he coiled into a drive like the keen golfer he became. There are any number of photographs of Sobers standing post-drive in the manner of someone who has just struck a three-wood down the fairway. 'His batting was utterly stylish and free, correct and dominating together,' said former England captain Mike Brearley. 'I once stood at extra cover at Cambridge to [him]. Apart from my alarm at the likelihood that he would middle one of his wonderful off-drives – played with the highest back-lift, the purest pendulum of bat-swing, and the most complete follow-through, sometimes slapping himself in the middle of the back at the end of the great arc of the stroke – straight at me, I have a vivid image from that afternoon 50 years ago of the style, the power, the classicism and freedom of his arms and hands, and recall it better than I remember most of the pictures I've seen in art galleries.'[18]

Barry Richards felt that Sobers was a '360-degree player' in spite of the era in which he played. 'He took his scoring opportunities within the laws of the day and was able to dominate attacks by doing that,' he argued. 'He could hit from outside off stump or leg. And in those days there were no rules to stop you bowling two feet down the leg side with eight fielders on the leg side. The laws of the game dictated who the geniuses were. Don't just look at the stats. I am vehemently against comparing people who wore helmets, or had particular laws during their playing time or particular pitches or field sizes being compared with people who didn't. Whatever way you look at it, Sobey was a genius.'[19]

Few batsmen have managed to marry technical correctness with flamboyance in the manner of Sobers. But it was that self-schooled orthodoxy that gave him the foundation to freelance at the crease. 'Sobers not only plays according to the book, he adds to it,' was how Charlie Griffith put it while they were team-mates. 'He has the ability to improvise on the spur of the moment. In full flight he cannot be contained. The difference between Garry and the others is that a ball which could cause any other batsman to play defensively would be hit for four by him. He is utterly fearless. I have often seen him open his eyes in amazement in the dressing room when some of our batsmen were making bowling look very difficult indeed. He would say,

"What the hell is going on out there?" When he went out to bat, the same bowling would become like child's play to him.'[20]

Sobers had an ability to shut out what had happened to previous deliveries or what might occur later. He cleared his head of everything but the next ball.

If it all added up to a seemingly invincible package, then that did not mean that opponents were completely devoid of hope when he came to the crease. A few theories circulated about the best way to get him out, even if they were generally accompanied by an acceptance that such ideas rarely came off. Len Hutton recalled, 'I suspected that if Sobers had a batting weakness it was outside the off stump, but he rarely got out in that area and when in form, which was normally the case, he was practically impossible to bowl to … I cannot recall seeing him indecisive and caught in two minds.'[21]

England opening bowler David Brown would explain how the 'weakness' Hutton identified was targeted in a Test in England in 1969. 'We aimed to get him caught at slip so we practised bowling wide of the off stump. We had a cordon of slips. We only had one man on the off side other than the slips and third man and that was John Edrich at extra cover. I bowled to Garry as wide as you like and he just smacked it straight into Edrich's hands. It wasn't supposed to work like that. The plan was to get him caught at slip, not at cover.'[22]

A spinner's view was offered, tentatively, by Prasanna. 'If there was any chink in his armour it was his tendency to withdraw and cut. This was to my advantage since I ran the ball away from a left-hander. Despite this, he was the one batsman who gave me butterflies in the stomach. There was a lurking fear of being smashed out of the attack, even before I had bowled an over at him.'[23]

Sometimes, the only way to combat Sobers was to hope that carelessness, boredom, showmanship or the match situation would be his undoing. Or the distraction of other interests. 'He always had a bet on the horses,' explained David Lloyd. 'Our plan to get him out was, if he had a bet on the three o'clock, we'd remind him that if he wanted he could watch the race in our changing room, where we had a telly. We got ours when Jack Simmons asked for it because he liked a bet too.'[24]

Birkenshaw offered a similar memory. 'In county matches you wanted to bowl at him early afternoon if he'd had a bet on a racehorse. He might just want to get back and watch the race. Ray Illingworth knew that was the case, so Illy got on to bowl before I did because it might be the only chance to get him out. A method that Illingworth used against him in the end was to put lots of men on the boundary. Garfield didn't enjoy that, didn't respect that. He thought Illy should be trying to get him out. If you made Garry bored he might give it away. He didn't like bashing it to long-off for one. And he would pick and choose his moments, as great players do. When he was playing against someone like Graham McKenzie or Illingworth, whom he respected, he set his stall out. If the challenge was on he was up for it. Great players don't like easy runs.'[25]

Sometimes a careless disregard of his surroundings could be his undoing. 'I played against Sobey quite a bit in county cricket,' recalled New Zealander Glenn Turner. 'One occasion, where Worcestershire were playing Nottinghamshire, he picked one ball and hit it down the fielder's throat at deep-backward square leg. When we came together as a group at the fall of his wicket, Basil D'Oliveira said to us, "I'll bet you when Sobey goes past the guy that caught him on the way to the pavilion he will say, 'I didn't see you down there, man.'" We asked the fielder and he confirmed that was exactly what Sobey said to him. He had such confidence in himself always that he was struggling with the fact that he could get out.'[26]

Birkenshaw suggested justifiably, 'Had he been more selfish, I don't know what his record might have been.' Certainly, opting to bat in the lower middle order for much of his Test career was a large reason why Sobers turned only two of his 26 Test hundreds into double centuries. Knight said, 'If the situation permitted after scoring a century, Garry would cut loose and play for the crowd. I was never crazy about the prospect of bowling to him when he was set, and I only thought about trying to contain him and avoid being hit for four or six.'[27]

According to Ian Chappell, 'You hope he gets a hundred and he gets bored with it. You don't want to upset him and guarantee that he gets 200. The last thing in the world you wanted to do was annoy Garry.'[28]

* * *

Sobers also had plenty to offer even on the occasions when his bat fell silent. England's Tom Graveney was not the only opponent who was 'always particularly wary of his bowling if he had failed with the bat'.[29]

Standing around in the field for hours on end was unthinkable to someone with Sobers's restless nature. 'I enjoyed bowling,' he said simply. 'If it meant bowling all day I would do it. Equally, if it meant fielding all day at short leg under the batsman's nose without a helmet, I would do that too. I always wanted to be in the game. That's probably why I developed three different styles of bowling. It meant there would always be a chance of the captain using me at some stage of the game.'[30]

Although starting out as a spinner, Sobers reckoned that fast bowling was in his blood. In the boyhood games where the player who got someone out was next to bat, it was the catcher who got that honour. Therefore bowling slow to entice someone to hit the ball in the air was a waste of time. Bowling them out with a faster ball was the way to get a bat.

At senior level, Sobers initially relied more on flight than turn with his orthodox finger-spin. As he rose higher in the game he found that the greater turn he achieved with wrist-spin posed more problems. Yet that took a toll on his shoulder. One specialist explained to him that getting into position to bowl the googly had stretched the tendons to the point where they were no longer holding the ball of the shoulder in the socket effectively. His faster bowling style began to dominate.

Statistical study of Sobers's career shows that his most successful period as a Test bowler was from 1961 to 1968, when he operated mostly as a swing bowler behind Hall and Griffith. In that eight-year spell, he took 125 wickets in 33 Tests. Only three men who topped 100 wickets in that same period – Fred Trueman, Lance Gibbs and South Africa's Peter Pollock – did so at a lower average than Sobers's 27.93. He was justified in believing that he might have taken more than his eventual total of 235 wickets had his great workload not restricted him to short spells on many occasions.

Sobers's swing was the perfect complement to the pace of Hall and Griffith. The general opinion among those who played against and with him was that it was the most dangerous of his bowling styles. 'He was the greatest swing bowler I have ever seen,' reckoned Alan Knott. 'He swung the ball very late and was deceptively quick. Your instinct was to move your feet right across the wicket to Sobers and if he made one swing back in you could be leg before. It seemed as if he was always bowling towards second slip but he had this great ability to make the ball dip in late.'[31]

Knott's England team-mate, D'Oliveira, said, 'No bowler ever gave me more trouble consistently; for a few years he was as quick as anybody I've faced, with a wicked, late in-ducker to the right-handed batsman.'[32]

Seam bowler Mike Taylor had the opportunity to observe Sobers from close quarters during several years together in the Nottinghamshire team. 'He had a great action,' he explained. 'He didn't bowl like they do now – chest-on and down the leg side. And at the end of the second finger of his left hand he had a little bit of hard skin, which was from pulling the finger back on delivery to make the ball go down the wicket with the seam up.'[33]

Graveney felt Sobers was under-appreciated as an opening bowler. 'I would rate Sobers more dangerous with the new ball than either Wes Hall or Charlie Griffith and when he went all out and slipped himself he could be just as fast, at least with the occasional delivery or over a short spell.' Sobers was also careful to disguise his bouncers, having noticed how Hall often signalled them. Graveney continued, 'Normally the left-arm quick bowler goes across the body, which can be awkward enough, but another whole dimension is added to the batsmen's problems if the ball comes back. Nothing is more worrying than having to guard against talent which can be so diversified. Garry also disconcerted with the way he was able to make the ball twist and swerve, and mix in a bouncer or two.'[34]

Interviewed by the BBC on the occasion of Sobers's 80th birthday, Geoffrey Boycott recalled, 'His seam bowling was fantastic. He picked up the ball and he had this lithe, fluid action and swung the ball late. I would say in his pomp he was like Jimmy Anderson. He was quite lively without being the fastest.'[35]

Few doubt that Sobers could be genuinely fast when he chose to be, although he admitted that he didn't have the stamina to do it over after over. 'He wasn't medium-paced when I faced him – he was sharp,' said Barry Knight. 'Garry's late in-swing bowling at pace was up there with Wasim Akram and late movement with Alan Davidson.'[36]

All-rounder Roger Knight, a county rival at Surrey and Gloucestershire, recalled Sobers teaching him his methods. '[He] explained how he swung the ball either way and how it was all to do with the position of the thumb, either on its edge for his left-arm in-swing deliveries or flat for the ball that left the right-handed batsman. That was often how we learnt the skills and it allowed me to develop the ability to swing the ball either way.'[37]

But not only could Sobers move the ball in the air, he could use the seam, too. 'On wet or damp wickets he bowled like Derek Underwood or Tony Lock,' said Barry Knight.[38]

And then there was his fielding, which was feline and fearless. As well as being able to catch the ball in any close position and swoop in the outfield, those who saw him keep wicket in Sunday exhibition matches believe he could have done an accomplished job at that – although an early blow in the mouth with a bail while keeping in a boys' game had put him off.

Simplifying his craft in typical fashion, Sobers put his success down to believing that every ball was destined for his hands, especially when at leg slip to Gibbs. The numbers bear out Sobers's belief, with 39 of his 109 Test catches being off the off-spinner. 'As soon as Lance bowled I would move up and sometimes take the ball off the face of the bat. Sometimes I would watch Lance turn and from the way he ran up I knew exactly what he was going to do. I also knew the batsmen and how they were going to shape up. I could quickly work out whether it was going to go fine or square.'[39] He remembered being struck only once, by Ian Chappell batting against Gibbs, and even then he managed to grasp the ball after it thudded into his chest.

Chappell had his own example of Sobers's remarkable feats in the field. With Victoria looking to rebuild after losing early wickets against South Australia, left-hander Ian Huntington attempted to block out leg-spinner Rex Sellers. 'Huntington played the first couple of deliveries with a dead bat and Sobers, fielding at leg-slip, took note,' Chappell explained. 'As Huntington prepared to play the third delivery in the same manner, Sobers walked forward and placed his right hand on the ground. Huntington's perfect forward defensive shot landed right in Sobers's accurately placed hand. It was pure genius resulting from an alert brain.'[40]

As Tony Cozier observed, 'Gibbs was a great off-spin bowler and Sobers around the corner was absolutely magnificent at snapping up balls that were a couple of inches off the ground. Gibbs would say that Sobers's anticipation at that short leg position was incredible.'[41]

It was an adjective that was never overused in discussion of Sobers's all-round ability.

12

A QUESTION OF LEADERSHIP

'The price of greatness is responsibility.'

Sir Winston Churchill

FOR ALL his qualities, Garry Sobers could be naïve, charmingly innocent, closed to nuance. It took a while, but by the end of the 1963 tour of England even he was beginning to take the hint about what was being planned. 'It's time you began to buckle down, to take life more seriously,' tour manager Berkeley Gaskin had told him quietly. 'You can make news in cricket. This has its penalties. You are not free to do as you please any more, you have a responsibility to others.'[1]

Sobers was not blind to his value to the team as an all-rounder, but had no ambition to be anything more. It was sign enough of his growth, he believed, that while sympathising with the younger players when they complained about being dragged off to an official function he could, as a senior player, see the importance of such events.

But then Frank Worrell began consulting him more often on the field, engaging in discussion over strategic decisions. His skipper had always been keen to talk to him about the game over

187

a beer, sharing his thoughts and telling Sobers that he was the most knowledgeable cricketer in his team. Now Sobers could feel Worrell 'drawing out of me things I never realised had sunk in during all my years of playing cricket'. In the fourth Test at Headingley, it had been Sobers's own idea that he should bowl the first over of the second innings, saying presciently, 'I've got a feeling I can get Micky Stewart out.'[2] Worrell's faith in his player's instinct had been immediately rewarded.

Forced to confront thoughts of responsibility, duty and maturity, Sobers could not escape the obvious conclusion. 'Frank Worrell himself, Berkeley Gaskin, Conrad Hunte and others were constantly drawing me out as well as feeding thoughts into me. [It was] a course of preparation – even of testing. A thought was placed in my mind that I might even be considered for captaincy.'[3]

With Worrell set to leave Test cricket to focus on the position he now held as Warden of the University of the West Indies in Jamaica and to move into politics, vice-captain Hunte might have been assumed to be next in line. Yet he was becoming increasingly involved in the Moral Re-Armament organisation, a peace movement developed in England by American minister Frank Buchman in the 1930s. Even though the players liked Hunte, Sobers felt that he was becoming remote, while there were suggestions that the WICBC feared he might use an elevated status to promote his own agenda.

Worrell had no doubt that Sobers was the man to succeed him and in the spring of 1964 a letter arrived in England, where he was preparing for another season of league cricket, inviting him to accept the captaincy of West Indies. Sobers felt equal to the task from a cricketing perspective. He understood that his knowledge, experience, achievements and instinct for the game placed him above other candidates. Yet two matters gave him pause. One was having to follow the great Worrell. Sport, he knew, was not often forgiving of those who traced the footsteps of the gods. The second factor was even more serious: the impact the position would have on his lifestyle. A free spirit, he was initially 'depressed at the thought of carefree days with the boys no longer being possible'.[4]

Sobers had rarely been one to adhere to minor details such as curfews. When captains had laid down such rules, he had told himself and team-mates that they didn't apply to him and continued his nocturnal existence, resolving that the later he got to bed the more determined he would be to perform well to avoid criticism.

Even when Worrell pushed back curfew to midnight, believing it was better for players to go out and get 'bombed' than sitting in the hotel worrying or expending mental and physical energy playing cards, he acknowledged that Sobers should be allowed to operate outside the regulations. 'When I'm on the field they have me totally, body and soul, but when I'm off the field I don't want them to tell me what to do,' was Sobers's attitude to his captains. Worrell, he knew, was able to live with that outlook.

As captain, Sobers could not impose a curfew to which he himself would not adhere. He was a partygoer, not a hypocrite. If he wanted to live life to the full he would have to let his team-mates do the same, even if he recognised that it might not be good for some of them, or even the team. Curfews would be consigned to history under his leadership.

These were the matters he got off his chest when he sat down with Jim Flannery, his captain at Norton, the Staffordshire-based team for whom he had signed in 1964. Flannery and other local friends stressed to him the honour of being chosen to lead one's country, and the rarity of such an opportunity. A few weeks after receiving the offer, he admitted to himself that he was 'exhilarated by the thought of possible honours to come, by the very challenge of the exciting way ahead'.[5] He wrote to the WICBC, telling them that he was honoured to have been asked and would accept the position. On 2 May, the new captain was announced.

Sobers never felt it himself − or if he did, he never acknowledged it − but his appointment was every bit as significant from a political and social perspective as that of Worrell. Perhaps even more so. 'So far its captains have been either English public school or university men,' said CLR James in 1964. 'So this is the first unambiguously native West Indian who has arrived at that exalted position.'[6]

Pointing out that Sobers 'neither attended a prestigious Barbados secondary school nor a university', Maurice St Pierre wrote, 'His elevation to the position of West Indian captain was achieved almost solely on the basis of all-round excellence in the game. Therefore Sobers succeeded to a position which had previously been occupied by a relatively educated West Indian of middle-class background.'

The political and social environment that provided the background to his appointment was also significant. St Pierre continued, 'Sobers was asked to perform during a time when West Indians, some of whom had recently attained political independence while others were struggling for this status, were questioning old values and seeking to create new ones. It was a period of serious cultural re-evaluation.'[7]

From a cricketing perspective, Sobers was about to carry a unique weight. The greatest of players, Don Bradman and Len Hutton for example, had been asked to lead teams, but had only batting to worry about when it came to personal performance. As EW Swanton wrote in *The Daily Telegraph*, 'There is no parallel in the whole story of Test cricket to a man who means quite so much to his side in every direction as a player also being entrusted with the captaincy.'

* * *

At the end of the 1964 season in England, Sobers was invited to play for Frank Worrell's XI in three matches against an England XI. It was effectively an unofficial England–West Indies contest and Worrell's team went into the final match at Lord's with a 1-0 lead. As they prepared to take the field for what proved to be the only day of a rain-ruined encounter, Worrell, about to make his final first-class appearance, approached Sobers. 'Well, you'll be skipper of the West Indies from now on, so how about starting here?' he said.[8] Having never previously been captain at any level, Sobers led the team on to the Lord's field.

Towards the end of that summer, Eric Williams, prime minister of Trinidad and Tobago, met Sobers while in London attending a conference of Commonwealth leaders. Williams asked him to become involved in a nationwide community programme designed to develop young people in a variety of areas outside the classroom, including in the sporting arena. Williams explained that Worrell and Rohan Kanhai, neither of them Trinidadians, were working for the scheme, nurturing cricket talent.

The approach left Sobers feeling conflicted, not because it was not his own island of Barbados but because he had intended to play some games for South Australia before leading West Indies in their home series against Australia. But over the next year or so, when his playing schedule allowed, Sobers travelled to towns and villages on the islands in a role that was 'expected to encourage and enthuse young minds in the schools and villages and perhaps others not so young'.[9] There was also discussion of Worrell and Sobers advising on the construction of a new national stadium.

But on a visit home, he recalled a government official challenging him about why he was not carrying out such work in Barbados instead of a neighbouring nation. His response was to ask why, if a similar programme was being developed, he had not been informed, and why it had taken word of his work for Trinidad for anyone in Barbados to approach him. 'I believe you did not think of me at all, but now try to blame me for not working with you,' he said, thinking he had been disregarded by his island rather than the other way around. 'I cannot know everything that is going on day by day at home unless somebody goes to the trouble to tell me.'[10] It would not be the last time Sobers and the authorities in his home country rubbed up against each other.

Immediately after the season, Sobers undertook one of the more curious engagements of his career, guesting for Yorkshire on the Bermuda leg of their tour of North America. Until 1992, the county would not take the field in a competitive match with anyone not born in the county, but were happy to add him to a squad that had been playing in Canada and the United States. According to skipper Brian Close, the intention had been for Sobers to play for the Bermudian teams to stiffen the opposition, but he declined the chance to face Fred Trueman and his colleagues on unpredictable matting wickets. Instead, in his first match, Sobers and a young, sunburnt Geoffrey Boycott – a new England international – both scored centuries against St George's Cricket Club.

'The pitch was matting on top of concrete, lightning fast and frankly dangerous if somebody decided he wanted to make a name for himself,' recalled Boycott, who was keen to avoid injury with a Test tour of South Africa coming up. 'There was an enormous amount of short stuff.' That was until Sobers received one that bounced in the bowler's half of the wicket. He warned the culprit, 'Cut it out.' Indicating Boycott, he added, 'Same goes for him.' Sobers was not a man to be disobeyed in his own part of the world.[11]

He also shared the new ball with Trueman, each of them taking four wickets in shooting out the home team for 48.

'He'll do for me, that lad,' Trueman remarked of his temporary colleague, while Close said at the end of the tour, 'I wish Sobers was a Yorkshireman.'[12]

* * *

Sobers could not have had tougher opposition for his first Test series as leader, with Australia's visit to the Caribbean early in 1965 considered a world championship bout. At least he had no concerns over his own form. His handful of first-class matches in 1964/65 had begun with scores of 83 and 102 for a Commonwealth XI against the Bengal Chief Minister's XI at Calcutta's Eden Gardens, where a few months earlier he'd recorded a six-wicket haul and a century for EW Swanton's XI against an Indian XI. He began 1965 by scoring heavily for both a Jamaican XI and Barbados against an International Cavaliers team.

When Sobers looked around the West Indies dressing room, he wished he had inherited a younger team who would have 'looked up to me and listened to what I had to say'.[13] Yet he would come to recognise the value of having seasoned players on the field, especially when, later in his captaincy, he experienced the problems created by leading a younger side in a period of transition.

For now he understood that several senior players had had their own designs on the captaincy. The most notable of them was Hunte, Worrell's vice-captain, although Sobers never had reason to doubt that the batsman was giving his all. He was surprised when Hunte, after his retirement, articulated the depth of the upset he'd felt at being overlooked for the leadership.

Yet former captain Jeff Stollmeyer, who would later be captain Sobers's first tour manager, felt that Hunte 'may have been rather too paternalistic and sanctimonious for [the players'] liking' and supported the more easy-going Sobers on the basis that 'West Indies players on the whole do not take kindly to rigid discipline off the field'.[14]

Interest in the series was enough that many English newspapers sent correspondents to the Caribbean. On the opening day of the series at Sabina Park, *Daily Mail* cartoon 'Jon's Sporting Types' depicted a football trainer leaving his charges in the pouring rain with the message, 'Carry on Cup training, boys, I am just going to listen to the Test score from Jamaica.'

Sobers won his first toss, but saw his team bowled out for 239. His contribution of 30 established a pattern for the series: good starts without a big score. Wes Hall's five wickets gave West Indies a first-innings lead and Australia were eventually set an unlikely 396 to win. Sobers was out for 27, tapping the ground with his bat to indicate to umpire Douglas Sang Hue that he thought the slip catch he had awarded had been a bump ball.

Australia's hopes flickered briefly at 144 for 4, with Neil Hawke and Brian Booth having added 69. According to former Australia captain Richie Benaud, 'It wasn't until Sobers produced a fine piece of captaincy by calling on [Joe] Solomon to bowl that the partnership was broken.'[15] Having aggravated a thigh injury when using the second new ball in the first innings, Sobers bowled spin for the remainder of the match, reaching a milestone with his one wicket in Australia's total of 216 – the first player with 4,000 Test runs and 100 wickets.

It was his first attempt at captaincy, however, that impressed Benaud, one of the game's great leaders. 'The game was a triumph for Garry Sobers,' he wrote in his book on the tour. '[He] led his side thoughtfully and with distinction, keeping them on their toes all the time and in the best traditions of that great captain Frank Worrell, making sure that the vagaries of the game neither had them in the heights of jubilation nor the depths of despair … On the last day he was hampered by a strained leg muscle but still managed to be everywhere to help his players.'[16]

Sobers had also found himself captaining a player being accused, not for the first time, of one of cricket's worst crimes. Charlie Griffith's bowling action had come under scrutiny in England in 1963, although he'd only ever been no-balled for throwing once in a first-class match, never in a Test. Nor was he called for it in this match, although Sang Hue had penalised him for over-stepping six times in two overs. But in the Australian dressing room, suspicions arose. Fast bowler Laurie Mayne recalled, 'A strange feeling came over me. This fellow chucks, pure and simple, I thought.'[17]

Benaud, in the Caribbean as newspaper reporter and author, said he 'didn't particularly like what I saw'. He felt that on some occasions Griffith pointed his front foot wide of the stumps, which made him very square at the point of delivery, and he was therefore throwing the ball. The photographs he took with a long lens were 'clear confirmation' that Griffith's arm was bent at the beginning of his delivery and straight at the end, which amounted to throwing.[18]

He wrote a story for the *Sydney Sun*, accompanied by his photographs, stating, 'Griffith throws. I am quite convinced of this.' The *Jamaica Gleaner* also ran the article, although sports editor LD Roberts hinted at a plot to unsettle the home team and argued, 'It is difficult for one to be convinced that Richie Benaud can really be sincere in his suggestion that the West Indies Board reopen the matter.'

Swanton, covering the series for *The Daily Telegraph* and *The Cricketer*, said, 'I detected no illegality.' The issue of throwing, he said later, carried 'implications of honour and national prestige which loom much larger than a technical consideration' and criticised Benaud for having 'blurted out his opinion … regardless of the consequences'.[19]

Yet, asked to analyse Griffith's action, renowned coach Alf Gover stated, 'There has never been any doubt in my mind that he throws both his bouncer and his yorker.' He explained, 'His arm goes away from his body in a bent position with his right elbow pointing in the direction of mid-on and his hand holding the ball close to his face. From that position he cannot bowl the ball, he must throw.'[20]

It would soon emerge, via a leak to the *Daily Mail*, that MCC – the game's lawmakers – had been alerted to new suspicions the previous September. At the end of the first day of the match at Edgbaston between the Frank Worrell XI and England XI, Australian umpire Cec Pepper wrote to MCC, saying, 'Having stood at square leg for the first time with Charles Griffith of the West Indies bowling, I should draw your attention to the fact that had it been other than an exhibition match I would have had no hesitation in calling him for throwing.' The fact that MCC had not alerted WICBC to the potential issue ahead of the Australian series was seen to have created a mess that might have been avoided.

If Sobers was seriously troubled by the controversy, he didn't speak much about it. He made no comment at the time and in 2002 he dismissed the incident by saying, 'It was water off a duck's back to Charlie,' and never wrote of any great stress it caused him as skipper. Swanton, however, felt it was significant that he had paid close attention to his bowler, often talking to him from mid-off or mid-on rather than occupying his preferred close-catching positions.

After West Indies' 179-run win in the first Test, the second, in Port-of-Spain, was a high-scoring draw. Sobers was run out for 69 in the first innings and scored 24 in the second. Benaud wondered about the impact of leadership. 'This was not the Sobers that I knew as one of the greatest stroke players the world has seen,' he said. 'Tactically he was matching Simpson, partly because he was a brainy cricketer and partly because he had the troops to command. His batting, once he settled down in his innings, had been fluent but not dynamic in the Sobers tradition.'[21]

Meanwhile, Mayne, who spent most of his time at third man or fine leg, recalled being asked constantly by the crowd who the best batsman in the world was. 'Before you had time to think, you were given no choice. "Sobers, man. Garry [is]

God,"' he explained, although he did try to play up to the fans by throwing in O'Neill, Simpson and Lawry. 'They love their cricket in that part of the world and they just think Sir Garfield is God.'[22]

While Australia were passing 500 in reply to West Indies' 429, Sobers took advantage of the home side's refusal to agree to a pre-series suggestion that leg-side fielders should be limited to five, as in many other countries, rather than six. Spinners Lance Gibbs and Tony White bowled a defensive leg-stump line with a packed field to support them. It proved that, for all his romanticism, Sobers could be a pragmatist when required.

West Indies won the third Test in Georgetown by 212 runs, Sobers continuing his unspectacular consistency with knocks of 45 and 42. Gibbs took six wickets in the second innings to help dismiss Australia for 144, and Sobers claimed four victims in the match.

Two up with two to play, Sobers was assured of a winning start to his captaincy when the fourth Test in Bridgetown was drawn. Going into the match on the back of an unbeaten 183 in Barbados's match against the tourists, Sobers lost the toss and saw the Australian openers, Lawry and Simpson, amass a first-wicket stand of 318. Griffith was warned by umpire Cecil Kippins for intimidatory bowling after sending down five bouncers in one over to Simpson, and he left Lawry groggy with a ball that grazed his cheekbone. The batsmen's heads had been in more danger than their wickets, however, and both went on to pass 200 in a total of 650 for 6. After a wicketless first day, Sobers worked hard to keep his players enthused and energetic on the second. According to Benaud, he 'whipped his men into some of their best and most fighting cricket of the tour'.[23]

West Indies responded with 573, Seymour Nurse becoming the game's third double centurion, Kanhai scoring 129 and Sobers adding a careful 55. Australia's final-day declaration was delayed by tight bowling, including Sobers going for only 29 in 20 overs, and the home side were set 253 to win in four and a half hours. At 183 for 3 and with 55 minutes remaining, Sobers promoted himself to number five ahead of Nurse, driving Graham McKenzie straight and slapping him past square leg for a pair of boundaries.

West Indies needed 39 in the final 35 minutes but lost two quick wickets against the new ball. Sobers – a batsman short with Jackie Hendricks having taken a blow to the head in the first innings – was gifted singles by a defensive field in order to keep him away from the strike. Solomon lacked the range of shots to compensate and the home side closed at 242 for 5, Sobers on 34. West Indies celebrated their first victory in five series against Australia and most of the following day's Caribbean newspapers used the phrase 'world champions'.

Those champions promptly lost the fifth Test in Trinidad. Sobers fell cheaply in both innings and another Kanhai century and a six-wicket performance by Griffith could not prevent a ten-wicket defeat.

Sobers accepted the Frank Worrell Trophy from Simpson at the end of a series which, while never matching the drama of 1960/61, had been worthy of its build-up. Sobers was critical of Simpson for not being attacking enough, although Benaud countered with, 'This was interesting reading because the two things on which the West Indians left themselves wide open to defensive criticism during the series were in the matter of the time taken by Hall and Griffith to bowl their overs and in the way the bowlers often operated down the line of leg stump to six on the on-side.'[24] Lawry thought Sobers's comments were 'unfair and incorrect'. He suggested, 'Sobers would have been better off if he had accepted the victory which the West Indies had deservedly won.'[25]

Benaud concluded that Sobers had 'handled his team well', but was fortunate that they had played well enough that he had not needed to be at the peak of his own form. He averaged 39.11 with the bat and took only 12 wickets at 41. Benaud wrote, 'No doubt the captaincy had some effect on him … though some of his batting was an absolute delight in miniature.'[26]

Team-mate Kanhai even suggested that West Indies had won 'because of the remarkable maturing of Garry Sobers'. Pointing out that the team had not fallen apart without the influence of Worrell, he said of Sobers, 'He's shrewd, popular, a deep thinker and a good leader. With Frank appointed team manager, the leadership was strengthened, not weakened.' He could also see Sobers becoming a better player, suggesting, 'Before he would go out to make a hundred flashy runs. Now he dropped himself down the order and went out with the idea of grafting for runs if necessary. His mental approach had completely changed.'[27]

For Sobers himself, the biggest revelation harked back to his initial fears of becoming detached from players with whom he had shared such good times. He found that he was no longer included in the gossip and tall stories that inhabit a changing room. Yet even though 'it was quite a surprise to find I am aloof from this' he also felt a sense of calm and pride from being in a position that made him privy to 'the true information and knowledge'.[28]

Wisden gave Sobers a good grade. 'He was three great players in one, and he seemed to thrive on his extra responsibilities of leadership,' it recorded. 'As a captain he showed an instinctive tactical sense which never let him down.'[29]

* * *

After his next season of league cricket in England in 1965, Sobers returned home for a long-awaited engagement. Thirteen years after his debut for Barbados, there was finally an opportunity to play competitively for his island with the introduction of the Shell Shield. Named after sponsors Royal Dutch Shell, the petroleum company, the tournament pitted Barbados against Trinidad, Jamaica, a Combined Islands team and British Guiana – soon to be Guyana after gaining independence from the United Kingdom. Unofficial regional competitions had been staged before, with the most recent edition in 1964 – a four-team league contested by the major islands – having attracted big crowds in the absence of any Test cricket. Sobers had been too busy in Australia to play in that event, the success of which hastened the introduction of the new officially recognised championship.

'I never could understand what the problem was in organising a West Indian tournament, since it seemed to be so essential to the development of our cricket,' said Sobers,[30] who would lead Barbados to the inaugural Shield title and see eight Barbadians picked to accompany him on the West Indies' tour of England later in 1966.

After a rain-hit draw against the combined Windward and Leeward team, Barbados continued their campaign in Bridgetown against Guiana. Sobers took six wickets in the visitors' 227 and went in the next day at 96 for 3. He should have been stumped in his 30s and, settling for steady accumulation of runs, shared a century stand with Peter Lashley and one of 214 with centurion Rawle Brancker before eventually being dismissed for 204. Former team-mate Clyde Walcott called it an innings of 'purpose and application'.[31] Barbados won by an innings and 15 runs, despite a maiden first-class century in Guiana's second innings by a tall, 21-year-old left-hander, Clive Lloyd.

Comfortable wins in their remaining two matches made Sobers and his men undisputed champions. As Tony Cozier remarked, 'Everything else in the series was overshadowed by the magnificent power of the Barbados team.'[32]

13

MAN FOR ALL SEASONS

*'The Sixties were a time when ordinary people could
do extraordinary things.'*

Model and actress Twiggy

THE SUMMER of 1966, which had seen England win
football's World Cup and 'Swinging London' make its claim
to be the cultural capital of the world, had just come to an end.
On the first day of October, Jimi Hendrix, an unorthodox left-
hander newly arrived from the United States, took the stage at
Regent Street Polytechnic to jam with Cream, who were about
to become one of music's biggest acts. Two numbers later, Eric
Clapton, Cream's guitarist, could only marvel at the virtuoso
performance he'd witnessed. 'He played every style you could
think of, and not in a flashy way,' he said. 'And then he walked
off and my life was never the same again.'[1]

Any cricketer who had shared the field with Garry Sobers
over the preceding few months would have recognised Clapton's
feelings. They were mere accompanists to the sport's undisputed
maestro as he travelled the country's Test grounds brandishing
his bat as Hendrix had wielded his guitar to deliver the lightest

of melodies, the heaviest rock or the smoothest of symphonies – whatever the situation desired. Rarely did he strike a bum note. Throw in his bowling and fielding and you had the greatest one-man band cricket had ever seen.

No less an authority than Neville Cardus, who had seen all the greats of the 20th century, proclaimed, 'We can safely agree that no player has proven versatility of skill as convincingly as Sobers has done, effortlessly, and after the manner born.'[2]

The biggest villain of an unforgettable summer of sport would turn out to be the Argentina captain, Antonio Rattin, sent off in the World Cup quarter-final against England at Wembley. Yet when the West Indies team arrived in the country in the spring, the title of public enemy number one belonged to their fast bowler, Charlie Griffith.

Late in the 1964 season, England batsman Ken Barrington had refused to play against Griffith in the Frank Worrell XI matches because he thought he was 'a blatant and dangerous thrower'.[3] The stories coming out of the Caribbean during Sobers's first series as captain had been a further reminder of the controversy over Griffith's action.

In the summer of 1965, MCC felt compelled to issue a statement saying they had not given instructions to umpires that Griffith should not be no-balled during the 1963 tour. Later it was announced by the MCC's Advisory Committee that the West Indies management had agreed that bowlers suspected of throwing on the 1966 tour could be reported to MCC by the umpires, even if not no-balled. Tour manager Jeff Stollmeyer would be informed of any reports.

Sobers had hoped that the subject would be dead and buried by the time his team arrived in England on 17 April. But, anticipating West Indies' arrival, Crawford White of the *Daily Express* said the tour could be 'the best Test series of the post-war era – or an international sporting disaster', adding, 'I call that disaster Hurricane Charlie.' Others, such as the *Daily Mirror*'s Brian Chapman, delighted in pointing out that Syd Buller, who had a record of calling no-balls for throwing, would umpire the tourists' opening first-class game against Worcestershire. 'Cricket faces possibly the most explosive start to a season in the history of the game in England,' he boomed in what Sobers called 'an article which was liable to start up the worst possible feeling'.[4]

At West Indies' first meeting with the media, Chapman described Sobers as being 'more nervous facing a press conference than any speed attack', although it was Stollmeyer who bore the brunt of the barrage of questions about Griffith. Sobers was grateful for Stollmeyer's composed dead-batting of the reporters' questions. If he had any apprehension ahead of the tour it was based on the absence of the calming influence of Frank Worrell. 'There were those fleeting moments when I wondered whether I was going to miss Sir Frank,' he admitted. 'He had encouraged me when I was low, advised me when I was bewildered, blasted me when he felt I was getting a bit too big for my cricket boots. Always he was there with a well-timed word when I needed him.'[5]

He and Stollmeyer had agreed the principles of their working relationship. Sobers would have complete charge on the field,

Stollmeyer was the boss away from it. Nobody would be allowed to come between them. The press conference had been the first test of their united front and it had been negotiated successfully.

Sobers turned his attention to raising the spirits of shivering team-mates, some of whom were experiencing the bitter chill of England for the first time. He reminded them of his first sight of mist when he'd arrived in 1957 and having to trust Worrell's word that the sun would come out eventually. He also promised them how much they would enjoy discovering London, which they could do before training began four days later at the indoor sports centre at Crystal Palace.

A month of cricket lay ahead before the first Test, although many days would be shortened or lost because of rain. At a reception during the opening match, Sobers told his audience, 'We always enjoy visiting Worcester. We always know we shall get a day off.'

In mid-May, he blasted 153 against Nottinghamshire. Shaking off the lack of quality practice time, his second fifty came off 44 balls, the third off 28, and he finished with five sixes and 20 fours in a 160-minute knock. Bagenal Harvey, by now working as Sobers's agent after looking after the likes of Denis Compton and footballer Johnny Haynes, made a mental note that Trent Bridge offered the most batsman-friendly surface in England.

John Clarke, in the tour book *Everything That's Cricket*,* recorded, 'The crowd of less than 5,000 was treated to

---

* Clarke died shortly after the first Test, and the book was continued by Brian Scovell.

a magnificent display of driving and of highly personal strokes,' adding, 'The big ground seemed almost too small to contain [him].'[6]

Against MCC at Lord's, Sobers made modest scores of 40 and 34, but his batting left a greater impression on Middlesex wicketkeeper John Murray than the second-day visit to the pavilion by world heavyweight boxing champion Muhammad Ali, in London to fight Henry Cooper. Describing an over from Glamorgan all-rounder Peter Walker, Murray recalled, 'He let Sobers have two or three balls and it looked like Garry was in real trouble with them, shuffling around like he'd never held a bat in his hands before. And after each one he'd call up the wicket, "Well bowled, Peter." So Walker gave him the exact same treatment again, and this time Garry banged it into the middle of the pavilion. No change of expression. "Well bowled, Pete."'[7]

A week later, Griffith was centre of attention again, no-balled for overstepping several times against Lancashire at Old Trafford. Yet, missed by the media on site, one of the calls had been by Arthur Fagg at square leg for throwing. Having expected to be besieged by reporters, Fagg was surprised to have left the ground unmolested and equally bemused when radio reports made no mention of the controversy for which everyone appeared to have been waiting. Sobers, who was sitting out the game, said of the media, 'Their chance came and they didn't just fumble it, ground it. They didn't even see it.'[8]

Fagg allegedly called certain reporters – 'for reasons best known to himself' according to Stollmeyer – and the manager's hotel room telephone was soon ringing off the hook. 'It is an isolated case and he was not called by an umpire chosen for the Tests so we are not paying any attention to it,' was Stollmeyer's stock reply.[9]

Sobers went into the first Test averaging 75 on tour with the bat and having just taken 6 for 11 in a victory over Derbyshire. His opposite number at Old Trafford was Mike 'MJK' Smith, who had led England in a drawn Ashes series the previous winter, but whose batting at Test level was frequently questioned. There were even stories flying around after he made 140 for MCC against the tourists at Lord's that Sobers had allowed him a big score to ensure he used up a place in the England order. Smith was known to be suspect against the fastest bowling, but Brian Scovell observed in the *Daily Sketch*, 'It was noticeable that Sobers did not attack him with pace when he first came in.'

The surface of the Manchester pitch was hard and dry enough for Sobers to have no hesitation in batting after he correctly called 'heads'. He had already seen his team reach 215, with Conrad Hunte scoring a century, by the time he strode out at number six. Sobers's position in the line-up had been the subject of much discussion among the tour selection committee, upon which captain and manager were joined by senior players Lance Gibbs, Wes Hall, Rohan Kanhai and Hunte. The majority wanted Sobers to bat inside the top four. 'But he preferred his chosen position, from which he claimed he could save the situation or push on, whichever was necessary,' Stollmeyer explained.[10]

According to EW Swanton in *The Daily Telegraph*, he 'did much as he pleased' in the evening session, reaching an unbeaten 83 by stumps. He batted with 'an exuberant mastery granted to few men on this level', said John Arlott.[11]

'Sobers,' wrote Scovell, 'began throwing his bat at the ball as though he hated it. Sometimes he played the wrong shot. His feet were in the wrong place or he was playing back to a yorker. But the end product was always the same – a searing, slashing boundary which left the fielders on the fence motionless.'[12]

It was a different story the next morning, however. The touch and timing had gone and he spent 45 minutes struggling through the 90s. He offered as many as four chances, yet it was a sign of Sobers's doggedness that he managed to advance his score to 161 in an innings that lasted 224 minutes and included 26 fours and a six.

By the time Gibbs had taken five wickets to dismiss England for 167, West Indies held a first-innings lead of 317 and Sobers enforced the follow-on. His three catches had included one effort at short leg to remove opener Eric Russell that defied physics, and now he took the new ball himself, ending up with three wickets.

England opener Colin Milburn, who made a second-innings 94, remembered, 'I marvelled at the all-round magnificence of Garry Sobers. Everything about this man was such world-class. Apart from his innings of 161, he bowled 49 overs of seamers and quick stuff, some orthodox left-arm leg-spin, some back-of-the-hand teasers … and took five catches, four of them in the leg trap. On top of this, he led his side with rare judgement for three days and still found time to give the racing pages a going over.'[13]

Gibbs claimed five more victims as England were bowled out for 277 before the end of the third day, the first time they had lost so quickly since being beaten by Australia at Headingley in 1938.

Before the teams arrived at Lord's for the second Test, West Indies had suffered a swift defeat of their own, skittled for 123 and 67 by Sussex in a nine-wicket loss at Hove. Twelfth man David Holford spilled a tray of drinks under the rush of reporters heading for the West Indies dressing room to speak to Sobers. 'It has not affected my morale in the slightest,' the skipper told them. 'In a long tour you have got to expect to come across a wicket like this. It was a typically green English wicket and Sussex had the right bowlers for it.' Sobers would come to consider the match as having benefited his team, ensuring they didn't succumb to complacency after their overwhelming success in the first Test.

What Sobers didn't welcome was more controversy around Griffith, who struck Sussex batsman Ken Suttle on the jaw in the one over he bowled when the home team batted for a second time, needing only six to win. Griffith was also accused of walking away without showing concern for his opponent. 'That hurt me more than anything else,' said Suttle.

After Suttle retired unsteadily to the pavilion, Griffith sent two more bouncers past the nose of England wicketkeeper Jim Parks, who said, 'Charlie came in like a steam engine.' Sobers claimed he had taken Griffith off after that one over because 'somebody might have got hurt'. Privately, he told Griffith, not for the first time, to ignore the noise of the media and continue to do his job.

Yet after the second day's play in the Lord's Test, Sobers would find Griffith knocking on his hotel-room door. Wicketless at the mid-point of England's first innings, events at Hove and the continued suspicions about his action had dominated the tabloid previews of the match. After sharing a drink, Griffith went silent and looked at his hands, before saying, 'These people are trying to destroy me. No matter what I do, somebody has to have a go at me. Maybe I should just pack my bags.'[14]

Sobers, who knew Griffith as a quiet man who 'doesn't go in for theatricals', was reminded of his own desire to go home from Pakistan in 1958.[15] He assured him that team-mates and management were on his side and urged him not to play into the hands of his critics. 'We'll continue to play you,' he assured his bowler. 'You are worth so much to this team.'[16]

Sobers recalled, 'That might not seem like much to tell a man who is on the verge of throwing away his career, his life. But these were words which Charlie could understand. He heaved himself out of that chair, gave me a nod and a sort of a grin and ambled off to bed.'[17]

On the field, Sobers would be called upon to avert another crisis. With Colin Cowdrey taking over from the discarded Smith as captain and 39-year-old Tom Graveney scoring 96 in his first Test for three years, England led by 86 on first innings. West Indies had been helped by the bizarre run-out of Basil D'Oliveira, who was making his Test debut. Having been dropped by wicketkeeper David Allan second ball off Sobers, he'd reached 27 when Parks – on his way to 91 – drove the ball down the pitch and saw it deflect off D'Oliveira's foot on to the stumps at the non-striker's end. Bowler Hall had the presence of mind to pick up the ball and pull a stump out of the broken wicket before D'Oliveira could get back to his crease.

By the fourth morning, West Indies had slumped to 95 for 5, only nine runs ahead. According to *The Times*, they were 'on the point of surrendering'. There were fears that the match might be over before the Queen arrived at the tea interval. Sobers had only just arrived at the crease and was not expected by the England fielders to be at his sharpest. 'Garry hadn't been to bed the night before that innings,' his close friend Barry Knight claimed, 'and everybody on the England team knew it. You only had to take one look at him, and you knew he had no sleep and was a shot duck.' Yet Knight also knew that 'on such occasions, to prove potential critics wrong, Garry always made an extra effort to make runs'.[18]

Sobers was joined by his cousin David Holford, a leg-spinning all-rounder who had made his Test debut at Old Trafford. Surveying the close fielders, Sobers determined that he needed to put Cowdrey on the defensive. 'I had to make him spread the field,' he said. 'And the only way to do that was to belt the hell out of his bowlers.'[19]

He told Holford to forget about attacking and to get his head down. Pointing at the brown pitch, he reminded him that it was no different to Kensington Oval. Sobers's plan worked to perfection. It took only a few aggressive shots for Cowdrey to set the field back when he was on strike, preferring to offer him a single and bowl at Holford. The West Indies captain was not the only one who felt Cowdrey had blundered. Scovell wrote, 'All he succeeded in doing was giving Sobers a lot of easy runs he would have had to work hard for.'[20]

What was now taking shape was the innings Sobers believed to be his finest in Test cricket – 'because of the state of the game, having to look after Holford and the tactical battle with Cowdrey'.[21]

Never shedding his long-sleeved jumper, 'Sobers moved on,' said Arlott, 'first protectively, always commandingly and gradually, too, Holford lengthened his stride. This was magnificent batting.'[22] Sobers reached his fifty from 85 balls and a cover drive off left-armer Jeff Jones brought him his century from 188 balls after 228 minutes. The only chance he had given was on 93 when he slashed Ken Higgs close to Cowdrey at slip. *The Times* said he 'was pacing the game as he wished'.

Once Holford had got over a nervy start, Sobers chose not to keep him away from the strike, eager to boost his growing confidence. 'I played the shots where I wanted to play them,' he said. 'I did not try to shield David, I let him get on with his game.'[23] Sobers had been too wrapped up in the challenge to remember that his century was a record 16th by a West Indian cricketer.[*]

---

[*] Sobers now occupies third place on that list, his 26 centuries ranking behind only Brian Lara (34) and Shivnarine Chanderpaul (30).

By the close of play, he was unbeaten on 121, with Holford on 71. At 288 for 5 – a lead above 200 – Sobers now had eyes on a declaration and was able to tell Holford to bat more freely. While Sobers reached 163, including 13 fours, Holford advanced to 105 in a 318-minute vigil and the partnership to an unbroken 274. The success of Holford, who held a degree in agriculture and was described by Sobers as 'the bright one in the family',[24] gave him particular satisfaction because he sensed that some within the team thought his cousin's place was down to blood more than ability.

With a lead of 283, Sobers felt his team couldn't lose the game with four hours to play. But 45 minutes lost to rain after they'd taken four wickets dented their chances of forcing victory. It may even have denied the opportunity of an unlikely triumph to England, who got to 197 for 4 as Milburn hit three sixes in a three-hour unbeaten 126.

Sobers called it one of the best Test matches he played in, while Scovell, perhaps falling prey to hyperbole, wrote in the *Daily Sketch* that West Indies' fightback was a 'cricketing Dunkirk unequalled in the history of retrieving last causes'. Even the crowd on Wimbledon's Centre Court showed their appreciation the next day when the West Indies team, smartly dressed in tour blazers, took their seats to a standing ovation.

West Indies took a 2-0 lead in the series with a 139-run victory in the third Test at Trent Bridge, a match that featured two episodes that angered and upset Sobers. All out for 235 after Sobers won the toss, West Indies surrendered a lead of 90 as Graveney this time made it to a century. He helped to rebuild after Sobers, who took four wickets, removed Geoffrey Boycott with the second ball of the innings, swinging one in exaggeratedly to trap him lbw. 'The best delivery I have ever faced in cricket,' was Boycott's description.[25]

Sobers walked away with the nonchalance of someone who had expected no other outcome. In fact, he always felt confident of dismissing the Yorkshireman, believing he was susceptible to the ball he brought in at him because he moved his front foot across the crease rather than down the pitch to meet the ball. The fact that Boycott prioritised defence over attack also offered Sobers the freedom to experiment with different deliveries without fear of a bad ball being severely punished.

West Indies approached their second innings knowing that they needed to knuckle down. It led to moments of unrest among the crowd and criticism from the press box as Basil Butcher and Rohan Kanhai shared a painstaking partnership of 110 for the third wicket. At one stage they took 20 overs to add 30 runs. Michael Melford in the *Sunday Telegraph* called it a 'dour, strokeless piece of batting', while the *Daily Sketch*'s headline was, 'THE BIG BORE TEST'. Reporter Scovell said, 'They did more damage to the game of cricket in 115 minutes of stalemate [after tea] than any other similar English crawl has done.'

The *Daily Mirror* really went to town, with Chapman claiming that the legend of West Indies as 'the gay Caribbean buccaneers, the calypso cavaliers' had been killed, along with the notion that 'Sobers is cricket's superman'. He continued, 'Enterprise of any sort was outlawed. By order of Sheriff Sobers.'

What angered Sobers was that the same critical voices that had previously accused West Indies of being too carefree and careless were now lambasting them for showing the kind of backbone that would be applauded if demonstrated by England batsmen. On Sunday's rest day, he warned, 'Tomorrow we may dig in even more. Do they want us to rush out there playing shots like mad when we are 90 behind? Just because we have created a reputation for playing a certain way, people shouldn't expect we always play like that irrespective of the state of the game.'

Sobers himself allayed some of the doomsayers' fears on the fourth day. While Butcher continued calmly towards a double century, Sobers hit 14 fours in scoring 94 off 138 balls before hitting Higgs to debutant Derek Underwood at mid-off. According to D'Oliveira, 'It was the best innings I saw that summer; he just devastated us in a couple of hours.' Noting that 'he gave it away with a slog', he added, 'That was the way Garry played the game.'[26] And when Stollmeyer told off Sobers for throwing away a century, he replied, 'Never you mind, Mr Manager. I want to pick up two or three [wickets] this afternoon.'[27]

A declaration at 482 for 5 left England needing 393 to win. They made only 253, Griffith taking four wickets and earning further disapproval by hitting Underwood on the head with a bouncer when only one wicket was needed. 'Griffith deserved every boo,' said the Daily Sketch. 'It was like tossing a hand grenade when the enemy had already surrendered.' In The Daily Telegraph, Swanton felt Griffth had 'gratuitously introduced a sour note' and the *Daily Mirror*'s Chapman said it was 'vicious, uncouth and utterly uncalled for'.

Sobers – who had been hit for six by Boycott – felt compelled to intervene, telling Griffith he didn't need to bowl bouncers at tailenders when there was plenty of time. 'He didn't offer any explanation; didn't say a word, in fact,' Sobers said. 'I was not suggesting in any way that he intended to hit Derek [and] I never mentioned the incident to him again.'[28]

Stollmeyer, however, persuaded Griffith to write a letter of apology to Underwood, and at the conclusion of the tour the WICBC withheld the bowler's bonus, an act the manager felt was unjustified.

Now came a month without Test cricket, the decks having been cleared for the three weeks of football's World Cup. In the meantime, West Indies played seven first-class games, the highlight for Sobers coming on the day after England opened their ultimately triumphant campaign with a 0-0 draw against Uruguay. Suffering from two sore fingers on his left hand and relying mostly on wrist-spin, his 9 for 49 in 19.4 overs to secure victory by an innings against Kent at Canterbury represented the best bowling figures by a West Indian in England, bettering the 8 for 52 Holford had achieved recently against Cambridge University.

Five days after Geoff Hurst's hat-trick against West Germany ensured it was all over and Bobby Moore had lifted the World Cup following a 4-2 win in the final, the host nation began a fourth Test that ensured the other major sporting contest of the summer would end in defeat.

On a Headingley wicket left green by several days of rain, Sobers dominated a partnership with centurion Seymour Nurse, scoring 174 of the 265 runs added for the fifth wicket. Sobers 'had the feeling that I could hit it anywhere I liked almost whenever I liked'.[29] Which is what he did, finding the boundary 24 times in a 240-minute innings. He became the first West Indian to reach 5,000 runs in Test cricket and he topped 100 runs in the session between lunch and tea. 'We'd seen it all before,' said Arlott. 'And it was as thrilling as ever.'[30]

'The Supremo!' was the *Daily Mirror*'s banner headline, under which Chapman began his report, 'It's that man again. The man England forgot while they cheered on their Wembley heroes.' In his column in the *Daily Sketch*, great West Indies all-rounder Sir Learie Constantine noted that Sobers 'has his own way of making good balls into bad balls' and marvelled at his assault on the new ball. 'He lashed into [John] Snow, hitting the ball against the fence so hard that it was bound to bruise it and take the shine off.'

After Sobers declared at 500 for 9, England were dismissed for 240 on the third day. Sobers's feat of mopping up the lower order to claim a five-wicket haul was overshadowed by yet more drama surrounding Griffith. This time he received a warning from umpire Charlie Elliott for throwing after delivering a bouncer to Graveney. Elliott told Griffith, 'You can bowl, Charlie, but any more like that I will have to call you. That delivery to Graveney was illegal.'

No one could understand why, if Elliott was so sure of what he had seen, he had not called a no-ball. Griffith believed it was because the umpire had been influenced more by the reaction of the England batsmen than the evidence of his own eyes. Griffith told Sobers, 'I saw them turning to Elliott as if they were saying, "What about that one?"'

Sobers approached the umpire. 'Was that your decision?' he challenged. 'Or did you make it because of the English players? If the players influenced you, I'll have to report you.' Sobers had to submit a post-match report on the umpire anyway, so that was not quite as dramatic as it sounds, but Elliott replied, 'It was my decision, Garry, and mine alone. I just didn't like the way he bowled that short ball.'[31]

It was not the end of the day's tetchiness, however. The West Indies players felt D'Oliveira was caught by a diving Hunte at midwicket off Gibbs, only for Elliott to rule it had not been a clean catch.

'Why didn't you walk?' Sobers called to D'Oliveira.

'I didn't think it was out. And the umpires didn't give me out.'

Sobers felt that 'an ugly feeling entered the match'[32] and when D'Oliveira was finally out for 88 after hitting four sixes, the fielding team refused to clap him off.

The follow-on was enforced and Sobers saw a hunch pay off with the wicket of Boycott before stumps on Saturday when occasional medium-pacer Peter Lashley had him caught behind. 'Everyone said that I was a genius,' said Sobers, 'but if the plan had failed I would have been an idiot.'[33]

England were bowled out for 205 in mid-afternoon on the fourth day – six wickets for Gibbs and three for Sobers

– leaving West Indies as winners by an innings and 55 runs and unassailable 3-0 leaders in the series. Hordes of fans raced across the field to gather below the pavilion balcony, where they chanted for Sobers, who appeared with champagne glass in hand.

The bubbly continued to flow on the team coach as it left the stadium, but it eventually left a sour taste. Griffith felt emboldened to air the frustration that had been building towards his captain for limiting his opportunities with the new ball. 'Too often he was willing to gamble with himself and I was made to bowl with a ball bereft of shine,' he said, admitting that 'my cup of pent-up emotion just flowed over'. A tearful Griffith told Sobers he didn't think he had given him enough support against the press criticism. It was a big turnaround from the pair's cosy chat during the Lord's Test. Sobers, observing the amount of alcohol that was flowing, sat quietly. When the players reached their hotel at the tour's next destination, Glasgow, a contrite and clear-headed Griffith apologised for having 'gone too far and said too many hurtful things'. Sobers forgave him.[34]

Meanwhile, the tourists quickly found out what their success had meant in the Caribbean. When copies of the *Barbados Advocate* reached England they were able to read, 'In Bridgetown yesterday jukeboxes time and again blared the music of Sparrow's calypso, "Sir Garfield Sobers, the greatest cricketer on Earth or Mars", and the Merrymen's version of "Archie (Break Them Up)", obviously reflecting the elation of West Indian supporters. Indeed, this was the pattern set by radio stations immediately after the match ended. Restaurants and liquor shops did a roaring trade – and in some instances one could hear the roar some distance away – and in some offices it was difficult to settle back down to normal routine duty.'

Sobers received telegrams of congratulation from WICBC president Noel Pierce and from Barbados Cricket Association president Eric Inniss, who noted, 'Your brilliant, inspired leadership and superb personal contributions supported by fine all-round team effort make all West Indians proud and happy.'

Barbados and its people had plenty to celebrate in 1966. The nation had been playing a larger role in its own affairs for the past couple of decades, with votes for all introduced in 1950. Grantley Adams, who had helped form the Barbados Labour Party, became the island's first prime minister in 1953 and his party held power for eight years. When the Democratic Labour Party came to office in 1961 under Errol Barrow a swifter path to independence from the UK was pursued. By the time Sobers was leading the Barbados-dominated West Indies squad to success in England in 1966, the country was waiting for the presentation of the Barbados Independence Bill in the House of Commons – which would eventually happen in late October. The Bill was passed in early November and on the final day of the month Barbados would follow Jamaica, Trinidad and Guyana in becoming an independent state, although retaining its British monarch.

Politically uninterested and geographically removed for the majority of his time, Sobers devoted little thought to such matters. Yet there was, according to manager Stollmeyer, an indirect impact on the party. He felt that 'more and more nationalism on the part of the individual territories that form the whole' had played a role in him being approached in Bradford early in the tour by a disgruntled group of non-Barbadians, who complained that the tour was being dominated by one group, even though that was a natural product of mere numbers. 'I had neither noticed nor conceived of any inclination to favouritism of the Barbadians,' recalled Stollmeyer, who called a team meeting to eradicate any resentment.[35]

* * *

For the second consecutive series, West Indies lost the final Test after the greater victory had been secured. An England team with its third captain of the summer, Brian Close, recovered from 166 for 7 to make 527, winning by an innings and 34 runs.

Sobers made 81 in a West Indies first-innings score of 268, hitting 12 fours and dominating his partnership with centurion Kanhai. He then captured three wickets as Graveney's 165 and a hundred by wicketkeeper John Murray drove England to an imposing 527, underscored by a tenth-wicket partnership of 128 between Snow and Higgs. Sobers's final total of 20 wickets for the series was bettered by only one team-mate, Gibbs with 21.

His final chance of adding to his haul of runs lasted only one ball on the fourth morning. Aiming a hook at Snow, he bottom-edged the ball into the top of his leg and into the hands of Close, breathing down his neck in typically fearless fashion at short leg. What caused Sobers to mistime his shot and suffer such an ignominious end to his triumphant series is unclear. In his version of events in *King Cricket*, he said, 'I was surprised to get a short fast ball so early in my innings.'[36] By the time he worked on *My Autobiography* more than three decades later, his memory had changed to, 'I knew what was going through his mind. "Bouncer, bouncer." Sure enough, Snowy bounced one at me and I quickly moved into position.' In both accounts, the ball dipped more quickly than Sobers expected.

The mishap did nothing to change the way in which history would remember his remarkable summer. A series victory as captain, and retention of the *Wisden* Trophy; 722 Test runs at an average of 103.14; 20 Test wickets at 27.25; more first-class runs (1,349) and wickets (60) than anyone on tour; and ten catches in the Tests, the most on either team. Almost six decades later, still no one taking 20 wickets in a series has come close to Sobers's haul of 700-plus runs, with South Africa's George Faulkner the only other to top 500, against England in 1910. Stollmeyer said, 'He never seemed capable of putting a foot wrong in anything he did on the field of play. His performances were superb in every department of the game, and I could only marvel at the quality of quantity of the superlative performances that he produced.'[37]

The dominance of Sobers might have reflected negatively on the overall view of the 1966 team, which was inevitably compared with the side of three years earlier. *Wisden* editor Norman Preston argued that 'this latest side was not so well balanced and relied too much on the all-round excellence of the captain'.[38] Even Stollmeyer admitted, 'Perhaps too much depended on the all-round skill of Garry Sobers.'[39]

Sobers, however, was well satisfied with the manner of his team's victory. 'On that tour of 1966 we shattered that folksy little picture of West Indian cricketers into tiny fragments,' he said. 'We produced a new image – of a team that could get its head down when the going was rough, and keep it down, even though others didn't like the sight very much.'[40]

* * *

Even though the Lord's Test had produced world-record receipts of £58,000, the overall tour profit had been around half of three years earlier, although the distraction of the World Cup was an undoubted factor.

English cricket's Board of Control, prompted by the success of one-day cricket since the 1963 launch of the Gillette Cup and perhaps inspired by football, promoted its own version of a 'World Cup'. With sponsorship from the Rothmans tobacco company, which had enjoyed the success of its series of International Cavaliers games against thecounties on Sundays, Lord's hosted a triangular series of games contested by a Rest of the World team, an England XI and a West Indian XI, the numerical qualification attached to signify the denial of full international status. The announcement of the event in March had coincided with the headline-grabbing theft of football's World Cup, the Jules Rimet trophy, from an exhibition in Westminster Central Hall, which meant the 50-over tournament was barely spoken about until the matches arrived almost a month after the final

Test. When the West Indies beat Warwickshire at Edgbaston in a warm-up game, the crowd of 10,000 eclipsed attendance at the real tournament, which attracted only 13,000 over three days at Lord's. Introducing the action on BBC TV, Peter West lamented the 'sorry lack of press publicity for the Lord's matches'.

The World team, led by Australia's Bobby Simpson and selected weeks earlier via voting forms in the *Radio Times*, lost to both the national teams, which meant the contest between England and the West Indies was, in effect, a final and could be said to have been the first one-day international – although that honour was reserved for the Australia–England clash in Melbourne in early 1971. England made 217 for 7 and captain Ted Dexter, mastermind of Sussex's victories in the first two Gillette Cups, set more defensive fields than Sobers had adopted and West Indies failed to end their tour with another trophy when they were bowled out for 150. Writing in *The Cricketer*, Michael Melford concluded, 'I am not a devotee of one-day cricket as such and I think a little of it goes a long way, but I do believe such a tournament may be worthwhile when played by the best.'

14

FUN, LOVE AND MONEY

*'This is a fiction adventure story created for
interest and entertainment and not a biography
nor a prophecy of how cricket of the future
might be played. It was fun to write. I hope it
will be fun to read.'*

Bonaventure and the Flashing Blade (Garry Sobers,
Pelham Books, 1967)

A COUPLE of weeks after departing England, the countdown
to West Indies' next engagement began with the announcement
of the party that would head to India in December for three
Tests. Garry Sobers had made it clear to the WICBC that he
wished to be rested, and that the tour should be used to look at
younger players. The Board reminded Sobers that India and its
cricket fans expected to see the West Indies captain.

In the end, he was grateful that his bosses stood their
ground. Even though the trip threw up the issues of comfort
and facilities that were typical of subcontinental visits at that
time, he had the satisfaction of another series victory as captain
– and he became engaged to be married.

The notable new name in Sobers's squad was Guyana batsman Clive Lloyd. Former West Indies fast bowler Prior Jones was appointed manager, although Frank Worrell would also spend much time in the team's company after travelling to India on a speaking tour.

In the first Test at Bombay's Brabourne Stadium the home side were limited to 296. A century by Conrad Hunte and consistent returns from the middle order, including 82 by debutant Lloyd and a laboured 50 for Sobers, earned a first-innings lead of 125. Eventually set only 192 to win, West Indies lost four wickets to leg-spinner Bhagwat Chandrasekhar with 90 on the board before Sobers joined Lloyd for an unbeaten century stand to seal the match, Lloyd adding 78 to his match tally and Sobers recording another half-century, this one full of confident, fluent strokeplay. 'I have to go – it's the [Indian 1,000] Guineas in half an hour,' he told Lloyd, dashing off without celebrating, keen to pursue a tip and fulfil a promise he'd made to English jockey Willie Snaith that he would be in attendance.[1] A bemused Lloyd recalled, 'Here I was playing in my first Test match and the captain was, apparently, more concerned about winning at the races than winning the Test.'[2]

Lloyd's memories of his captain on his first tour remained mixed, and not just because he insisted on calling him 'Clyde', a habit he never relinquished. 'I was still in awe of Garry,' he said, recalling being invited into his room for a nightcap. 'I wasn't much of a drinker but he would pour me a small whisky from the little jug he kept. It was difficult to believe I was sitting here listening to him talk about the game.' Yet bonhomie went only so far. 'I think at that stage of my career I would have enjoyed a little more guidance,' he said.[3]

The second Test at Calcutta saw West Indies total 390 – with another 70 for Sobers – before Lance Gibbs bagged five wickets to shoot out India for 167. Sobers enforced the follow-on and took four wickets as India failed by 45 runs to make West Indies bat again. It sounds straightforward, but there was plenty of unwanted drama.

The Indian team was taking the field in front of a packed Eden Gardens crowd on the second morning, New Year's Day, when it became apparent that thousands of fans were unable to access the seats for which they had tickets. At first, they attempted to secure any possible vantage point and then they began flinging missiles of various descriptions at the police. When one spectator crossed the field in an apparent attempt to calm the others, police mistook him for another agitator and, according to Indian captain the Nawab of Pataudi, he was 'beaten up by half a dozen men in uniform'.[4]

At that point, thousands of fans entered the playing field, prompting officers to use canes and tear-gas. Stones and bottles were thrown at the police, and fences and chairs were ripped apart before being set alight in the stands. By this time, both teams were in the dressing rooms, suffering the sting of tear-gas. Then Hunte decided that he needed to rescue the West Indian flag from on top of the pavilion.

Outside, where buses were being burned, fans sheltered players as they looked for cars to carry them to safety. Sobers was one of five West Indians who squeezed into a Ford Prefect while stones were being thrown at the team bus. Back in their hotel, the tourists were of a mind to call off the tour. It needed the calm diplomacy of Worrell and Pataudi, along with assurances from West Bengal chief minister PC Sen that the match could continue safely, before play resumed two days later and the tour was rescued.

Wes Hall remembered the match not just for the tear-gas but for the assistance Sobers gave him in combating the mysteries of Chandrasekhar. When Hall was on strike Sobers would watch the bowler's grip and hand position and, when he detected a googly, would move his bat to indicate to Hall that he could play the ball with the spin to the leg side. The fast bowler scored 35 before falling to Chandrasekhar shortly after the loss of his eagle-eyed partner.

More was happening in Sobers's life, however, than cricket and crowd trouble. He had become engaged for the first time, to 17-year-old actress Anju Mahendru, whom he met at a party. Sobers said he 'fell head over heels in love' and thought 'why not?' when the subject of engagement arose. If that hardly sounds like the deepest of passions, then neither does the fact that he couldn't correctly remember her name in future years – calling her 'Anju Mahindu' in his autobiography. More than 500 people attended an engagement party and local media delighted in taking photographs of this power couple; the world's greatest cricketer and the girl who had been modelling since the age of 13 and had recently undertaken her first major film roles. 'The people in the West Indies must have wondered what was going on,' he admitted.[5]

When Sobers left India to continue his career in England, it was with the full intention that their relationship should continue towards marriage, but it soon became obvious that it would never happen. There were reports that Anju's parents did not approve of the alliance and she would eventually speak about the relationship in the manner of someone swept off their feet rather than a woman in love. 'I was very young and sports people had a certain aura about them,' she said on one occasion. Another time, she said on television that Sobers possessed 'everything that a little young girl would look up to', adding, 'Unfortunately Sobers fell in love with me because I wasn't in love with him.'[6]

Sobers, with his charm, status and good looks, would continue to attract admiration from women all over the world throughout his life. Interestingly, many of the photographs he received from unknown, admiring females – innocent portraits, not shots of the racy variety – were retained and appeared in the collection of memorabilia he offered to the Barbados Museum and Historical Society when he was in his late 80s.

Back on the field, the Test series concluded with a high-scoring draw in Madras, where both teams topped 400 in their first innings, Sobers falling five runs short of a century. Needing 322 to win, West Indies settled for a draw at 270 for 7. Sobers maintained his record of making a fifty in every innings without going on to three figures by scoring an unbeaten 74 – for a final series average of 114. 'That man Sobers was a marvel,' said Indian spinner Erapalli Prasanna. 'Bowling to him one often wondered whether he was human.'[7]

Witnessing the series for *Playfair Cricket Monthly*, Rusi Modi exclaimed, 'What a magnificent player Sobers is! Take him away from the West Indies side and the world champions would be reduced to an ordinary team. Considering the variety of strokes he plays, his consistency is amazing.'[8]

Three series as captain. Three series victories. Thirteen Test matches played, seven won and only two defeats. And no loss of personal form. 'The conversion to captaincy had been painless,' Sobers recorded. 'Everything was going well and all the time I was captain and winning, everyone was with me.'[9]

But Pataudi had felt that 'this once great Caribbean combination seemed to be in decline'[10] and, indeed, Sobers would not win another series. He won only two of 26 more Test matches as captain. 'The day I stopped winning,' he admitted, 'many of those same people were against me.'[11]

* * *

Sir Frank Worrell did not live to see another West Indies Test match. Even before the end of the Indian tour he was taken ill and sent home to Jamaica, where it was discovered that he was suffering from leukaemia. On 13 March 1967, at the age of 42, he died in hospital.

'I lost a friend, whose wisdom guided me for many years,' Sobers said shortly after the news broke. 'I – and countless other West Indies cricketers – owe to him a debt which can never be repaid, and the players of the future will benefit from his greatness too.'[12]

That comment was a hasty addition to later editions of *King Cricket*, the book about the 1966 tour of England that was released in January 1967. Its publication came during a busy period for Sobers the 'author' as his agent, Bagenal Harvey, looked to maximise his position as one of the most famous sportsmen in the world.

In 1965, London-based Pelham Books – about to embark on a series of named football annuals with the likes of George Best, Denis Law, Alan Ball and others – had published *Cricket, Advance!* Across 108 pages, Sobers – or someone writing in his name – offered advice on playing the game, complete with a series of technical photographs.

The following year Pelham put out *Cricket Crusader*, the first Sobers autobiography, ghost-written by Reginald Martin, a prolific author of children's science fiction and western novels under a variety of pseudonyms. It was the first of several volumes of Sobers memoirs, including *My Most Memorable Matches*, with Tony Cozier in 1984; *Twenty Years at the Top*, penned by Brian Scovell in 1988; and *My Autobiography*, with Bob Harris in 2002. There was also *The Changing Face of Cricket*, in collaboration with cricket writer Ivo Tennant, in 1996, in which Sobers mixed memoir with thoughts on the modern game.

None of the autobiographies can be considered classics of the genre, despite the credentials of the collaborators, largely because of Sobers's sketchy recollections, absence of deep insight and his lack of interest in considering the context and legacy of his own career. The first, *Cricket Crusader*, is the one that contains some of the most revealing passages – for example, around the death of Collie Smith – and the greatest effort to give Sobers some kind of voice, which one might expect from an author of fiction such as Martin. There is some crossing of the line, however, and the flights of fantasy taken by the writer on occasions make it sound like he was sharing the same stimulants that The Beatles were experimenting with while creating the *Sergeant Pepper* album around the same time.

Pelham published *King Cricket* early in 1967 with the boast that it was 'one of the most outspoken books ever written about cricket', although the amount of first-person revelation that Sobers adds to the functional match reports of the 1966 series make that a tenuous claim.

Later in the year came the most bizarre of all Sobers's literary endeavours when he was listed as the author of another Pelham publication, *Bonaventure and the Flashing Blade: A Novel about Cricket*. The actual writer was Martin, who also penned sports-themed tales for Law and motor-racing driver Graham Hill. Martin created a story about a computer buff called Clyde St Joseph Bonaventure who was rubbish at cricket but developed a program to give him match-winning skills, bringing him to the unwanted attention of foreign enemies. It is the name of Sobers only that appears on the cover.

It prompted journalist Will Buckley to take a copy with him when given the chance to interview Sobers in London in 2001, a decision that didn't bear fruit. 'Hoping to start on a high note, I produce the book,' Buckley recalled. 'Sir Garry, recoiling, looks at the dust jacket as if it were a picture of Alan Knott in his underwear. "I've never seen one of them," he says.

And, after closer inspection: "I think I may have read it." It's not going to provide a talking point.'[13]

* * *

Sobers had rounded off his 1966/67 tour with a century in the final first-class match against Ceylon in Colombo, before returning to Shell Shield duty for Barbados with an unbeaten run-a-minute 97 against the Leeward Islands, newcomers to the tournament. Two matches later he made 165, batting at number seven, to ensure a draw against Guyana in Georgetown, the only one of four matches Barbados failed to win as they topped the table again.

After a month off, Sobers was back in England to ply his trade for another summer. He might have been exhausted enough to ask his country for a winter break, but there was no question of him missing the more lucrative bread-and-butter of his professional career.

While playing for Norton on Saturdays, most of his Sundays were taken up representing the International Cavaliers. Sobers hardly set the country alight in these games, his only half-century – a score of 86 in a partnership of 159 with Clive Lloyd – coming when the Cavaliers took on the Indian tourists at Southport. He was a little more productive with the ball, including a best of 5 for 21 against Leicestershire.

It was lucrative, gentle knockabout stuff. But when Sobers returned to the Caribbean to renew rivalry with England things became tougher than he could have imagined.

15

A GAMBLE TOO FAR

'Infamy! Infamy! They've all got it in for me.'

Kenneth Williams as Julius Caesar, *Carry on Cleo*
(Anglo-Amalgamated, 1964)

EASTER 1968 was still a month away, yet Trinidad's Good Friday ritual had been initiated early. Tradition called for an effigy – a 'bobolee' as it was called – of Judas Iscariot to be hung in a public place, or positioned on a chair, so that passers-by could beat it with sticks or any other implements that were to hand. On the evening of 19 March youngsters in the capital city of Port-of-Spain fashioned their own figure upon which popular wrath could be exacted and hung it in Independence Square. In the image of Garry Sobers.

The West Indies captain's crime had been another betrayal of sorts. He had let down the sport that united and defined the Caribbean by treating a Test match with outright recklessness. The declaration that had allowed England to win at Queen's Park Oval in the fourth match of a tight series was either horrible miscalculation or extreme neglect. Either way, Sobers had descended from deity to devil in the space of 215 England runs.

'Sobers's status as West Indian folk hero was considerably diminished,' was writer JS Barker's understated summary,[1] while Henry Blofeld, visiting from England, observed, 'The Caribbean was left in dismay and many people had an immediate desire to crucify Sobers. In some places it was obviously felt that he had gambled with nationalism.'[2]

The MCC team arrived in the latter days of 1967 to talk that Sobers's team was past its peak, with Conrad Hunte retired and Wes Hall and Charlie Griffith, 29 and 28 respectively, increasingly fragile. England had their own issues, meanwhile, not least the fact that they were being led by a man widely accepted as being third choice.

Brian Close, unbeaten in seven Test matches as captain, was favoured by the selectors but the blatant time-wasting tactics that ensured his Yorkshire team achieved a draw against Warwickshire at Edgbaston had turned officialdom against him. An executive committee of former county captains had officially censured him for his actions and that was enough for England to look elsewhere, especially when he said unrepentantly, 'My conscience is clear. My job was to prevent the other side from winning.'

As John Arlott commented, 'He placed authority in an intolerable position and one from which it was impossible for him to be appointed England captain again if by definition he refused to accept its definition of fair play.'[3]

MJK Smith, the first of three England captains to oppose Sobers in England in 1966, would have been asked to return to the role but he promptly announced his retirement from first-class cricket.* That left Colin Cowdrey, whose defensive approach in the three Tests he'd led that summer had not impressed Sobers. This time, according to EM Wellings's tour report in *Wisden*, Cowdrey 'led England much more skilfully than Sobers had led the West Indies'.[4] And England batsman Tom Graveney believed, 'No unbiased judge could possibly fail to put Cowdrey ahead of Sobers in all the accepted arts of captaincy in that series.'[5]

It was the beginning of a period that exposed Sobers's shortcomings as a captain – beyond the controversial Trinidad declaration. In his history of West Indies cricket, Michael Manley recorded that West Indies were 'quite capable of defeating the Englishmen' but added, 'It is the captain who has to provide the chemistry of unity, of fellowship, of discipline; in short, the ingredients that pull a collection of talented individuals together and turn them into a great team.'[6] By implication, and by dint of the 1-0 scoreline to England, Sobers failed.

His led his team into the field in the first Test in Trinidad after losing the toss. 'From that moment until the last hour or so of the fifth day Cowdrey's leadership was more assured, more shrewd and more inspiring by personal example than that of Sobers,' Barker recorded.[7] Three different bowlers shared the first three overs – 'the first of a number of eccentricities from the West Indies skipper', according to Barker – as confusion surrounded their preferred choice of ends.

---

* He returned to the Warwickshire in 1970 and played for England again as a batsman against Australia in 1972.

England's innings closed on the third morning with 568 on the board. Ken Barrington and Graveney reached three figures, while Griffith was the pick of the bowlers with 5 for 69. Sobers caused more raised eyebrows by failing to put pressure on England's batsmen by using his best bowlers at high-pressure moments. Uncharacteristically, he missed a couple of catches and then looked painfully out of form in scoring only 17 in a West Indies reply that relied on Clive Lloyd's 118 to get them to 363. 'The Invisible Man in this Test match so far had been Garfield Sobers,' said Barker. 'His touch as captain had been as unsure as his batting, his bowling had been unremarkable.'[8]

Following on, West Indies reached 164 for 2 before a clatter of six wickets for 16 runs. Sobers had dropped himself to number seven, a surprising decision even in light of his bruised little finger. There were 90 minutes remaining when Hall joined his captain and after he prodded down the wrong line at every ball in a Titmus over, Sobers ensured that he took the bulk of the off-spinner's deliveries. Stubbornly, the pair took West Indies to safety with a partnership of 63, Sobers ending unbeaten on 33 in 115 minutes.

Describing the scene as stumps were drawn, Blofeld said, 'Spectators invaded the field and swarmed round Sobers and Hall as if they were cheering a two-wicket victory. Some of them were singing calypsos. They had not had much to cheer during the five days and this was their moment.'[9] Close, on tour as a journalist and author, observed that the 'cosy, almost smug, picture of Caribbean supremacy' was no longer 'unsmudged'.[10]

It became even more stained at the second Test in Jamaica, where West Indies were forced to follow on for their third match in a row. Cowdrey scored his 19th Test hundred in a total of 376, his team losing only two wickets on the first day. Sobers appeared intent merely on keeping the score down to manageable proportions, giving up only 14 runs in 11 overs on the second morning.

The absence of Hunte was driven home when West Indies slipped to 5 for 2, Sobers having experimented by sending wicketkeeper Deryck Murray in first. By the third day, the dry pitch was heavily cracked. 'The wicket,' Close noted, 'was not suitable for a club match, let alone an international game.'[11] Sobers was hopelessly lbw first ball to a John Snow delivery that shot along the deck. He left the field to shocked silence.

With a lead of 233 and the rest day looming to help his bowlers, Cowdrey sent West Indies back in. Seymour Nurse and Stephen Camacho had shared a century opening partnership by the fourth morning, but things were about to get ugly. At 204 for 4, Basil Butcher feathered Basil D'Oliveira down the leg side and, after a slight pause while he confirmed that wicketkeeper Jim Parks had taken a clean catch, headed to the pavilion, sparing Douglas Sang Hue the need to make a decision. David Holford was taking guard when bottles began flying over the eight-foot mesh fencing around the boundary. A chant went up: 'We want Butcher.'

Police with batons gathered, while Sobers, Cowdrey and Graveney approached the unruliest section of the crowd to point out that there was no dispute about the validity of Butcher's dismissal. 'The noise was so deafening that any reasonable exchange of words was impossible,' Cowdrey recalled.[12] Sobers turned to the English players and shrugged. 'They're so mad no one is going to pacify them.'[13] As Graveney commented, 'If Garry could not get a hearing, what chance had we?'[14]

There was, though, a sense that the protest was losing momentum until the white-helmeted riot police arrived. Close thought they 'acted as bait for the bottle throwers'.[15] Suggestions circulated later that political disruptors were behind the unrest. The chief of police said as much to the players as he warned them that he was about to employ tear gas and told them to return to the dressing rooms.

They might have been safer in the open. 'The police threw their gas bombs straight in the path of the prevailing north-east winds,' reported Alan Ross in the *Observer*. 'Those whom they wished to flush out escaped almost scot-free while the players, the TV cameramen, the cowering members and their friends in the pavilion were obliged to undergo the mild equivalent of a Somme gas attack.'

Allowing for the taking of tea, 75 minutes were lost. Officials approached Cowdrey and assured him that the time would be made up on a sixth day if necessary so that England were not disadvantaged. Yet when play resumed, the momentum of the match had changed. 'The whole episode knocked the stuffing out of us,' argued Cowdrey.[16]

English opinion was, understandably, that their team had lost enthusiasm; fielders watching for missiles as much as shots by the batsmen. Sobers had almost fallen for his second golden duck of the match when a lifter from David Brown flew off the splice of his bat and dropped just short of Edrich. Then he was dropped by D'Oliveira on 7. But now he hit Brown's first ball after the stoppage for a straight four. Manley recorded that 'Sobers proceeded to give one of those performances that set him aside as a player completely extraordinary in the history of cricket'.[17]

Ending the day on 48, Sobers went steadily to his 18th Test century – his fifth at Sabina Park – after rain shortened the fifth morning. He hit Titmus for a straight six on his way to scoring 16 in an over after lunch, but his progress from 88 to 100 was entirely in singles, serving to make the game safe. His innings was all the more meritorious on an unpredictable surface whose cracks were extreme enough for Graveney to joke with the slender Gibbs that he'd better not walk on the pitch for fear of disappearing.

'Mastering the fading England attack was not a serious problem for Sobers,' said Barker. 'Mastering the eccentricities of the pitch was another matter, and perhaps only Sobers, whose unique virtue is that his cricket is at least as much by instinct as technique, of all living batsmen could have done it.'[18] Chapman's tabloid offering in the *Mirror* was, 'As a Houdini, he should be offered life membership of the Escapers' Club.'

Keith Miller would rate Sobers's effort as his finest Test-match innings and the best in bad conditions that he'd ever seen. 'I examined the pitch and found I could insert all the fingers of one hand, finger length, into these huge cracks,' he explained. '[He] somehow dismissed the torments of the pitch from his mind and played strokes as though it was a plumb, easy batting pitch.'[19]

At 391 for 9, Sobers declared – 113 not out – leaving England needing to score 159 runs to win or, in reality, bat out a maximum of 155 minutes to draw. After holding the initiative for almost the entire match, England suddenly found themselves on the defensive. Sobers took the ball under thickening cloud and his first two deliveries swung down Boycott's leg side. The third was straighter and was jabbed away in defence. The fourth ball again swung towards leg, prompting Boycott to leave it alone. Yet the ball spat off the seam and bowled him behind his legs. Cowdrey survived an lbw appeal first ball and was trapped by the final delivery. One over gone: 0 for 2.

By the time bad light stopped play 38 minutes early, England were 19 for 4. Sobers visited Cowdrey in the dressing room and informed him he would be making use of the additional 75 minutes originally earmarked so as not to disadvantage the away team. Some felt that, in the circumstances, the more sporting gesture would have been to shake Cowdrey's hand and call it a draw.

After Griffith hit Parks in the throat early on the extra day Sobers used himself and Gibbs to attempt to prise out the last six wickets, giving up only when two wickets were still needed with only one ball left. England might have been the ones fighting for their lives in the end, but Peter Smith aired a typical view in *Playfair Cricket Monthly*, when he wrote, 'I have no doubt that but for the mistaken use of tear-gas, which harmed only the many innocent people in the crowd and delayed the clearing-up operations, England would never have been in danger of defeat. After the riots Sobers was a changed man.'[20]

Barbados hosted the third Test after an eventful few days of build-up. Boycott scored 243 in MCC's warm-up game against the island, but the more serious headlines were those concerning an accident in which Titmus lost four toes after having his left foot slashed by a speedboat's propeller. Remarkably, he would continue his cricket career later in the year and even earn an England recall in 1974/75 at the age of 42.

West Indies scored 349 – Sobers contributing 68 – around the first rain in a Bridgetown Test for 20 years. Significantly, given the comments Sobers would offer in later weeks about England's negative approach, they had begun by scoring four runs in 45 minutes and only 37 in the first 30 overs. Boycott and Edrich responded with an opening partnership of 190 before Sobers had Boycott leg-before on 90 after the Yorkshireman offered no shot to an inswinger. Edrich scored 146 in a total of 449 – another England first-innings lead of three figures. Lloyd entertained the final-day crowd with a century as the game petered out into a draw.

And so the series returned to Trinidad, where for more than four days' play the stalemate continued. Having left out Hall, it was West Indies' turn to extend their first innings into the third day before Sobers declared at 526 for 7. Nurse and Kanhai reached centuries and it was left to Lloyd and Sobers, who both fell in the 40s, to add a little urgency.

England made painful progress to 404 in 175.4 overs. Cowdrey scored 148 on what he called the best pitch he'd batted on, but against an attack that included the erratic leg-spin of Willie Rodriguez and the part-time offerings of Joey Carew, who reeled off 15 consecutive maidens, there was no ambition beyond maintaining parity in the series. After the third day, Barker noted that 'the habitués at the pavilion bar argued earnestly whether it had or had not been quite the worst day they had ever endured'.[21]

England collapsed late on the fourth day from 373 for 5 when Sobers, in desperation, gave Butcher his first bowl in Test cricket for ten years and saw him rip out the last five wickets. Bad light meant there was time for the home team to add only six runs to their lead of 122 before close of play. 'The fourth Test was now not only dead,' said Barker. 'It was embalmed.'[22]

There was no attempt at resuscitation on the fifth morning. By early afternoon, two and a half hours' pedestrian batting had taken West Indies to 92 for 2, a lead of 214. Yet England's 12th man, Essex spinner Robin Hobbs, had got wind of something. 'I was sitting on the side in my whites,' he recalled, although his memory of England being 'flogged all round the park' is hardly accurate. Hobbs heard Sobers announce, 'All right, lads, get changed' and he immediately ran to the middle to tell Cowdrey, 'Hey, skip, they're going to declare.'[23]

Out of the blue, England's batsmen found themselves padding up for a run chase of 215 in 165 minutes. 'We thought, "Bloody hell, this is a bit generous,"' recalled Pat Pocock, who had been left out the England team.[24] It was a tougher equation than Sobers had set them in Jamaica, but there was no comparison between the two pitches. Blofeld recalled the small numbers of spectators being 'shocked into silence'.[25]

West Indies were without their only specialist fast bowler after Griffith had pulled a muscle three overs into his first-innings work, with Pocock suggesting, 'That was Garry's biggest mistake, not allowing for Charlie not being fit enough to bowl. Not only did he not have the force of his bowling, but without him they bowled a lot more overs than they might have done otherwise.'[26] As Barker pointed out, Sobers 'had at his disposal what must surely be the oddest collection of unseasoned bowlers ever to attempt to win a Test match'.[27]

West Indies never looked like pulling it off. England rarely looked unlikely to fail in a run chase that Cowdrey, according to some, had been reluctant to pursue. Hobbs remembered, 'Cowdrey sat in his chair and said, "Well that's it. Well done, lads. Play it out for a draw." And Edrich and Barrington were aghast. "A draw? They've only got three bowlers ... We can walk this."'[28]

Cowdrey's own explanation did not entirely contradict Hobbs. 'I did not want to have to fight a rearguard action against Rodriguez when neither Tom Graveney, Basil D'Oliveira nor myself could guarantee to pick his googly,' he said. 'My whole approach was to keep the temperature down and see how we went.'[29]

They went well. Edrich was first out at 55 and Cowdrey entered to play a match-winning innings of 71 in 75 minutes, including ten boundaries. Close recorded, 'Sobers was at a loss where to place his field.'[30] Nor was he inclined to limit the number of overs his team bowled once the runs began to flow. Without any fast bowlers' run-ups to eat up time, his team reached 20 overs in only 58 minutes. England scored 58 in the first half-hour after tea, Boycott adding calm support to his captain, and 85 runs were needed in the final hour, 40 in the final 30 minutes. Even Gibbs's removal of Cowdrey and Graveney could not halt the victory march. There were three minutes and eight balls remaining when D'Oliveira hit the winning runs, with Boycott unbeaten on 80.

'The sky fell in on Sobers's head,' Cowdrey remembered. 'For days afterwards his motives, his character, even his right to continue captaining the West Indies were fiercely debated throughout the islands. They had lost and Sobers was solely to blame.'[31]

West Indies had given away a match in which they had lost only nine wickets, made more than 500 in their first innings and had never been under pressure until Sobers interfered with the inevitable course of the match. He told reporters, 'I've taken gambles before – but this is the first time I have lost. When things pay off you are great and when they don't you are an idiot. This is a game of cricket and if every game is drawn what is the sense of playing it?'

Yet none of that addressed the main criticisms of Sobers's actions, most of which seem perfectly valid well over half a century later, despite Wellings having argued in *Wisden* that 'those who blamed him were being wise after the event'.[32]

EW Swanton might have observed in *The Cricketer* that 'the indication that Sobers acted in a sudden impulse is contrary to one's general impression of his captaincy', but there is no other conclusion to reach. He could even be accused of an act of petulance as he became increasingly angered by England's reluctance to bowl more than 22 overs in the two hours before lunch. 'Colin Cowdrey looked for a draw first and a win second,' he would complain. 'The series was very, very dull. It probably forced me as captain to try to inject something into the cricket.'[33] When he played golf with Close two days later he admitted to him that his heart had ruled his head.

If Sobers had thought about declaring any earlier than when Hobbs overheard his instructions to his team – if it had not been purely impulsive – why had he allowed his batsmen to meander with no instruction to increase the scoring rate? 'It didn't make any sense,' Lloyd recalled. 'We were all quite mystified about what Sobey was up to … There had never been any consultation among the senior players.'[34]

No one loved to gamble more than Sobers, whether it was on the racecourse, in the casino or on the field. But – a few hours after the UK government had announced that punters such as Sobers would now have to pay an increased tax rate of one shilling (5 pence) in the pound – this was a bet for which he'd spent no time studying form or calculating odds. If he had, he would surely have concluded that everything was stacked against him. Comments such as Blofeld's that 'if the West Indies had won he would have been feted' miss the point that there was virtually no chance of success.[35] As John Woodcock wrote in *The Times*, 'The side that lays the odds should always leave itself with an even chance of winning. This Sobers failed to do with the attack he had.' West Indian-born TV journalist Trevor McDonald concluded some years later, 'Sobers had acted with total disregard for professionalism.'[36]

Manley suggested, 'Sobers miscalculated, assuming perhaps that he could work another personal miracle. Miracles are fine when they succeed. When they fail, however, one is entitled to examine the question of probability.'[37] D'Oliveira, meanwhile, recalled one West Indian player saying to him, 'The trouble with Garry is that, despite his genius, he thinks he's God on the field and nothing can go wrong.'[38]

Not only had it been unlikely that West Indies could take ten quick wickets, Sobers failed to appreciate the risk that an England line-up used to chasing targets in county cricket would feel comfortable in replicating that on the easy Port-of-Spain surface. Edrich likened the task to the kind of limited-overs challenge English players faced in the Gillette Cup, calling it 'ten to one on an England victory'.[39] Close pointed out that English batsmen were 'the best in the world at this type of cricket'.[40]

Not only had Sobers misjudged the match equation, he appeared to have misread the mood of the public. No one could argue when he said, 'There was a lot of time-wasting. It was not conducive to good cricket or the entertainment of the paying public.' Nor can one take issue with his belief that 'the spectators always have to be considered'.[41] But there was something more important to the cricket fans of the Caribbean, which was to not give away a Test match.

It was easy for those in the England camp to applaud a 'sporting' declaration – using the same language that resurfaced when Hansie Cronje made his infamous move on behalf of the bookmakers in the South Africa–England Test at Centurion in 2000.

Swanton, for example, wrote in *The Cricketer*, 'All followers of cricket must applaud Sobers for snapping his fingers at the tradition of Test cricket that maintains one must never give the enemy a chink of a chance of winning.'

Trevor Bailey, not one to say a word against Sobers, felt that the critics 'entirely missed what his gesture meant to cricket'.[42] Yet Manley argued, 'Sportsmanship does not mean inviting the other guy to a victory which is clearly beyond your own reach … The decision turned out to be a disaster.'[43]

* * *

While the MCC tour party, the 21 journalists who had travelled with them, and numerous expat and holidaying English fans celebrated at the Queen's Park Hotel and the nearby Pelican Inn, the Caribbean digested news of defeat. As Sobers's effigy was being booted around and strung up in Port-of-Spain, fights broke out in other major population centres in the region, people spilling into the street from the homes, shops and pubs where they had been listening on the radio.

Leaving his colleagues at the team hotel, Sobers sat alone in a local nightclub, oblivious to the singer on stage. All he could do to redeem himself, he realised, was to ensure that his team tied the series in the fifth Test in Guyana. He proceeded to give a performance that Manley said 'rates as possibly the greatest single-handed effort in all cricket history'.[44]

With the match scheduled for six days and Georgetown offering a good-looking strip and a fast outfield, Sobers chose to bat, moving himself up to number five for the first time in the series and joining Kanhai with 72 on the board. A partnership that reached three figures in two hours advanced to 250 on the second day, with Kanhai out for 150 and Sobers continuing on to 152. While Kanhai had reached his century in 177 balls, Sobers took 286. '[He] played a conscientious and sensible second fiddle,' said Barker. 'Perhaps too conscientious. He played half-volleys back to the bowlers with a care that managed to convey only qualified approval of Kanhai's uninhibited onslaught.'[45] According to Close, 'It was a crisis made for a player of Sobers's class and calibre. He had Kanhai to supply the aggression at one end while he did the thinking for both of them at the other.'[46]

His departure hastened his side from 385 for 4 to 414 all out, but Sobers again struck quickly with the new ball, trapping Edrich lbw without scoring. Rain and Boycott's assured hundred looked like undermining West Indian hopes of victory, even with Sobers removing Cowdrey and Barrington with the second new ball. England were only 43 runs behind when their innings ended on the fifth day.

At 83 for 3, Sobers took charge of West Indies' second innings, reaching his fifty in only 54 balls, including a monstrous straight six off Pocock that landed in the Regent Street canal. He hit him into the road before being left 95 not out from 118 balls when the last wicket fell at 264, seven minutes before the scheduled close of play. Close described

Sobers as 'the king fighting for his crown' and called it 'an innings which proved beyond all doubt he is the greatest batsman in the world'.[47]

Needing 308 to win, England looked beaten at 41 for 5, Sobers accounting for Edrich again and Gibbs taking four wickets. At tea, West Indies were still seeking another breakthrough as Cowdrey found support in 21-year-old wicketkeeper Alan Knott, who hit only 24 scoring shots in 260 balls. Sobers, meanwhile, was again becoming frustrated by the pragmatic – or cynical – approach of Cowdrey, who spent time calling for and adjusting new pads among other delaying activities. 'It was never built into me to go out there and do something that is contrary to the game, like wasting time,' he said.[48]

Gibbs at last removed Cowdrey in the sixth over after tea, before Sobers took out Snow and Lock with his wrist-spin. When Gibbs had Pocock caught, England's last pair had to survive six minutes. Barker described the crowd as a 'positive hurricane of roaring, whistling, howling pandemonium'.[49] Knott, unbeaten on 73, negotiated a maiden over from Sobers, and Jeff Jones had to play at only one ball from Gibbs in the final over to save the match.

England had recorded only their second series victory in the West Indies and the spectators at the Bourda ground were not about to take it good-naturedly. Once more police batons had to be drawn as fans swarmed over the ground, jeered outside the pavilion and then began throwing objects at the England dressing room, the press box and the television stand. Tony

Lock was hit on the head by a stone and police escorts were needed to return the team safely to their hotel.

The conclusion of Wellings in *Wisden* was that 'the tour focused a spotlight on unpleasant aspects of West Indies cricket'[50] and, even without the furore over his Trinidad declaration, it had not been an enjoyable few weeks for Sobers. 'That series was not played in the spirit in which I expected it to be played,' he said. 'I always thought cricket should be a game with people challenging each other, not looking to see how you can draw.'[51]

But there are two sides to every story, especially a sporting contest. No one involved with English cricket shared Sobers's gloomy view. Even *Wisden*'s negativity related to the crowds and umpiring, not the nature of the matches. The view of Chapman in the *Daily Mirror* was, 'For sustained excitement and for magnificent cricket I rank this tour equal to Frank Worrell's in Australia seven years ago. Indeed for sheer somersaults of fortune and crackling finishes it takes precedence.'

Given more time to consider events, Blofeld concurred. 'This had been one of the most exciting Test series ever to have been played, with four matches out of five going to the last half-hour,' he wrote. 'There were none of those dull days.'[52]

Take away the Trinidad declaration and the snatching of an unlikely victory and maybe English opinion would have been closer to that of Sobers. And perhaps West Indian memories would have been different if their team had rescued the series. 'If we had won that last match, I suppose I would still have been considered a great captain,' Sobers said, which might have been an overstatement but would have balanced the scales a little.[53]

As it was, Sobers was to be saddled with his decision forever. 'Not all his brilliance as a player,' wrote Barker, 'could compensate his fellow-countrymen for that disastrous false step.'[54]

16

CAPTAIN UNDER PRESSURE

'It matters not how strait the gate, how charged
with punishments the scroll;
I am the master of my fate: I am the
captain of my soul.'

English poet William Ernest Henley

WHILE EVENTS of the fourth Test against England shone the most unflattering light on the leadership of Garry Sobers, the series had already been notable for closer examination of his captaincy. It was an inevitable consequence of the fact that West Indies could no longer dominate opponents as they had in recent years and, therefore, would rely more on any edge their skipper could provide. The scrutiny would intensify.

'At the end of this series Sobers would no longer be considered a great leader,' read Michael Manley's history of West Indies cricket. 'As a captain he was to have opportunities to redeem himself, but he did not in fact take them.'[1]

When Sobers's period in charge of the team ended in 1972 – after failure to win any of five home Tests against New Zealand – few could dispute that his time was up. 'For several years we were the best team in the world,' he argued. 'I do not think my record was a bad one.'[2] Yet little happened after Trinidad to offer mitigation against criticism of his captaincy.

His idealistic approach to the game might have made him a wonderful sight to behold on the field, yet it did not always best serve the team's needs. Colin Cowdrey, smiling and affable, and enough of a gentleman that MCC ended up naming its annual lecture on the spirit of cricket after him, had offered an interesting comparison. Having previously lost the England captaincy because of defeats at the hands of his rival, Cowdrey was not beyond stooping to what Sobers felt was gamesmanship in order to win a series. Sobers was a fierce competitor and not averse to pragmatism in his own batting, but Cowdrey's time-wasting in the field and at the crease trying to save a game were anathema to him. As commendable as that might be, a tendency towards romantic principles is not usually compatible with success as a Test captain. It allowed JS Barker, summarising the MCC tour, to write, 'Cowdrey worked harder and more intelligently at the business of winning it than did Sobers.'[3]

But it went deeper than that. Sobers struggled to relate to players who were not as gifted as him, which meant most of his team. This manifested itself in an inability to get the best out of them, especially if they were going through the dips in form or crises of confidence to which he had rarely been subjected. Henry Blofeld noted that Sobers had never had to 'work out the game for himself in the way of all other cricketers and this has meant that he is unaware of many of cricket's problems'.

When great players were replaced by lesser, more fallible recruits Sobers 'was unable to understand and advise'.[4]

Instead, he shrugged off the challenges faced by others in the belief he could win games himself; Port-of-Spain being a prime example. 'He has taken up cricket matches and remoulded them to his design,' wrote John Arlott.[5] And Blofeld observed, 'Sobers appears not to acknowledge the impossible for he has no need.'[6]

Clive Lloyd argued, 'He was a great man and he just knew that he was great ... He was a guy who didn't like draws, he just wanted to win. Nothing fazed him. I've been there when it was flying around and then seen Garry go out with that walk of his and he just made it look like a different game. If fellows were having a rough time, he'd just do his own thing for them.'[7]

According to West Indies stalwart Michael Holding, Sobers took gambles that were beyond other captains 'because [he] knew his ability and thought others had his ability, too'.[8] Perhaps more accurately, he either forgot or didn't care that they didn't.

His unshakeable self-belief also exposed him to accusations of batting too far down the order at number six, believing he could still influence events from that position – which he frequently did. Sobers faced the paradox that the more runs he scored in that position the more, in his mind, it justified leaving himself there. To others it was a sign that he was the best batsman and should therefore promote himself. It became such a talking point midway through the 1968/69 Australian tour that manager Berkeley Gaskin was forced to address it. 'It would be impertinent for a manager to try to captain a team,' he told journalists, before adding, 'If I were in charge I would bat Sobers as the trend of the game dictates. With his great authority he should take charge. It is difficult to take charge with authority at number six in positions that have presented themselves so far.'

In Sobers's defence, he played such an important role in the bowling attack that it was perhaps the only way he could prevent his burden becoming overwhelming. Few great all-rounders have found the magic formula of maintaining personal performance while achieving team success as captain. For every Imran Khan and Kapil Dev there is Ian Botham and Andrew Flintoff, and neither Imran nor Kapil, both World Cup winners, had the weight of being their team's best batsman on top of bowling responsibilities.

Barker wrote after the MCC tour in 1968, 'From the first to last Sobers the player was too much in the game to allow Sobers the captain to detach himself from the long, cool, captain's look at its developments.'[9]

Which bring us to Sobers's qualities as a tactician; stunted not just by his workload but his natural feel for the game. Manley suggested, 'Sobers, the brilliant and largely instinctive athlete, did not need to be analytical or even particularly thoughtful about the game. Indeed, his intense physical attributes were almost a disadvantage in that regard, enabling him to overcome challenges with physical rather than mental accommodation.' Sobers's knack of picking the right bowler at the right time – especially early in his captaincy, and particularly when it concerned his own introduction into the attack – might make that a somewhat exaggerated viewpoint, but it has its basis in truth.

Blofeld, who watched West Indies lose three successive series under Sobers, said, 'As a captain the sharp instinct on which his whole game is based leaves him ... Once a man is captain of a side, and a losing side at that, instinct has to give way to practicality based on deliberate thoughts which must be directed at solving the problem.'[10]

Barry Richards, who played under Sobers on a winning Rest of the World team in England in 1970, remembered, 'He did so much that it was hard to judge whether he was put under pressure as a captain. But I have always thought that somebody who is a genius isn't the best person to captain. You want more of a Mike Brearley, a thoughtful, analytical bloke. Garry played very much from the heart. He wasn't a person who analysed or asked, "Where do these players score? Where do we get these guys out?" His cricket was more spontaneous.'[11]

According to Tom Graveney, 'Garry ran the game. He hardly needed a team. That was perhaps the beginning and the end of his strategy.'[12] Lloyd confirmed that 'there was not much talk about strategy', suggesting, 'Garry's view was that these players were big enough to know what to do.' And his own status as a player meant 'you didn't question too many things' when it came to what he believed would benefit the team.[13]

As a captain, it could often appear as though he was doing things by numbers. Trevor Bailey suggested that he was more like the prosaic Len Hutton in his captaincy than the intuitive

Richie Benaud. 'He seldom did the tactically unusual, and to that extent was predictable.'[14] He also observed that Sobers was such a good bowler that he found it difficult to set fields for the inaccurate bowling of team-mates.

'I never felt he had a real feeling for the problems of his bowlers, or any insight in to how they were feeling,' England's John Snow concurred. 'Then again he always had his own outstanding ability to extract himself from difficult situations he may have created by not quite utilising fully the talents of those under him.'[15]

As Nottinghamshire captain in later years, facing the challenge of squeezing a result out of three days' play and sometimes frustrated by the daily grind of the county game, he could be too eager for results. 'He was always impatient for things to happen,' said Pat Pocock, an opponent at Surrey. 'When he was leading Notts and they had a side at, say, 40 for 4 on a green wicket you could see Garry snapping his fingers if another half-dozen overs went by without a wicket falling. Most captains, quite correctly, would stay with the seamers, wait for their wicket then attack the new batsman with pace and movement. That was far too clinical for Garry. He would remove the seamers, put on an occasional leg-spinner and hope that the change would work the trick.'[16]

* * *

When West Indies visited Australia for five Tests in 1968/69, Sobers became even more exposed as captain. It is almost impossible to find a review of his leadership – either contemporaneous or reflective – that is not damning. Australian writer Phil Tressider, in his tour book, concluded, 'To put it bluntly, Garry Sobers was no match for Bill Lawry. The Australians were well drilled and well led; the West Indies never looked an integrated combination.'[17]

One particular recurring theme highlights another perceived weakness. It is the art of man-management where evaluation of Sobers's captaincy is the most unfavourable. Tressider, pointing out that Frank Worrell 'had welded his teams with infinite care, understanding and affection for his men's welfare', felt that Sobers 'lacked the great man's warmth and breadth of vision'. He argued, 'Sobers should have spent more time with his players. He should have been on hand to arrest the lethargy that crept insidiously into the side's play.'[18]

Whereas Worrell's advanced years and healthy distance from his younger charges generated an atmosphere of respect and affection, Sobers was unwilling to impose discipline on players he had grown up with. Nor was he inclined to offer mentoring to the younger ones. 'He failed to provide the guidance and inspiration which was so necessary,' said Tony Cozier,[19] while Lloyd felt that a more forceful manager than Gaskin could have provided the 'strong hand' that was needed.[20]

By the mid-point of the tour, according to Manley, 'West Indies were dangerously demoralised. Stories began to leak of increasing disaffection. The main problem was Sobers. A genius, an ultimately professional player himself, Sobers lacked the one quality that might have rescued the leadership. Insight is not easy to define.'[21]

But there are those who believe he might have achieved it had he paid closer attention to his players.

From the opposition camp, batsman Keith Stackpole questioned West Indies' unity. 'You sensed rivalry between them, especially Sobers and [Rohan] Kanhai. The fact was they were a collection of brilliant individuals led by a casual genius who was not disciplined enough to be a strong captain. Sobers at times seemed more interested in playing golf than forging team spirit.'[22]

That was not just a rival scoring cheap points, it was a common observation. Citing his 'remoteness', Blofeld said, 'On free days Sobers was hardly ever seen with his players, he seldom practised with them, spending a great deal of time on the golf course, and therefore did not lead by example.'[23]

Having just played a year of non-stop cricket – including his first county season – and suffering from increasing knee and shoulder pains, Sobers took every opportunity to escape the game. It sounds reasonable enough, except that he had accepted the responsibility of captaincy and now had a commitment to fulfil. As Tressider pointed out, 'Sobers treasured his golfing hours as an outlet for tensions, as any freelance virtuoso might do. But Sobers was no free agent.'[24]

His forgiving biographer Bailey suggested that the problem was exacerbated by the fact that 'his keenness and considerable skill at golf was not shared by most of his compatriots'.[25] So it was their fault, he seems to imply, rather than wondering whether Sobers might have, in that case, curtailed his on-course excursions.

An easy indicator of a team falling apart is poor fielding and, having watched the whole series, journalist Murray Tippett declared, 'As a captain [Sobers] was unable to produce the enthusiasm from his players, and this was borne out by their pitiful fielding. Possibly this was the worst fielding by an international team to visit Australia.'[26]

Sobers was subsequently informed that West Indies dropped at least 34 catches in five Tests. 'What did he do to rectify it?' posed Tressider. 'How could he justify absences on the golf courses when he could have been directing intensive fielding workouts at practice sessions?'[27] As Manley pointed out, 'None of this seemed to occur to Sobers at the time.'[28]

Under Sobers, there was no expectation for the team to work on physical conditioning, no running or weight training. According to Manley, 'It was not unusual to see players in that era knocking back a brandy during the lunch or tea intervals.'[29]

But Sobers is not without support. One of the finest of all Test leaders, Australia's Ian Chappell, has little truck with those who dismiss his captaincy. 'A lot of codswallop is spoken about Garry's captaincy, especially in the Caribbean,' he argued. 'Garry was an excellent captain; he knew the game well and he was always looking for a result. He was great to captain against because you knew unless weather intervened there was going to be a result. Garry was always around for a drink and in 1968/69 it was his players who were often missing from the dressing room gatherings. Garry can't be blamed because Wes [Hall] and Charlie [Griffith]'s best days were behind them and his fielders dropped a lot of catches.'[30]

Sobers, however, had invited criticism by spending the days leading up to the first Test, played in Brisbane, taking what was then described as a business trip to Melbourne, missing a pair of warm-up games. 'This was, of course, big news, a captain deserting his side just before the first Test,' said Blofeld.[31] The *Melbourne Age* reported that only Gaskin and Sobers himself knew his whereabouts in the city and even Gaskin was unsure when he would rejoin the team, although he added that Sobers was on a mission that 'could be of great benefit to the whole team'.

A captain going missing a few days before a Test series was something of an embarrassment, although the story was forgotten when West Indies won in Brisbane for their only victory of the series. But as the months went by, Sobers tended to travel on his own more frequently, accepting lifts from friends while team-mates went by train or plane. He had often driven himself on previous England tours, but in a large country where travelling is a greater burden and during a tour where results were going badly, it was not a good look. 'Even as the admiration for Sobers as a player and the affection for him as a genuinely pleasant man were unbounded, disaffection was growing concerning his captaincy,' said Manley, who argued that Sobers was 'not aware of the mounting difficulties'.[32]

Having ordered extra nets after a ten-wicket defeat by South Australia in an early match, and told his players that the tour was 'not fun nor a spree', he had undermined his authority by allowing himself to be accused of treating it exactly like that – or as 'a golfing holiday', as Tressider put it. And after West

Indies went 2-1 down in the series with another ten-wicket defeat in Sydney, Sobers again left himself open to accusations of hypocrisy when he was publicly critical of his team. 'What is very clear is that we must have more serious practice,' he told reporters. 'We must work as hard in the practice nets as in the middle of a match.'

Tressider, who was following the tourists around Australia, relayed Sobers's comments to one of the team and received an incredulous reply. 'Did Garry Sobers really say that? You must print that!' The author remembered, 'The tour was nearing the end of its third month and only now had he gone all out for dedicated attention to practice. And from a skipper who could claim only a passing acquaintance with the geography of Australian practice nets.'[33]

It was all very well for Sobers to argue that he was acting no differently than on previous, more successful, tours. He failed to recognise that the demands on the captain were different when his team was no longer sweeping all before it. Even Bailey was forced to admit that leading by example was not always enough, especially, he might have added, when those actions were less than exemplary. 'It did not always work where the side was short of class and consequently inclined to seek excuses for their own deficiencies,' Bailey suggested. 'Small details have never been his strong point, and it followed that on tour he really needed to be a manager to tie up the loose ends and occasionally to crack the whip.'[34]

Playfair Cricket Monthly columnist Rex Alston suggested in 1969, 'He has not matured as a leader – another example of captaincy not necessarily sitting naturally on the shoulders of a great player.'[35]

Yet one must not overlook an important question when it comes to the analysis of Sobers as Test captain. That is, the fundamental issue of whether history judges him too harshly. We weigh him up as Sobers the great all-rounder and compare his achievements in charge of his team to his superhuman contributions as a playing member. Anyone else with his won–lost record would be remembered as a serviceable, if unspectacular, captain.

Then there is the factor of having to follow Worrell. Not only did that bring an imperative to continue winning matches, but Worrell had recalibrated the expectations of a West Indies captain. Sobers got the job mostly because he was the best player. 'Sobers was therefore asked to do a job for which his main qualification was individual performance, but which required much more,' was the summary of Caribbean sociologist Maurice St Pierre. 'It may be said, therefore, that he was underqualified for the job and his employers were not sympathetic to his shortcomings.'[36]

Wrapped up in that is the question of whether Sobers deserves more credit for the success he achieved with what is often described as 'Worrell's team' in his early years as captain and, equally, whether he is blamed too much for failing to arrest its decline when the raw material at his disposal was diminishing. The success West Indies achieved under Lloyd and Viv Richards in the post-Sobers decades also makes for an unflattering comparison.

Chappell continued, 'The codswallop spoken, particularly in the Caribbean, centred around Garry's declaration in Trinidad. He was probably bored with England's cricket and I think he banked on there being enough spin to bowl England out and win the game. Garry's generous declaration was later blamed for some of Clive Lloyd and Viv Richards's non-declarations in games where West Indies batted too long, saying they wanted plenty of runs so they could maintain attacking fields. Blaming Garry was a cover-up for captaincy insecurity. Sobers was a better captain than both Lloyd and Richards.'[37]

Next comes the matter of his leadership – as historically significant as it was – being viewed in a wider context than the environment of West Indies cricket. Sobers, as we will discuss later, rarely saw himself as having a role to play as champion for his people. Interesting, then, is the importance he attached to being a champion of Test cricket; certainly in the manner in which his own team played it. It is unfair to condemn him for that, certainly in the view of Cozier, the great Caribbean journalist and broadcaster, who said, 'As captain, he enhanced … the reputation of West Indian cricket, not, let it be admitted, by his tactical reading of the game, but by his approach to and deep affection for it. In whatever Sobers did, he gave the distinct impression that the game was to be enjoyed, its image glorified, never sullied.'[38]

Tony Greig, who played under Sobers for a World team and against him in Test and county cricket, concurred. 'Garry Sobers may not be considered by many people to be the best captain of all time, but I can tell you in my experience in every single thing he did, he did [it] in the best interests of the game,' he said. 'He always tried to win.'[39]

Blofeld made a good point when he said, 'Sobers is the man he is and therefore the cricketer he is and no one would want it to be any other way.'[40] It also made him the captain he was. And would anyone who witnessed Sobers at his magnificent best want to risk a dilution of his brilliance by injecting more of the Ray Illingworth, for example, into his character?

Perhaps Sobers could have found ways to achieve improvement in his captaincy. But it might have come at too high a price.

17

JOINING THE COUNTY SET

'I should like to save the Shire, if I could.'

Frodo Baggins (*Fellowship of the Ring,*
JRR Tolkien, 1954)

AT THE end of 1967, the Advisory County Cricket Committee met at Lord's and made a decision that would change the landscape of the English game, and the career of Garry Sobers. From now on, it was determined, overseas players could appear in the County Championship without serving a period of residential qualification. No county would be allowed to have more than one import or sign a second within three years; and no team could have more than two overseas players in total, although after five years they would lose their overseas designation.

Domestic English cricket had again been diagnosed as needing a fillip, five years after the Gillette Cup had been introduced to generate interest, excitement and income. 'The presence of world stars in the County Championship should act as an enormous stimulant to the competition, and the counties are to be congratulated for progressive thinking,' said

Playfair Cricket Monthly editor Gordon Ross. 'The only fly in the ointment may be the feelings of our own home-bred players when they hear what some of the overseas players are to be paid.'[1]

Yet Roger Davis, the young Glamorgan batsman who was to play an important bit-part in Sobers's first county season, countered that final point by recalling, 'For me, it was a thrill because I was starting to play against all my heroes. You try to explain to today's players who we were playing against, they wouldn't believe it. You don't get overseas players of that stature and for a whole season.'[2]

According to Lancashire's David Lloyd, 'It was totally different then than anything that we've got now in that the overseas players were there for years. People like Clive Lloyd and Farokh Engineer would live in the area, and they've still got places there. You had nine local lads and two bits of stardust and sometimes it was a question of whether our stardust was better than yours. As batsmen, we would aspire to pick up little bits that you would get from watching Garry or Barry Richards or Gordon Greenidge. Garry lifted your game somehow. He was a joy to play against. He always had a smile on his face and he was fabulous company. He had no edge to him at all. He was just one of the lads in the teams that he played with and against.'[3]

Sobers, who would have jumped happily into county cricket earlier but for the regulations, was the prize among the overseas candidates. During 1967, as counties got wind of the changes to come, he found representatives of Lancashire, Gloucestershire, Leicestershire and Northamptonshire knocking on the door of the pavilion at Norton. Initially, he could imagine no other destination than Lancashire after his years there in league cricket. But it was Nottinghamshire who announced in December 1967 that Sobers was joining them as captain, once they had agreed compensation to Norton for buying him out of his contract. Sobers considered himself the first cricketer to be 'transferred'.

Having just finished 16th out of 17 teams in the Championship without winning a single match,* Nottinghamshire chairman Dick Milnes promised members that 'my committee means business' and looked forward to a 'new era for things at Trent Bridge'.[4] Notts presented to Sobers's agent, Bagenal Harvey, a package worth between £5,000 and £7,000 a year for three years – depending on which source one trusts – plus accommodation, use of a car and return tickets to Barbados. Sobers formally signed the contract during the England tour of the Caribbean the following March. Only the very best First Division footballers in England could achieve such a level of salary. 'One may ask, where is the money coming from to pay these expensive stars with county cricket in its present parlous financial state?' pondered *Wisden* editor Norman Preston.[5]

Ross said of the new recruits, 'It will be interesting to see how they can adapt themselves to performing at full pitch for six days a week. One thinks particularly of Sobers, who will be expected to bat, bowl and field better than anyone else. But he

---

* They lost only four of their 28 matches, one fewer than eventual champions Yorkshire, but drew 22 and suffered two no-results.

must do something like this for Notts in order to give them a fair return on their investment.'[6]

Sobers, who confidently told friends that he could lift Notts into the top four, arrived for his first day of work at Trent Bridge to a barrage of news cameras, to whom he offered a cheery comment about the British spring weather. 'He met the players on a very cold day in the nets at Trent Bridge,' recalled new team-mate, seam bowler Mike Taylor. 'He had a sheepskin coat on and he never took it off. He was just introduced to all the players and we didn't see him again until the first match. I think he went off and played a bit of golf with Ted Dexter.'

That Nottinghamshire debut was at home in a first-round Gillette Cup match against Lancashire, 'It was chilly Saturday in late April,' said Taylor. 'He never had a net and he never warmed up. In the dressing room he touched his toes half a dozen times and they gave him his Notts sweaters and that was it.' Sobers went out and took 3 for 28 in more than 11 overs of swing bowling and hit an unbeaten 75 as his team overhauled the visitors' 168. Taylor continued, 'I was batting with him and it was getting very drizzly and dark. He came down the wicket and said, "What are we going to do?"' I said it was up to him. He replied, 'I have got a Rothmans Cavaliers game at Cambridge tomorrow so we'd better carry on.'[7]

In the second round of the Gillette Cup he scored 95 and took 4 for 15 in 11 overs in a victory at Worcestershire. The run came to an end in the quarter-final, when Sobers's 76 was not enough to get Notts to their target against Gloucestershire at Trent Bridge.

The knockout matches were icing on the cake; it was the bread and butter of three-day cricket where Sobers and Nottinghamshire most desired improvement. After six draws, Sobers took 5 for 31 at Taunton in a victory over Somerset – who featured a young Greg Chappell – although he missed the team's first home win of the season a week later while nursing a groin injury. Later in the summer Sobers's quick-fire 77 and an ambitious declaration paid off with a win against Lancashire, signalling the start of a late-season surge. Gordon Ross wrote, 'His mere presence in the side has probably made each player just that little bit better. As a side they can now believe in themselves and one day soon Sobers is going to cut loose with the bat as only he can.'[8]

That day came early in August during a victory over Kent at Dover in which Sobers produced what Derek Underwood described as 'the most incredible innings I have seen'. The England man added, 'This was Sobers with a difference. A rare moment when he was motivated by anger.'

Kent captain Alan Dixon delayed his second-innings declaration to set Notts 186 to win in 135 minutes. Sensing that Sobers, who had taken 11 wickets in the match, felt Dixon should have closed earlier, Underwood recalled, 'He came in at number three and from that moment the match was lost.' Sobers smashed 105 out of 148 in 77 minutes, reaching the fastest century of the season, and Nottinghamshire cruised home by five wickets with five overs to spare. 'He hit so powerfully through the line of the ball, off both front and back foot, that it was a treat to watch,' Underwood added.[9]

On site for *The Daily Telegraph*, EW Swanton reported, 'For the most part his two sixes and 18 fours came from hits made with the bat swinging vertically, off either front or back foot, into and through the line of the ball. When, occasionally, he took something of a liberty, his eye was seemingly unaffected by dreadful light. It truly was a superlative innings.'

Up to fifth place in the table, another win against Gloucestershire took them into their final match at Swansea's St Helen's ground on the final day of August in sight of clinching that top-four place. The home team, Glamorgan, had spent the season trying to catch eventual champions Yorkshire.

After winning the toss, Sobers was happy to let his batsmen get on with it while he kicked back in the pavilion. By now, team-mates had become used to their skipper's casual preparations. 'He was a very relaxed bloke,' Taylor explained. 'Before we batted he often used to be asleep. He never got nervous about who was bowling. He lay there on the treatment table and closed his eyes.' Taylor knew better than anyone why Sobers seized upon opportunities to grab a nap. 'Bob White and I travelled with him that year. We drove him, in his Australian car, because he didn't like driving. He never slept much – he didn't want to miss anything. He never drank excessively, but in those days every club had a casino. I have never had a bet in my life but I went in a few casinos with him. He liked to have a bet.'[10]

Opener Brian Bolus advanced to a century and Notts made steady, unspectacular progress. 'One or two middle-order players sensed a declaration coming from their captain and selfishly blocked to make sure they would be not out and so improve their personal batting averages,' suggested Glamorgan captain Tony Lewis. 'They were using up valuable time.'[11]

Even when the fourth wicket went down during the afternoon, Sobers stayed put. BBC's *Grandstand* was showing racing from Newcastle while ITV's *World of Sport* was at Goodwood. Neither had shown its final race yet. 'I went in before him because he wasn't ready to bat,' said John Parkin, an occasional first-teamer who was about to see history made from the best seat in the house.[12]

At 308 for 5, after Deryck Murray was bowled by Malcolm Nash without scoring, Sobers stirred himself to walk down the 80-odd concrete steps that led from the pavilion. He headed back for tea five overs later with 25 against his name. 'I was going in to have a little look at the bowling and then make as many runs as possible so I could make a declaration,' was his approach. 'I was about to throw my bat at the ball. It didn't matter whether I got out or not.'[13]

After the interval, BBC Wales, which had been televising parts of the game during the day, had taken the cricket off the air, going instead with *Grandstand*'s offering of athletics and powerboat racing. By good fortune, it was decided to keep the cameras rolling and for Wilfred Wooller, Glamorgan secretary as well as broadcaster, to continue his commentary. Whatever sixth sense the producer might have had, it cannot possibly have been that cricket was about to witness a feat never before performed.

By the time the over that would reverberate around the world began, Sobers had rattled along to 40. Alan Jones, waiting to open the Glamorgan innings, recalled, 'He had already played some fantastic shots. Alan Rees was at cover and was highly rated as one of the best in the world in that position. He said some of the shots that went past him on the ground were absolutely brilliant.'[14]

At the non-striker's end, Parkin was eager for his own piece of the action. 'I spent the over in which he hit the six sixes just waiting, ready to run. When he came to the middle he said to me, "Let's have a quick ten minutes," so I knew he was going to be looking for boundaries but I was keen to get on strike.'[15]

Nash was a good enough left-arm seamer to collect 993 wickets in his first-class career, playing in England Test trials. 'He was a most dangerous bowler with the new ball,' said Lewis, yet on this day he was 'trying to copy Underwood'. The Kent man's briskly delivered left-arm spin had skittled the Australians a few days earlier on a rain-soaked track at The Oval and Nash thought he could achieve success in the same style.

'I was bowling left-arm orthodox round the wicket as I had been for seven or eight overs prior to tea and I got a couple of wickets so I carried on pitching it up,' Nash recalled. 'The best way to get [Sobers] out is let him have a go at it. We'll see if we can get him to whack one up in the air and get caught.'[16]

Jones continued, 'Malcolm was a very good seam bowler with great control. He used to bowl his left-arm spin in the nets quite often. He was a very confident boy and that day he thought he had a chance of getting Garry out, no matter what he bowled.'[17]

Delivering the entire over from round the wicket, Nash pitched the first ball full and, with the merest of foot movement, Sobers swung it over long-on. 'They had a very short boundary on the leg side,' Sobers explained, 'and [with] Malcolm being a left-arm spinner the ball was coming in to me.'[18] It meant that when the second ball pitched a little shorter, Sobers had no hesitation in sitting back in his crease and flaying it over the midwicket boundary on the Gorse Lane side of the ground into the wall of The Cricketers pub. 'Goodness, gracious me,' Wooller gasped in the commentary box, while Nash's thought was, 'He is going to mishit one any time now.'[19]

Ball three, around off stump, disappeared into the spectators behind long-off. Former England all-rounder Peter Walker, fielding at slip, heard wicketkeeper Eifion Jones say to Sobers, 'I bet you can't hit the next three for six.'[20] It was a dangerous comment to make to such an inveterate gambler.

The fourth ball was too short, swung over square leg, the arc of Sobers's bat becoming more extravagant with every shot. 'Garry just took him apart,' said Alan Jones. 'Nashy was no mug. It wasn't as if someone was lobbing them up. He was bowling them properly. He believed until the very last ball he could get Garry out. But he just middled everything. They weren't slogs, they were good cricket shots.'[21]

Skipper Lewis invited Nash to bowl over the wicket and fire in yorker-length seamers. 'That was after the third or fourth six,' he said. 'But other than those vague memories I am just left with images of the ball being blitzed with a coil of the body and a lash of the bat.'[22]

By now Sobers's team-mates were gathered together excitedly in their pavilion viewing area. 'He'd had a fantastic season,' said Taylor. 'But surely he couldn't do this, could he?'[23] The last man to cotton on to the potentially historic nature of what was happening, was non-striker Parkin.

Ball five. And if not for the margin of a few inches people would remember Ravi Shastri as the first man to hit six sixes in an over 17 years later. 'I gave it a little more air,' Nash recalled. 'It wasn't quite such a full length, and Sobers went through his shot and got underneath it.'[24]

Davis, usually a close fielder, was at long-off, conscious of the hazard behind him. 'I had played for Swansea, so I got to know the wall about a metre behind the boundary,' he explained. 'From the other end you could just see a small wall but, if you went over it, it was a six-foot drop. I had seen club players go over, and you could get a nasty injury. So when Nashy came on to bowl his stupid left-arm spinners my thought was, "They are going for a declaration so it doesn't matter if it goes for six or four. I am not going over the wall."

'That is how I set myself up, which might not be very team-spirited but I was thinking more of my life than where the ball was going. I stood about a foot inside the boundary and I was not going to move because if I went backwards the ball would take you with it. Whatever happened I was going forwards or sideways.'[25]

Sobers's shot descended towards Davis, who stood his ground, caught the ball and toppled backwards towards the boundary, which was marked by a painted line. Sobers left the crease. 'The crowd started shouting, "You're not out,"' he remembered. 'I think they were enjoying it even more than I was.'[26]

Davis continued, 'The ball went very high. The spin takes it away from you sometimes and I dived to my right and thought I had caught it because my feet were inside. I didn't know the law had changed. In 1967, if you caught the ball inside the boundary it was out whether you went outside or not. I don't think half our side knew that you couldn't do that now. Tony Cordle came across and said it was out. But when I got up there was all the bloody fuss about: did I go over the boundary? The crowd all wanted six sixes even though they were Glamorgan supporters. I couldn't care whether it was six or not – as far as I was concerned, they had got too many runs already.'[27]

While umpires Eddie Phillipson and John Langridge wondered what signal to give, Lewis, with thoughts on winning the match, was more concerned about the minutes ticking away. 'We are wasting time here,' he told them. 'Give a six.' Phillipson's arms went into the air and play continued. Jones explained, 'You can imagine the crowd going absolutely mad at that time. It didn't matter where Malcolm bowled that last one, he was going to hit it out of the ground.'[28]

Davis's near-miss, meanwhile, would end up as his 'claim to fame'. He added, 'My friends don't stop talking about it, so I have lived on it although I have never brought it up myself. My friends will get talking to somebody we have never met and they will say, "That is the guy who caught Garry Sobers." It has carried me my whole life and it comes up every few weeks.'[29]

According to Sobers, it was only after the fifth ball that the idea of making history took over. 'I have got to give it a go,' he thought. 'I can't let it slip now.'[30] Expecting the final ball to be bowled flatter and quicker, he decided to target the short leg-side boundary rather than risk being caught on a straight hit. 'I ran in and bowled a seamer off a short run, round the wicket, something I'd never ever done before,' said Nash, 'and it was the worst ball of the day, let alone the over.'[31]

Sobers remembered, 'He dropped it halfway down the wicket. My eyes opened as big as a football. I had one eye on the ball and one eye on the short boundary and I swung at it. I swung so hard that even if it had hit the top edge it would have still gone for six.'[32]

The ball flew off the middle of the bat and within a split-second Wooller was declaring, 'He's done it, he's done it.' As the ball disappeared over the stands and along the narrow street that led away from the ground he added the famous line, 'And my goodness, it's gone way down to Swansea.'

According to Walker, 'Sobers's wind-up for the last ball is one of the most indelible memories I retain from 18 years as a first-class cricketer.'[33]

Remarkably, batting partner Parkin was perhaps the last person in the ground to realise what had just happened. 'It didn't really register with me that he'd hit five consecutive sixes,' he admitted, 'and so when he hit the sixth and I saw him walk down the wicket and take the applause I was quite surprised.'[34]

Sobers declared and, once Glamorgan had begun their reply, the close of play presented an opportunity for events to sink in. Nash didn't fully appreciate that history had been made, but the ribbing of team-mates and a request from the BBC for a joint interview with Sobers emphasised the enormity of what had happened. The cash-conscious Sobers reminded Nash to make sure he got paid for his appearance. 'He got double the fee that I did, of course,' Nash remembered.[35]

In the St Helen's bar that evening, Sobers was surrounded by Glamorgan members and committee men. 'All of them wanted to talk about the six sixes,' Parkin recalled, 'but Garry did not want all that. He was not that sort of person. He told us players, "Come on, lads, let us go back to the old tavern." He did not want to make too much of a fuss about the record.'[36]

Nottinghamshire went on to win by 166 runs, Taylor taking five second-innings wickets to finish the season with 99. 'Garry was a very positive captain and I got the most wickets I ever got that year,' he said. 'He set attacking fields and I had people caught where I never had before.'[37]

A finishing position of fourth place earned Sobers a case of champagne after winning a bet with Bunty Ames, the wife of former England wicketkeeper Les, who had doubted his prediction of hauling Notts that far up the table.[*] He finished the season with 1,570 Championship runs at 44.85, scoring only two centuries but adding 13 half-centuries. He took 83 wickets at 22.67.

'The advent of Sobers completely transformed Nottinghamshire,' said Rex Alston in *Playfair Cricket Monthly*'s

---

[*] Glamorgan would have to wait another year to win the County Championship in 1969.

review of the season. 'Sobers was half the side, playing the two most brilliant innings of the summer.'[38]

Preston would write in *Wisden*, 'For too long county cricket had been stifled by dour, safety-first methods. The overseas players by their enterprise and natural approach brought a breath of life into the three-day match. Garfield Sobers, as befitted his reputation, was the outstanding personality, and in bringing about the revival of Nottinghamshire by his own inspiring deeds he induced a new faith in the cricket ability of all the other members of his side.'[39]

In his summary of the season, Notts chairman Milnes said of Sobers, 'His leadership was exemplary; his personal performance magnificent.'[40]

Sobers admitted that the county circuit had been hard work and he would end up reflecting on his Nottinghamshire career with regrets that his appearances in future years were restricted by injury and touring commitments. He found the daily grind 'too taxing, almost boring in some respects'.[41] It was not an uncommon sentiment. Barry Richards, who scored 2,395 runs in 1968 at the start of an 11-year stint with Hampshire, admitted to waking some days with the thought, 'Oh no, not another day of cricket.'

He explained, 'I think Garry used to pick his moments, as I did. You don't like to admit it at the time because everyone thinks you are putting in 100 per cent all the time. And you just can't do it. Some of us left England in September and were playing in Johannesburg or somewhere two days later. County players couldn't grasp that they wouldn't play for six months but we continued playing. I found some games tedious and when I said that in my book in 1977 I got absolutely roasted for it. Without the lure of Test cricket, it just made it harder for me. Gordon [Greenidge] and Andy [Roberts] were sneaking off every so often to play in front of a full house at Lord's and here you are at Derby with five people you can introduce yourself to. Garry would have had times where he would have got himself motivated but I don't think he could do it every day.'[42]

David Lloyd added, however, 'I understand that about Garry having to lift his game for certain matches, but he didn't have to lift it very much.'[43]

Playing against West Indies team-mate Clive Lloyd at Lancashire was the kind of motivation that Sobers enjoyed. 'Garry always loved a fight,' recalled wicketkeeper Engineer. 'Clive and myself were hitting the old ball easily. The new ball was taken and Garry came on to bowl. We just needed one further run to get [another] bonus point. Garry bowled six of the most beautiful left-arm outswingers. Clive was batting, I think, in the 70s. He tried to drive, did not get a touch on a single ball.'[44]

Yet the presence of Sobers could enliven some of the quieter matches for his opponents. Surrey's Pat Pocock remembered Sobers helping Nottinghamshire bat out the remaining overs before an inevitable draw. Approaching seam-bowling team-mate Robin Jackman, Pocock ordered, 'Don't try to get him out, otherwise we've got to watch a load of other guys scratching around. I'd rather watch Garry.'[45]

Pocock also recalled Nottinghamshire players telling him about their captain's forgiving attitude when they were dispatched to the boundary. 'That's all right,' was a typical response. 'It'd be a miserable old game if nobody ever hit a four.'[46]

* * *

In 1969, with Sobers missing half the season on West Indies duty, Nottinghamshire finished eighth in the Championship and 13th in the inaugural season of the 40-over John Player League on Sunday afternoons. In the Gillette Cup, they came within one game of Lord's, losing to eventual winners Yorkshire in the semi-final at Scarborough, even though Sobers gave up only 12 runs in his 12 overs.

He had undoubtedly contributed to improved Notts performance, but the club made a loss of £7,540 in 1969 as fewer than 10,000 fans paid to attend their three-day matches. Of the 4,000 average crowd for Sunday matches, 3,000 were members. A sum of £22,053 received from a bequest from the estate of Cyril Lowther kept the club's head above water.

In between games for the Rest of the World Team in 1970, Sobers played 14 Championship matches and scored 1,154 runs at 76.93, including five hundreds, but Notts won only four games to finish tenth. The club, forced to make savings, had reduced the roster of professional players to 13, plus Sobers. They still lost £10,540 on the season, leaving an overall deficit above £30,000.

By 1971, 'the constant cricket was wearing out his talent',[47] according to the club's official history, even though he took

53 wickets and scored 1,485 first-class runs at 46.40 – good numbers for mere mortals – as Notts finished 12th in both the Championship and John Player League. Only one match was won as Sobers missed the majority of 1972 and even with him averaging 45.45 in 15 matches in 1973 that total of victories could not be exceeded and Notts could not lift themselves from the bottom of the table.

By 1974, Sobers had one year remaining on his extended contract. Leadership of the team passed to Jack Bond, the 41-year-old captain-manager who had just led Lancashire to three Gillette Cups and two John Player Leagues. But for the third straight year, Notts could muster only a single three-day victory. Sobers played 15 Championship games and his 1,110 runs included four centuries, one scored in only 83 minutes against Derbyshire at Ilkeston, earning him the Walter Lawrence Trophy for the fastest hundred of the season. His 29 wickets cost more than 30 each.

Sobers ended his Nottinghamshire career without helping them to any tangible success. Off the field, county membership was down to 3,794, its lowest level since 1946 – a trend affecting many cricket and football teams as economic challenges made the post-war attendance boom an even more distant memory.

But his influence was felt beyond the league tables. Derek Randall, who would establish himself in the Notts team in the early 1970s before going on to play for England, said, 'Sobers was out of this world, a god. Just to watch him play was fantastic, and he had a big influence on my play and my attitude.' Randall called him 'a firm believer in encouraging young people to play their natural game' but always willing to offer advice.

'At first I was very shy and nervous: I would sit quietly in a corner of the dressing room listening to every word the senior players had to say, but Sobers helped me to come out of my shell and to feel a full-fledged member of the team … He was not the type to nag us and correct our techniques because he was a great believer in the theory that the game should be played naturally. He never tried to change me or water down the extravagances in my style.'[48]

And even within other counties, Sobers was creating memories that would last his opponents' lifetime. Typical was the story recounted by former Essex all-rounder Keith Pont, describing his Championship debut against Nottinghamshire in 1971. 'As an 18-year-old to be able to walk on the field and play against Garry Sobers … Strangely enough, Robin Hobbs bowled to Sobers and he ran down the wicket and smashed it straight at me and I caught it at mid-off. Up until that point I didn't realise how hard professional players hit the ball. I managed to hang on to it, much to the delight of Hobbs and the rest of the team. That was my introduction to county cricket.'[49]

18

DECLINE AND FALL

'While the music has begun, I drink to
memories in the gloom.
Though the music's still the same, It has a
bittersweet refrain.'

Engelbert Humperdinck, 'The Way It Used to Be' (Roger
Cook, Roger Greenaway, 1969)

GARRY SOBERS sat in his hotel room in Perth. It was little more than a month since the conclusion of his first English county season and now another 11 months of cricket in the next year stretched ahead of him. Reporters gathered round as though waiting for a sermon from cricket's high priest, yet the man who could make spirits soar with his feats on the field was in the mood only for a confessional.

'I am weary of cricket,' he admitted. 'It is no longer a game to me. I am a professional and I play cricket as a job, just as a working man goes to work each day.' For that reason he had arrived in Australia ahead of most of his team in order to partner Wes Hall in a double-wicket competition, spread across the five major cricketing centres over a period of two

287

weeks. They earned A$6,000 each for finishing as the top team, ahead of second-placed Graeme Pollock and brother Peter and six other combinations. Ironically, Sobers had needed to win a battle in the selection room several months earlier to secure Hall's services for Australia, threatening that if he was left out, as the committee suggested, they could look for a new captain.

Tiredness was not considered a good enough excuse by locals when Sobers opted to miss the opening game of the tour, remaining in the big city while his colleagues travelled to the traditional up-country one-dayer in Kalgoorlie. It was the first time the touring captain, they pointed out, had failed to participate.

Once again the tourists carried the burden of being saviours of the sport in someone else's country. 'To say Australia needed the tonic of another West Indian tour was the understatement of the decade,' said author Phil Tressider, referring to the decline in attendance that had forced the Australian Cricket Board to trial Sunday play. 'In a prosperous society where cars are banked bumper to bumper along seaside roads and surfboards perched precariously above, it was so easy to give cricket the go-by.'[1]

In the opening first-class contest Sobers smashed 25 boundaries in scoring 132 in 113 minutes against Western Australia. 'It was batting mayhem,' said Tressider, 'a succession of thunderous drives, pulls, cuts and lifted strokes that left bowlers and fieldsmen paralysed.'[2] Broadcaster Alan McGilvray reckoned he had never seen a finer innings in Perth. Unknown to most observers was that Sobers had again performed at the highest level after being out all night. To catch up on lost sleep, he had strapped on his pads on arrival in the dressing room and dozed off on a bench, giving team-mates instructions to wake him when it was time to bat.

In Adelaide, Sir Donald Bradman welcomed Sobers in a Town Hall reception by pleading, 'As an old South Australian player we expect you to take it a bit easy on us.' Sobers was in no mood for favours, recording a five-wicket haul, but his team surrendered tamely by ten wickets. 'If we don't pull together we will be beaten all the time,' he said. 'Some of our players are taking things too light-heartedly.' He then fell four short of another century against Victoria and rounded off his preparation for the first Test by taking the New South Wales bowling for 130 off 138 balls.

But, with his words to his players in Adelaide still resounding in their ears, Sobers then did his disappearing act while the team prepared in Brisbane for the first Test, eventually showing up on the final day of the first-class game against Queensland. Quite apart from the mixed message his trip to Melbourne sent to his team about commitment to the cause, it was not received well by his hosts. 'Queensland cricket – its administrators and its followers – have been snubbed and insulted over the mystery of the missing West Indies captain,' said Brisbane's local paper, the *Courier Mail*, arguing that 'it smacks of indifference and insult to cricket in this state'.

* * *

So where was he? What was this 'mission' that tour manager Berkeley Gaskin had said would ultimately benefit the team? The truth was that he was following his heart.

Sobers had met Pru Kirby during the summer of 1968 while she was working in England for a public relations company, promoting the Australian canned fruit industry. Pru, from Melbourne, had Sobers on her target list of public figures to be filmed discussing their connections to and love of Australia. After the interview in Nottingham, Sobers asked her out to dinner and they saw each other frequently over the next few weeks.

After arriving in Australia for the West Indies tour, Sobers visited Pru's home address, knowing she had not yet returned from England, but keen to meet her parents, which he did on several more occasions. To Pru's surprise, he was alongside her father, John, to greet her in Sydney after her long boat trip home. 'He was part of the family by the time she arrived,' John explained.[3]

Sobers, who 'loved her very much',[4] was keen for their relationship to become long-term, but Pru had doubts. He was coming to accept that they were destined not to be together when, in Brisbane, he received a call from her. Her sister had persuaded her that, if she loved him, she should find a way to make things work. They needed to talk. Sobers left his team while he and Pru spent time in Melbourne discussing their future.

It was on New Year's Eve that they resolved to marry, although there was still the matter of Sobers's previous betrothal to the Indian actress, Anju Mahendru, to be dealt with. For that he needed to call her in India, explain the situation and wait for a letter from her releasing him from their engagement. Even after that, the impending marriage remained private until only a few days before the ceremony in England the following September. 'He's just a very nice young man,' Pru's mother said when the news broke. And, responding to a question that appeared relevant at the time, she added, 'He's just Garry. The fact that he has a dark brown skin didn't enter into it at all.'

Meanwhile, Garry's mother, Thelma, who at this point had never left Barbados, was merely a distant observer. 'I am glad Garry has found the girl he wants to settle down with and I am looking forward to meeting her,' she said. 'I am sure they will be happy.'

* * *

The immediate impact of Sobers's compassionate leave on his team appeared to be limited. The West Indies players ended the first Test match standing outside the Gabba singing the reggae hit 'Mister Walker' in celebration of a 125-run victory. 'It turned out to be a poignant moment,' said Henry Blofeld, 'for it was the final hour of triumph for these West Indians.'[5]

Having batted first, West Indies achieved a first-innings lead of 12, despite Australian centuries by captain Bill Lawry and vice-captain Ian Chappell. Both had been dismissed by Sobers catches off the part-time bowling of Clive Lloyd, who hit 129 to propel his team to a second-innings total of 353. Then Sobers produced one of his more remarkable performances as a bowler.

After the late decision to omit Hall, Sobers took the new ball with Charlie Griffith, despite the discomfort in his shoulder. On the fourth morning of the match, it was revealed that Sobers had undergone an x-ray that revealed a piece of floating bone in the joint. It made it too painful to get into position to deliver the left-hander's 'wrong 'un' when he bowled wrist-spin. If all he could do was turn the ball in to the right-handed batsmen, it was not worth bothering. Instead, after his opening spell, he reverted to the finger-spin that had originally got him into the West Indies team.

Clasping a beer in the dressing room a few hours later, he explained he couldn't remember when he had last bowled orthodox slow left-armers, but his figures of 6 for 73, including the final two wickets to secure victory, proved that he hadn't forgotten the skill completely. Former England fast-bowler-turned-journalist, Frank Tyson, called it 'a triumph for the triumvirate of cricketers that is Sobers'.[6]

Put in at Melbourne, West Indies were rolled over by burly fast bowler Graham McKenzie. Known as 'Garth', the Western Australian numbered Sobers among his eight victims – bowled by a shooter – as the tourists managed only 200. Then Lawry (205) and Chappell (165) shared a partnership of 298 in a total of 510. With neither Hall nor Griffith to call upon, Sobers shared the bulk of the bowling with Gibbs – taking four wickets apiece – but often appeared bereft tactically. 'Sobers's main hope was to contain and hope that the batsmen would get themselves out, but so often he seemed to have no idea how to do this and no plan which he was trying to put into action,' said Blofeld. 'Sobers, wandering from mid-off to mid-off, appeared to have lost control.'[7]

Batting again, a total of 280 meant West Indies lost by an innings. Leg-spinner John Gleeson cast a spell over their batsmen – taking five wickets in the second innings for the second consecutive match – and the only real resistance came when Sobers, who scored 67, shared a sixth-wicket partnership of 124 with Seymour Nurse. Sobers, after a slow start, had decided that the best method against Gleeson was attack, once hitting him for three successive boundaries.

Sobers caused raised eyebrows when he turned up at the Sydney Cricket Ground on the eve of the third Test in a tangerine golf shirt, having come direct from the Royal Sydney course, and created more comment when deciding to leave Griffith out of the 12 originally selected, bringing back Hall instead.

Again, West Indies batted disappointingly – Sobers falling one short of a half-century – before Australia racked up another mammoth score. Doug Walters's 118 included five fours in a single over off Sobers, who returned figures of 0 for 109 after suffering a thigh strain, and Australia's 547 gave them a first-innings lead of 283. A slightly better effort second time around included a Butcher century and another brief Sobers counter-attack against Gleeson, but it still only left Australia needing to knock off 42 for a ten-wicket victory.

A series that had struggled to live up to the nail-biting excitement of eight years previously finally delivered a thriller at the Adelaide Oval. Sobers, who'd scored an unbeaten 121 against a Tasmanian XI between Tests, took only 132 minutes to hammer 110, with boundaries accounting for 72 of his runs – 15 fours and two sixes being fired in all directions. 'This was to start an uninhibited and magnificent onslaught,' wrote Murray Tippett in *Playfair Cricket Monthly*. 'He seemed to release all his pent-up emotions as he took to Gleeson.'[8] A four and six off Alan Connolly took him to 50 in only 44 minutes.

'It seems that all he has to do is to be in the mood,' said Blofeld. 'He half strode, half sauntered out to the wicket [and] batted like a cultured tidal wave.' Sobers had displayed 'the elegance, the grace and freedom and the natural movement of which Nureyev would have been proud'.[9]

Yet again, Sobers had succeeded without great preparation. When Tony Cozier received news on the eve of the match that his wife had given birth to their first child, a son, Sobers ignored the fact his team-mates had gone to bed and told Cozier they should celebrate. 'We should not allow a Test to spoil the occasion,' he said as they headed out in the company of Rudi Webster. 'Guiltily, I tried to persuade Garry, in the wee hours of the morning, that enough was enough, but he would have none of it,' Cozier added. Sobers told his companion, 'I'm feeling good. Don't worry about me,' and went out next day and proved it.[10]

Yet his efforts only gave West Indies a score of 276 and the game seemed to be following a familiar pattern when Australia passed 500 for the third match running. Walters reached three figures again and Redpath, out for 45, was the only one of the top six not to notch a half-century. McKenzie even managed to add 59 in a total of 533.

Finally, West Indies offered a solid response, batting more than 137 overs for 616. Butcher led the way with another hundred and Joey Carew (90), Rohan Kanhai and David Holford (80 each) all fell just short. Sobers contributed a brisk 52. With his team 614 for 9 at the end of the fourth day, Sobers chose to keep the innings going on the fifth morning so that he could ask for the heavy roller to administer one final piece of punishment to a deteriorating pitch before unleashing Gibbs as Australia chased a target of 360. But the off-spinner took only two wickets. Sobers went for 37 in his first three overs and, at 304 for 3 with just under an hour remaining, the home side were threatening a famous victory. Chappell was lbw to Griffith on 96 and then came a sequence of run-outs that saw Walters, Eric Freeman and Barry Jarman sent back in the space of 14 runs. Sobers was the fielder for the first and last of those, obliterating Jarman's stumps with a brilliant pick-up and throw on the run.

There had already been one controversial earlier run-out in the last over before tea when non-striker Redpath was caught wandering outside the crease by Griffith, who pulled up in his delivery stride and took off the bails. Umpire Lou Rowan had no choice but to give him out. Sobers went to the Australian dressing room to apologise to skipper Lawry, although to some it seemed an empty gesture. As a man who always espoused good sportsmanship, Sobers said he was 'disgusted' that Griffith did not give Redpath a warning but felt 'there was little I could do about it'.[11] The other view was that had Sobers really felt guilty about it he could have withdrawn the appeal.

McKenzie and Gleeson both fell on 333, before Connolly joined Paul Sheahan for a nerve-wracking final 17 minutes. West Indies had 26 deliveries to take the final wicket and

Sobers took the new ball, but Sheahan played out the final over to achieve a draw that maintained Australia's 2-1 lead.

As was often the case in a series as yet undecided, six days were allocated for the fifth Test at the SCG. Australia surpassed their own prolific efforts in the series by batting for more than 13 hours and posting 619 after being sent in by Sobers, who had consulted team-mates after winning the toss. Walters marched to 242 and Lawry 151 as the first sighting of Hall and Griffith as a pairing in the series produced no upturn in West Indies' fortunes. The poor performance in the field – including a number of missed chances – was evidence of a side resigned to its fate, while the captain's tactical decisions rarely stood up to examination. Blofeld concluded, 'The effect of his captaincy, or lack of it, was that his side disintegrated as a team and became 11 individuals.'[12]

The extremity of the situation prompted Sobers to move up to four in the order – Cozier called it 'folly' that it had taken so long – but he managed only 13 as West Indies were left facing a deficit of 340. Lawry chose to pile on the misery before declaring at 394 for 8, Redpath and Walters, again, having posted hundreds. Sobers, unhappy with his opposite number's ruthlessness, argued, 'Declarations like that drive the crowds away.'[13]

Walters – the first man to score a double century and century in the same Test – had achieved a sequence of 76, 118, 110, 50, 242 and 103 in the series, while Australia's haul of 1,013 runs in the match was then the third-highest in Test cricket history, and remains fourth at the time of writing.

A victory target of 735 was unrealistic, as was batting almost two days for survival once three wickets fell for 30. Sobers, at number five, chose the moment for his final batting exhibition of the tour. He passed 1,000 first-class runs for the season as he took only 99 balls to reach a century that seemed like a release of his frustrations at Lawry's approach, West Indies' performance and the media's criticism. 'Sobers decided he had had enough of this tomfoolery,' wrote Tressider. 'He treated Gleeson like a whipping boy. Was there ever such gallant heroics when all was lost?' He concluded, 'He was still king, though his empire had fallen in ruins around him.'[14]

Out for 113 after hitting 20 fours, Sobers left Nurse to reach his century and carry the match into the sixth morning before seeing his team bowled out for 352 in front of a meagre crowd of a few hundred. A 382-run margin of defeat and a 3-1 scoreline in Australia's favour offered a miserably accurate picture of West Indies' efforts. 'We have turned full circle and we are now at the bottom,' Gaskin sighed.

So a series that began for West Indies with the music of victory – the players joining in that jubilant chorus of celebration in Brisbane – ended as British crooner Engelbert Humperdinck was climbing the charts around the world with a lament for happier times, 'The Way Things Used To Be'. In his case, it was the love of a woman that had been lost. The West Indies, meanwhile, appeared to have lost their passion for the sport.

'It was sad to watch these once famous West Indians trying vainly to recapture their former powers,' was Blofeld's summary for *Wisden*. 'When things began to go wrong they were unable to regroup mentally and take a cool look at their problems. Sobers, their captain, might, with his ability and experience, have been able to stop this, but he seemed to be unaware of what was happening.'[15]

Sobers's own batting showed no sign of decline, producing 497 runs at 49.7. His bowling, however, hampered by injury, was less effective. His 18 wickets arrived at an average of 40.7. But there was no chance for him to rest his aching body, with the first of three four-day Tests in New Zealand starting a week later. His team arrived 'tired and disillusioned', according to Cozier, who noted that 'their lack of spirit was clear from their cricket'.[16]

Having inserted New Zealand on a green-looking Auckland pitch, Sobers found his team replying to a total of 323, achieved by number eight Bruce Taylor clubbing a thrilling hundred in 86 minutes. Despite a century by Carew and 95 by Nurse, West Indies trailed by 47. New Zealand skipper Graham Dowling was then able to declare at 297 for 8, leaving West Indies chasing 345 to win in two and a half sessions of the final day. Nurse batted beautifully again, scoring 168 to see his team home by five wickets with three overs remaining. No one in New Zealand, Sobers might have noted ruefully, was kicking effigies of their captain around the streets after Dowling's declaration.

The pattern was reversed in the second Test at Wellington's Basin Reserve, New Zealand inserting West Indies and finding themselves needing only 164 to win after bowling them out for 148 in their second innings. The target was reached with four wickets down.

Christchurch hosted a draw in the third Test, Nurse dominating the first two days by batting for almost eight hours for 258. Apart from Carew's 91, there was no other support in a total of 417. Sobers was out without scoring for the second successive innings. The West Indies bowlers earned a lead of 200, leaving New Zealand to survive almost a day and half to save the game. An unbeaten century by Brian Hastings ensured they did so after Sobers took three of the six wickets to fall. It took his total for the series to seven, at the cost of 43 each. Meanwhile, his batting had collapsed, with only 70 runs in five innings.

* * *

Sobers was exhausted, carrying injuries and in desperate need of rest. But he was a professional cricketer who needed to earn money. So he would begin another tour in a month's time, a three-Test trip to England, before returning to Nottinghamshire for the remainder of the 1969 season.

'The time has come for some tree-shaking to let the old fruit drop,' Don Norville had written in the *Barbados Advocate* after the latest tour. He got his wish, with only five of the 1966 tour party to England returning in 1969. Kanhai, who had opted out of New Zealand, would again be missing, as would Nurse, who surprised Sobers by retiring after his prolific New Zealand tour.

Sobers was angry that the party was selected before his captain's report on the tour of Australia had reached the WICBC. There would be no Hall or Griffith this time, both left at home, along with Richard 'Prof' Edwards, who had taken 15 wickets in New Zealand. In their place were three uncapped pacemen: Barbadian Vanburn Holder, who had experienced English conditions with Worcestershire; Guyana's Philbert Blair; and Grayson Shillingford, a Dominican with only three first-class matches behind him. Sobers would find himself taking the new ball throughout the series, along with his other duties.

'What was obvious,' said Cozier, 'was the fact that the West Indies were in for hard times.'[17] None more than Sobers himself. *Wisden*'s Norman Preston would conclude that 'Sobers was absolutely stale' and had lost his appetite for cricket. 'His efforts over the years had now begun to tell. At times Sobers seemed to lose concentration.'[18]

He arrived at the first Test at Old Trafford at the start of a summer heatwave with more first-class ducks (two) than fifties (one) on his tour record. England ground out 413, with Geoffrey Boycott taking 332 minutes for his 128, while Kent and Barbados all-rounder John Shepherd took five wickets on his Test debut.

West Indies collapsed for 147, before making 275 in their second innings. Sobers contributed 48 in 140 minutes. A brief assault on Snow, whom he hit for four fours in two overs, contained 'a hint of desperation', according to *Playfair Cricket Monthly*'s Basil Easterbrook. 'Perhaps the most significant thing to emerge from the match was the inability of Sobers to be, as so often in the past, a one-man team,' he said. 'It is as if Garfield Sobers, rising 33, no longer relishes the role of Atlas.'[19] England duly completed a ten-wicket win, continuing the worrying trend that when West Indies lost, they did so by wide margins.

In front of a five-day attendance of 100,500, Lord's produced a more evenly contested draw. West Indies scored 380 – including a century for Charlie Davis – and 295 for 9, Sobers declaring after he had scored an unbeaten 50. Davis had been responsible for Sobers being run out in the first innings, but the captain assured him generously at the next break, 'It was as much my fault as yours, go on and make a hundred.' Peter Short, tour treasurer, said, 'I could visibly see the burden of responsibility lift from the young shoulders of Davis.'[20]

England made 344 in their first innings, rescued by centuries from Yorkshire's John Hampshire – the first Englishman to score a Test debut ton at Lord's – and skipper Ray Illingworth, leading the side after Colin Cowdrey ruptured an Achilles tendon.

Sobers had been unable to bowl in the later stages of the innings because of an injured thigh muscle. Having then been allowed to bat with Camacho as his runner, there were raised eyebrows in some quarters when he was suddenly able to send down 29 overs in a row when England batted again. John Woodcock suggested, 'The legality of this was not in question, only the ethics.'[21] Having been set 332 to win in four hours plus 20 overs, England needed 61 from the final ten overs and settled for a draw at 295 for 7, Boycott reaching three figures again.

Spared a trip to Ireland, Sobers missed the embarrassment that befell his colleagues at Sion Mills. An Irish team still decades away from becoming a credible presence in world cricket blew West Indies away for an astonishing total of 25, not a single batsman having reached double figures. The final score represented something of a recovery after they were 12 for 9. Ireland lost only one wicket in winning the game, before batting on to give the crowd some additional value for money.

It was more erratic batting that saw West Indies blow a golden opportunity to level the Test series at Headingley after limiting England to 223 and 240, Sobers taking 5 for 42 in the second innings after what *Wisden* called 'two very fine spells of fast-medium bowling'.[22]

West Indies batted poorly in their first attempt, all out for 161, but were well placed to chase down 303 to win when they stood at 219 for 3 late on the fourth day. Then came a tumble of four wickets before stumps, including Sobers being bowled for a duck by Barry Knight. 'The way to victory had been established,' said Preston. 'Sobers had only to complete the task, but before getting a proper sight of the ball he stood, leaden-footed, head in the air, as he aimed to drive and Knight bowled him comprehensively. That was the end as far as West Indies were concerned.'[23] The tourists were all out on the fifth day for 272.

Sobers finished the series with only 150 runs, at an average of 30, along with 11 wickets. Not until the last week of August did he score his only two first-class hundreds of the season, against Surrey and Leicestershire after returning to Nottinghamshire.

At last, Sobers could rest and recuperate, with no meaningful cricket in his diary until the end of January. By the time he returned to English fields in the spring of 1970 he had played only two further first-class matches, one for the International Cavaliers against Jamaica and one for Barbados against Guyana in the Shell Shield, making an unbeaten 116. If crowds were wondering if Sobers still had anything to offer at the top level, then events on the wider political and sporting landscape were about to provide the platform for him to give an emphatic answer.

19

BACK ON TOP OF THE WORLD

'The struggle is the struggle of life itself,
upward and forever upward.'

English mountaineer George Mallory

THEY MIGHT have been the greatest team never to play Test cricket, at least until Australian tycoon Kerry Packer corralled the world's best players at the end of the 1970s. But when the Rest of the World side led by Garry Sobers beat England 4-1 in the first summer of the decade they were, at the time, playing officially recognised Tests. The record books, at the insistence of the International Cricket Conference, would soon change, yet the memories of Sobers back to his magnificent best at the highest level could not be erased. 'Sobers has returned to England irresistibly refreshed,' said John Woodcock. 'Even in a side composed of the best cricketers in the world, Sobers was like a giant.'[1]

The relatively relaxed period Sobers had enjoyed over the winter might have been somewhat busier had the International Cavaliers team he'd been selected for not been barred from playing matches in South Africa by the apartheid government because it contained black players. It was the same political issue that led to the matches in England that re-established Sobers at the pinnacle of his sport.

Once the West Indies and New Zealand cricketers had left English shores at the end of the 1969 summer, the next major sporting visitors were South Africa's rugby players. Already banned from the Olympics and football's World Cup, the country was facing further sporting isolation. South Africa's rugby tour of Britain in 1969/70 was less significant as a series of sporting contests than it was as the backdrop for the 'Stop The 70 Tour' movement's efforts to prevent the republic's cricketers following the same path the next summer. The group's supporters staged pitch invasions and left a trail of arrests and battle scars in their wake, using weedkiller to paint slogans on cricket grounds.

While debate raged over the visit of a cricket team that was about to beat Australia 4-0 to stake a claim as the best in the world, English cricket braced itself. Barbed wire went up around the Lord's square, and the new season began with a reduced programme of 12 tour matches – down from 28 – having been scheduled at eight of the country's most secure venues.

Such was the fallout from the controversy that Sobers could not avoid being caught up in it. A group called the West Indian Campaign Against Apartheid Cricket announced that any Caribbean county cricketers who played against the South African tourists would be 'pilloried'. Sobers, who had said he would have no problem playing against the tourists, got a sense of what exactly that meant when he arrived at The Oval on 20

May for Nottinghamshire's three-day match against Surrey to find protestors, including anti-tour campaign leader Peter Hain, outside the ground with banners. 'One way ticket for Sobers to Bantuland', read one, while another said, 'Send the Uncle Toms to the reserves'. Such was his ability to be single-minded about his cricket that he went out and scored 160 of his team's total of 281. By the time he'd added a second-innings century and seen Surrey achieve their run chase, the tour was off.

With a general election less than a month away, Harold Wilson's Labour government felt compelled to instruct the Cricket Council to rescind the South Africans' invitation. A major motivation had been fears that African and Caribbean countries would boycott the forthcoming Commonwealth Games in Edinburgh if the tour went ahead. The Test and County Cricket Board was left staring into a £100,000 hole of lost revenue and a potentially blank summer for the England team ahead of an Ashes winter in Australia. The solution was to be found scattered around the counties; the overseas cricketers who would be asked to form a Rest of the World team to play five Test matches.

Freddie Brown and Les Ames were appointed as managers and would help Sobers, the obvious choice as captain, to select the team. There was no shortage of talent already in the country, including West Indians Rohan Kanhai, Clive Lloyd, Deryck Murray and Lance Gibbs; Pakistan's Intikhab Alam; and India's Farokh Engineer. England-based South Africans Barry Richards and Mike Procter would be joined by fellow-countrymen Graeme Pollock, Eddie Barlow and Peter Pollock, while seamer Graham McKenzie provided an Australian presence. Guinness signed up as sponsors of the series, donating a trophy and £20,000 in prize money.

With the country engrossed in England's ultimately unsuccessful football World Cup defence in Mexico, interest was slow in building and it was not until the fourth and fifth games that crowds woke up to what was on offer, by which time Sobers had helped his team to a 2-1 lead.

The first Test of the summer began, unusually for the era, on a Wednesday – so as to avoid play on Thursday, 18 June, the day on which the country upset the opinion polls by voting Ted Heath's Conservative Party into power. Sobers's last spell of bowling under the old prime minister had been a devastating display of swing bowling at pace. He had five wickets by lunch and finished with figures of 20-11-21-6 as England, missing Geoffrey Boycott and Colin Cowdrey, were shot out for 127. Sobers reckoned he bowled better at Headingley later in the summer for no reward, while *Playfair Cricket Monthly* editor Gordon Ross stated, 'Those quite close to Sobers had suggested that whilst his batting still burgeoned his quick bowling was nothing like as effective as it used to be, and he may not pay as much attention to that particular one of his many facets in the future. Sobers proved that this theory can be thrown to the four winds.'[2]

EW Swanton felt the early exchanges had proved the manner in which the matches would be contested. 'The Rest went at their opponents as though their lives depended on it,' he wrote in *The Daily Telegraph*.

Barlow, chosen to open the batting in spite of the presence of Pakistan's Majid Khan and New Zealander Glenn Turner in the country, made a century in the World's first innings before leaving the stage for Sobers. In 280 minutes he hit 30 fours and scorched 183 runs in a total of 546, cutting loose after reaching three figures by swinging John Snow into the Mound Stand for one of his two sixes.

'It lived in the mind and memory for some of the most glorious stroke-making by Sobers that Lord's has seen for years,' said Ross.[3] Despite Illingworth's dogged 94, the game was over in four days as Intikhab spun out six England batsmen in a total of 339.

'Sobey played out of his skin,' was Procter's memory of that match. 'I knew him from county cricket, but just to see him play like that against the best in the world, as England were then, he was unbelievable. He got wickets with seam, with spin. In the end we won. And the best part came when at the end he just said, "Okay, guys, see you at Trent Bridge." It was like nothing had happened.'[4]

The England fightback that the series badly needed as sports fans turned their attention from World Cup to Commonwealth Games was forthcoming in Nottingham, where the home team, showing five changes, won by eight wickets. Lloyd and Barlow were centurions in the first and second innings respectively, but their side managed scores of only 276 and 286 as Basil D'Oliveira and newcomer Tony Greig, who dismissed Sobers twice, finished the match with seven wickets apiece. England's second-innings 284 for 2, including an unbeaten seven-hour

Brian Luckhurst hundred, was higher than any total they had previously made to win a Test in England.

Illingworth had again narrowly missed out on a century and Woodcock felt that teamwork under his leadership had been a big part of England's win, 'something which the Rest, however hard they try, find it difficult to achieve'.[5] This time it was not a knock on Sobers's captaincy, more a realistic reflection of an invitation team who had never played together and who disappeared back to their counties between Test matches.

During the third match at Edgbaston, Illingworth was named as captain for England's forthcoming Ashes tour – Cowdrey again confined to the role of deputy – and his side were beaten by five wickets. The home team made a solid start until Sobers, as Ross put it, 'threw the custard into the fan' by taking three wickets for only six runs, removing Cowdrey and Keith Fletcher without scoring. After England's 294, Sobers scored 80 and shared an exhilarating partnership with centurion Lloyd before declaring at 563 for 9, the most runs England had ever conceded on this ground. Sobers took four wickets in England's second innings.

A thrilling fourth Test at Headingley got closer to the kind of crowd it deserved, an overall attendance above 45,000 prompting EW Swanton to reflect that 'the series had finally triumphed over its detractors'.[6]

Those present on the first day saw an incredible display of medium-paced cutters by Barlow, who took 7 for 64. 'All I did was bowl straight,' he said simply. His spell concluded with a sequence of four wickets in five balls, including a hat-trick with the first three of those deliveries, the victims being Alan Knott, Chris Old and Don Wilson. The makeshift nature of Sobers's team was demonstrated by the fact that the short-leg catch to complete the hat-trick was taken by England's 12th man, future captain Mike Denness, who was subbing for the Rest.

Sobers hit 16 fours and a six in scoring 114 in just over four hours to help his team achieve a first-innings lead of 154, despite Richards being unable to bat after injuring his back. Glamorgan's Roger Davis remembered, 'I did 12th man for England at Headingley and Brian Davis was doing it for the Rest of the World. Garry was not out overnight on Friday and it was an 11.30 start the next morning. Brian was in the dressing room and at 11.10 there was no sign of Garry. Then he walked in with his dinner jacket on, got changed and went out and completed his century.'[7]

Barlow took another five wickets as England scored 376, identical to the World's total, leaving a target of 223 to win. At 82 for 5, it seemed a tough task, although it might have been worse if Greig had held a chance offered by Intikhab, who helped Sobers add 115 for the sixth wicket. 'He gave glamour the miss,' said Woodcock of the determined Sobers. 'None of the overseas cricketers has been keener than Sobers to win the Guinness Trophy and all the rewards that went with it.'[8]

Sobers eventually fell for 59, but with the score 183 for 8 the ridiculous strength of the World's batting was demonstrated by Procter and the crocked Richards coming together to share a match-winning partnership of 43, leaving a relieved Gibbs unused in the pavilion. Basil Easterbrook was left to tell *Playfair*

Cricket Monthly readers, 'If Sobers had played for England I believe we would have gone to The Oval 3-1 up instead of 1-3 down.'[9]

Richards believed that playing alongside so many men from the Test nation against whom he had been unable to measure himself helped motivate Sobers. 'I think the fact that he had five South Africans in the team, he just wanted to prove how good the West Indies were,' he recalled. 'He was just spectacular in that series. I must admit that for me it was a vehicle to play cricket, one of the first times you are not actually representing anything. Some of us took it with a pinch of salt at the time, but Garry just won the games on his own and we just rode on his back.'[10]

Among the World's array of stars, Graeme Pollock was the one who had most notably failed to take a turn in the spotlight. He rectified that at The Oval, where, after England were all out for 294, he cut and drove his way to 114. *Wisden* called the partnership of 165 between him and Sobers 'a batting spectacle that will live long in the minds of those privileged to see it'.[11]*

Lancashire fast bowler Peter Lever kept England in the match by taking seven wickets before Boycott's 157 left the World needing 284 to win on a wicket becoming increasingly dusty. 'It would probably have been beyond the capacity of any normal batting line-up,' said Easterbrook.[12] Sobers had no thought of playing safe. Kanhai, another who had yet to be seen at his best, made 100 and it was appropriate that it was

---

* Among those lucky spectators was the nine-year-old author, sitting on the boundary grass at his first day of international cricket.

Sobers (40 not out) who hit Lever to the third-man boundary to complete a four-wicket win on the fifth day.

'I was privileged to join him at the end,' said Procter. 'He was again so natural, dealing with the bowling on a very, very difficult wicket. He did not exaggerate his shots, just played them, knocked off the winning runs and away he went. His attitude was unbelievable.'[13]

'The improvised Test series proved a better substitute than almost anyone hoped,' said Swanton, while his fellow columnist on *The Cricketer*, Woodcock, added, 'From a section of the press box came a plea not to recognise these as official Test matches. But the editor of *Wisden* intends to include them among the official records and Lord's are in full agreement with that.'[14]

Yet in due course the ICC would rule otherwise, announcing, 'This conference reaffirms that matches played by individual member countries against a World XI are not official Test matches and therefore should not be included in Test match records.' Thus Sobers had 588 runs and 21 wickets erased from his Test record; the unfortunate Alan Jones was robbed of his only England cap; and everyone else was left lamenting their losses.

England fast bowler John Snow offered a typical view from the English camp when he said, 'I am very proud of the 19 wickets I took, even though, laughably, they have now been officially deducted from my Test-playing record. They were earned the hard way against the best batsmen in the world.'[15]

And Procter, whose close friendship with Sobers grew from that summer, argued, 'That series as a whole was a great advertisement for Test cricket … how that didn't warrant Test status I will never know.'[16] Conversely, Barlow believed that 'the matches paled in comparison to the real cut and thrust of Test cricket'.[17]

When you look at many of the uncompetitive Test matches since the expansion of the ICC's list of full members – not to mention the spurious, knockabout Australia versus World XI 'Super Series' game of 2005 that was afforded Test status – it is easy to share the frustration that Sobers and his band of merry men go unrecognised and largely forgotten. But maybe the assessment of Woodcock is legacy enough, especially given the environment that created the games. 'As an exercise in international relations the series was an object lesson,' he said. 'No friction, no clenched fists, no jealousy, no discrimination.'[18]

It was what cricket needed. And it was what Sobers needed to disprove the impression that he was becoming a spent force. What he didn't need was what happened next.

20

'AFRO-SAXON': THE RHODESIA AFFAIR

MALCOLM X: Brothers like you and Sam
[Cooke] and Cassius [Clay], you all are our
greatest weapons.
JIM BROWN: We're not anyone's
weapons, Malcolm.
MALCOLM X: You need to be, Jimmy.
You need to be for us to win.

One Night in Miami (Kemp Powers; Amazon
Studios, 2020)

GARRY SOBERS called it 'the worst period of my cricketing life'. One weekend of meaningless cricket, undertaken without a thought to its consequences other than the money it earned, turned him from national treasure to public enemy. His actions put Caribbean politicians at each other's throats; prompted a flurry of correspondence at senior diplomatic levels; and threatened to create a rift between him and his own government in Barbados.

It all stemmed from an invitation delivered by the South African all-rounders, Eddie Barlow and Mike Procter, towards the end of the England–Rest of the World series. 'The West Indian lads and South African lads got on so well that we had already discussed the need to get Garry to come over to Southern Africa,' Procter recalled. 'Getting him to South Africa was out of the question, given the political climate, but we figured that Rhodesia wouldn't be too much of an issue … We felt his visit would provide a major boost to cricket in Rhodesia.'[1]

It was suggested that Sobers participated in a double-wicket tournament in early September. Staged in the capital city (now Harare), the Salisbury Sports Club competition was being held on Pioneers Day – which commemorated the raising of the Union Jack by Cecil Rhodes's Pioneer Column of troops at the site of Fort Salisbury in 1890.

Having just led a team in a series that resulted from opposition to apartheid in neighbouring South Africa – and having been banned from playing there with an International Cavaliers team – Sobers might have been expected to have a greater inkling of the political status of Rhodesia, run by Ian Smith's white minority government. Smith had declared independence from the United Kingdom in 1965 after disagreeing with the UK's insistence on setting a timetable to hand government to the black majority as part of its granting of independence. United Nations sanctions followed, along with the banning of multi-racial Rhodesian teams from the Olympic movement. In cricket, an all-white Rhodesia team continued to compete in South Africa's provincial championship, the Currie Cup.

Meanwhile, forces loyal to black leaders Robert Mugabe (Zimbabwe African National Union) and Joshua Nkomo

(Zimbabwe African People's Union) were taking a bloody fight to Smith's regime. 'Black opinion in particular and progressive opinion in general were strongly focused on the struggle in southern Rhodesia as a companion piece to the anti-apartheid movement directed against an even more profound racism to the south,' said Michael Manley, at the time the leader of Jamaica's opposition People's National Party and two years away from becoming prime minister.[2]

All of which had evidently passed Sobers by. 'It is not that Sobers was merely apolitical. This implies someone who has thought about it and taken a neutral position,' suggested Manley in his role as West Indies cricket historian. 'Sobers was divorced from politics in the sense of being largely unaware of them.'[3] Which, as it happened, was not totally out of character for Barbadians of Sobers's generation. In 1950, during Sobers's formative teenage years, William James Hughes, Bishop of Barbados, gave a farewell sermon in which he accused his Anglican audience of living 'cyst-like, in a little world' and told them they knew 'nothing of the social and political awakening of the West Indian masses.'

Rumours of the participation of Sobers in the Rhodesian tournament spread in the first week of September. When he arrived at The Oval to play for Nottinghamshire in a John Player League game he was greeted by reporters, to whom he offered no comment. His trip was confirmed the next day.

The following weekend he received a warm welcome in Rhodesia and within a few hours of arrival he was partnering former South Africa Test captain Ali Bacher in Salisbury. A standing ovation from the predominantly white crowd and a chorus of 'For He's a Jolly Good Fellow' accompanied him to the middle.

Rival player Don Mackay-Coghill had joked with Sobers, 'The organisers are very clever. They've totally nullified your ability by giving you Bacher as a partner.' Bacher, who never bowled a ball in Test cricket and ended his first-class career with only two wickets, said, 'I'm told that when I bowled my first ball, Garry, standing behind me at mid-on, just shook his head.'[4] Sobers did not perform well and his partnership didn't win, but such was his stature that the other teams gave him a guard of honour as he left the field. And the organisers paid him a reported £600.

Sobers attracted further disapproval by chatting with Smith in the stands. Smith said he'd had a 'lovely day discussing the great men of cricket'.[5] Smith assured Sobers that he was welcome back any time. Having been in Rhodesia for less than 48 hours, Sobers headed for Barbados, where he landed on 15 September to be greeted by a hostile crowd of media.

He seemed genuinely unaware of the storm into which he was flying, despite the interest generated by the announcement of his involvement in the event. He had convinced himself that as the participants in the tournament had been invited along non-racial lines there was nothing controversial about it. 'To say there was an uproar in the Caribbean is comprehensively to understate what took place,' Manley recorded. 'Caribbean political leadership in government, in opposition and, of course in the lunatic fringe, found one voice in which to denounce Sobers for going to Ian Smith's rebel, racist nation.'[6]

Sobers's first comment was to declare blithely, 'I've been moving into a new house and have not been reading the newspapers. I have heard a few rumours about the criticisms but nothing more.'

Then he announced happily that Smith had asked him to return any time. 'The door is open,' he declared, adding how warmly he had been received. When it was made clear to him how widespread the condemnation had been, he said, 'I have never been bothered by criticism,' and doubled down on his participation because he felt that going 'would do some good' even though he conceded that it had been mostly a white crowd who attended.

He argued that Rhodesian sport was largely non-racial and that South African cricketers were happy to play with and against blacks. Eventually he took refuge in declaring, 'I am a professional cricketer and a sportsman, not a politician.'

Unless you believe that Sobers was fully aware of the consequences of his actions and simply didn't care, you have to concede that he was politically naïve enough to miss the point of what isolating regimes such as Rhodesia and South Africa might achieve. He did not appear to understand that his participation in the Rhodesia event could be politicised. As Manley, among the most vocal opponents of apartheid, accepted, 'Here was no case of a man taking blood money in the sense that he was going to defy world opinion and silence his own conscience for filthy lucre.'[7]

Even so, there was now music to be faced. 'In much the same way that West Indian people rose up against apartheid in West Indies cricket and assured Frank Worrell the captaincy, they swiftly moved against Captain Sobers,' Caribbean historian Hilary Beckles explained. 'It had taken black West Indians a century of intense struggle to place their cricket leadership in the hands of a working-class player. They did not take too kindly to Sobers's trip which was conceived as offering support and legitimacy to a racist regime ... How could the leader of the only popular black West Indian institution – the cricket team – not recognise that since the 1920s the region's cricket culture had been highly politicised and ideologically charged to resist racial injustice?'[8]

Antiguan newspaper *The Workers' Voice* described Sobers as 'a white black man' and said he had 'abdicated his loyalty to Africans everywhere, and all West Indians in particular'. Raymond Sharpe, sports editor of the *Jamaica Gleaner*, felt Sobers had shown an 'apparent unwillingness to become fully aware of his responsibility to the West Indies nations as West Indies captain'. The *Antigua Star* said, 'His deed was most unkind to all those dedicated to the struggle against racism,' calling him 'an Afro-Saxon'.

Reuters reported, 'He has ventured into Rhodesia, where the racial oppression of his own African people has shocked even whites in the old colonial countries.' The *Jamaica Star* argued that Sobers had set back the movement to isolate Rhodesia and South Africa from top-level sport, putting it down to 'some naivete and a lack of recognition of the political aspect'.

Meanwhile, suggestions emanated from Rhodesia that Sobers would be asked to return with two full teams for a pair of first-class matches. The *Rhodesian Herald* argued, 'Rhodesians wanted Sobers to see that sportsmen of all races and creeds are welcome here. Colour doesn't matter a damn. It's a man's talent that counts.'

Not in the eyes of tennis player Arthur Ashe, the first black man to win a Grand Slam event when he lifted the US Open title in 1968. He had turned down an invitation to include Rhodesia on the itinerary of his upcoming tour of Africa.

Nor in the view of various groups and individuals across the Caribbean who suggested Sobers should forfeit the West Indian captaincy. They included Frank Walcott, general secretary of the Barbados Workers' Union, who stated, '[He] represents the heart and soul of millions of people in the West Indies, who see their national identity manifested in cricket, and their symbol of pride and equality with nations is Garry Sobers. He cannot lapse into any area which is an offence to the dignity and character of West Indians.'

Sobers's response was, 'This was a personal matter. I am a professional cricketer and I went to play cricket. I don't see why this should affect my position as captain of the West Indian team.' He also repeated his argument that 'I thought I would be aiding the cause of multi-racial sport in Africa'.

Errol Barrow, prime minister of Barbados, supported Sobers's right to pursue his career wherever he chose. Speaking at a seminar at the Centre for Multi-Racial Studies at the University of the West Indies, he said that most of Sobers's critics would have gone to Rhodesia without hesitation if offered that amount of money.

Letters to the *Barbados Advocate*, and the general feeling on the streets, showed the level of support Sobers retained from his own people. This was largely mirrored in Trinidad, where Sobers had held ambassadorial and community roles. Leader of the opposition, Vernon Jamadar of the Democratic Labour Party, said Sobers had shown 'calm dignity in response to the primitive savagery of West Indian gutter politicians'.

Yet the attacks continued to mount from other regions. Jamaican government minister Hector Wynter said Sobers should be forced to apologise. Then, on 10 October, Forbes Burnham, the prime minister of Guyana – whose country was a regular Caribbean Test-match venue – spoke to reporters on his return from a meeting in Lusaka, Zambia, at which opposition to states such as Rhodesia and South Africa had been top of the agenda. Asked about Sobers by the Guyana Broadcasting Service, Burnham launched into an attack. 'In my view,' he began, 'and in the view of my cabinet colleagues, Garfield Sobers should no longer be captain of the West Indies cricket team unless he recants and apologises for his foolish and ill-advised stand. He would be unwelcome in Guyana. Indeed it is tragic that a man so outstanding in the field of sport is not sufficiently intelligent to understand the relationship between international sport and international politics, and politics generally. He ought to remember that had it not been for politics, people like him would never have been captains of West Indian teams. I am doubtful whether Mr Sobers would be welcome in Guyana.'

The region's *Sunday Chronicle* joined the call for Sobers to lose the captaincy and Kenny Wishart, president of the Guyana Cricket Board of Control, echoed Burnham's comments, which were also endorsed by the United Negro Improvement Association.

The WICBC could easily imagine the reaction, especially among the Barbados players, if they simply deselected Sobers for future games in Guyana to avoid a political storm. Secretary Peter Short did little to clarify the Board's position when he said that Sobers had no need to apologise and doubted it would come to him being barred from playing in Guyana, before adding that they would have to 'take up this serious matter at top level'.

A few days later, the ruling Jamaican Labour Party became the latest group to call for Sobers to resign. And Manley, as leader of the opposition, warned that Sobers 'might not be welcome anywhere in the world by people who believe that justice is bigger even than sport'.

Barbados's deputy prime minister, Cameron Tudor – who disapproved both of Sobers's actions and the strength of the suggested sanctions against him – called it 'an affront to the people of Barbados' to suggest that someone might be refused entry to Guyana and condemned the 'implied denigration of Mr Sobers by responsible people who now choose to divorce politics from common sense'.

Apart from the personal ramifications for Sobers, whose home was under siege from journalists and public, he had created a new fault line in the always delicate geology of West Indies cricket. Barrow phoned him from a trip to the United Nations in New York, telling him to do nothing until he returned.

The fallout was not restricted to the Caribbean. In England, where Sobers earned the bulk of his living, there was embarrassment that the man chosen to lead the Rest of the World team in a series that was, in essence, a celebration of all things non-apartheid could head off to play in an outwardly oppressive, racist nation as soon as it was finished. Not all the reaction was critical, however. The *Daily Express*, for example, claimed, 'The great majority of British sports fans will applaud him for making a personal decision without prejudice.'

At government level, the actions of one of the country's highest-profile resident sportsmen at a time of delicate relationships with Smith and his Rhodesian regime, as well as with post-independence Barbados, generated a flurry of inter-departmental and trans-Atlantic correspondence. Letters flew between the British High Commission in Bridgetown and the Foreign and Commonwealth Office in Whitehall under the heading 'The Sobers Affair' and featuring such phrases as 'this sorry saga'. In one memo, John Bennett of the High Commission, warned, 'This affair is not conducive to Caribbean cooperation and is likely to remain prominent as a talking point,' although he added, 'In the Caribbean there is a tendency for statements which in Europe would lead to strained relations between states here being accepted in a much more relaxed manner.' Bennett concluded, 'One hopes that wiser counsel will prevail and that the whole affair will be allowed to die a natural death.'[9]

English cricket had some previous with Smith, dating back to an invitation in 1967 for champion county Yorkshire to tour Rhodesia. On that occasion, George Thomas, secretary of state for the Commonwealth Relations Office, wrote to various Yorkshire MPs to remind them that the government's policy 'has always been to deplore organised sporting tours of Rhodesia while the state of illegality exists'. Thomas feared potential damage to the UK's relationships with 'Afro-Asian peoples'.[10]

This latest episode led Indian prime minister Indira Gandhi to hint that her country might not consider the West Indies a suitable destination for its proposed 1970/71 tour if the matter was not resolved satisfactorily. She shared that view with Trinidad prime minister Eric Williams, who asked Wes Hall to ensure Sobers knew what was at stake. Sobers recalled Hall urging him to 'get someone to write something that sounds like an apology'.[11]

Yet Sobers, as Manley pointed out, was 'not a man easily given to apology',[12] while Blofeld noted, 'He has a strong will coupled with a streak of obstinacy.'[13] Former team-mate Everton Weekes had recognised early on that Sobers 'had a mind of his own and never really felt comfortable conforming with what was accepted as the "right" thing to do'. He continued, 'One always felt he had the tendency to act suddenly without reflection.'[14]

Sobers wondered why no one at the WICBC or in government had advised him to refuse his invitation if it was such a poisoned one. And the Barbados Advocate suggested that he might have been helped more by the Board since the controversy erupted. On Short's rush to oppose calls for a Sobers apology, the paper said, 'In an emotional situation such as the one we are experiencing what is required is someone to "cool it", not to add fuel to the fire. It could make it tougher for Garry to back down.'

In his hurry to accept the Rhodesian money, Sobers had created a situation that now threatened his career, or at least might change the course of it. How he handled the situation represented what the *Advocate* called 'the most important cricketing decision of his career'. The publication wondered whether he might be forced to 'turn his back on West Indies cricket once and for all and be the strict professional', although in noting that England would be the best place for that it added that many West Indians in Britain were 'not hiding their militancy'.

Eventually, Sobers realised he had to say something for the sake of his sport and to salvage his reputation. On Sunday, 25 October, he delivered a letter to Noel Pierce, president of the WICBC, with copies to the prime ministers of Barbados, Guyana, Jamaica and Trinidad and Tobago, and the chairman of the council of the West Indies Associated States. It was then released to the public, who were able to read the following:

Dear Mr President,

When I accepted an invitation to take part in a two-day, double-wicket competition in Rhodesia I was assured that there was no segregation in sport in that country but I was not made aware of the deep feelings of the West Indies people.

I have since learnt of this feeling and the wider international issues involved.

I am naturally deeply distressed by and concerned over the tremendous controversy and bitterness which have arisen after my return from Salisbury.

As I was not aware of the serious repercussions I may have expressed myself in such a way as to create the impression of indifference to these issues.

Mr President, I wish to inform you in all sincerity that this is far from my true feelings as the prestige of West Indies cricket and the unity and dignity of the West Indian and African people are interests I have always served.

I therefore wish to convey to you and the members of the Board my sincere regrets for any embarrassment which my action may have caused and to assure you of my unqualified dedication whenever I may be called upon to represent the West Indies, my country and my people.

G St A Sobers

There is much to unpack there. The detached reference in the first paragraph to the 'deep feelings of the West Indies people' poses the question of how far Sobers had now grown apart from them after a decade in his bubble as a 'global cricketer'. Then there is the issue of whether a letter that spends most of its time being defensive and self-justifying and contains a single mention of 'regret' in its final paragraph actually constitutes the apology that had been demanded. Short certainly believed so, saying he hoped the letter would bring the controversy to an end.

The majority, who, despite their anger, would really rather not have been forced to burn down an icon and surrender the prestige he bestowed upon them, happily accepted the letter for what it purported to be. Burnham paid tribute to Sobers's 'West Indianism and his bigness' and said he was 'assured of an enthusiastic welcome to Guyana'. From Trinidad, Williams confirmed his approval.

According to Manley, 'A grateful Caribbean grabbed the apology with both hands. He was, after all, the first complete Caribbean folk hero, after George Headley. The thought that he might be lost as a consequence of a political gaffe was intolerable. For the great majority the incident was forgiven and promptly forgotten.'[15]

But not, ironically, in Barbados, where Barrow and his cabinet had agreed that Sobers did not need to issue an outright apology and had made a statement to that effect. In what was interpreted as a show of support, Sobers and wife Pru had been guests at a lunch given in honour of Charles, the Prince of Wales, the day before the letter was released. Deputy prime minister Tudor even told the High Commissioner, Sir Lionel Luckoo, that this was the government's way of responding to Burnham.

The prime minister, therefore, was blindsided by the final content of the letter. When the text was agreed between Sobers, representatives of the WICBC, and Algy Simmonds of the Ministry of Home Affairs later on the Saturday afternoon, and run past Barrow for his approval, the final paragraph – the only vaguely apologetic part of it – was absent. Barrow explained that he heard of the 'apology' via the BBC and said of the version he had seen, 'At no time did I take it to be [anything] other than a dignified and restrained statement of his position.'

A revealing letter sent by John Stewart, of the British High Commission, to Dennis Mitchell at the FCO's Caribbean Department, sheds light on the apparent turn of events. 'It looks as if Barrow has in fact been fooled,' Stewart said, explaining that the original wording had been agreed around 6 p.m. 'Sobers was then left alone and sometime after 6.30 apparently transmitted to the WICBC the text of his letter, which had suddenly acquired the last paragraph offering outright apology.' Notwithstanding the question of whether Sobers had truly apologised, Barrow was 'furious'.

Stewart continued with some interesting conjecture:

Somehow or other, Sobers was got at between 6 p.m. Saturday and 6.30. The most likely solution is that pressure had during the whole of the previous week been brought to bear on Sobers's Australian wife, (I have been told by several people close to Sobers that she was very distressed about the affair and that she was in fact considering persuading Sobers to leave the West Indies forever and take up permanent residence in Australia), that she succumbed to the pressure which had been put on her and in her turn persuaded Sobers on Saturday evening to throw in the towel and insert the apology which eventually appeared in his statement.

It now appears that Sobers by his action has averted the crisis in West Indian cricket affairs, but at the price of seriously offending Barrow, the Barbados government and several of the senior members of the Barbados Cricket Association. A miserable tale and we can only hope that we have now heard the last of this and that the Barbados government will eventually forgive and forget.[16]

Regardless of what one thinks about the depth of sincerity in Sobers's letter, the question remains of whether, given the global status he carried and the position he held in the hearts and minds of black people in the Caribbean, United Kingdom and beyond, he did himself a disservice by settling to be forgiven for lack of political awareness. The option of making himself a voice for change, rather than an uninterested non-participant, does not appear to be one his easy-going character allowed him to consider.

Allister Hughes, columnist in the *Virgin Island Daily News*, was among those who saw, not just a missed opportunity but a dereliction of duty:

He thinks about cricket and not about the political fact that a minority of white people hold millions of black Rhodesians in subjugation. Garry is the hero of every West Indian boy playing backyard cricket. Like nobody else, he is the symbol of unity in the Commonwealth Caribbean. As West Indies captain his image transcends national boundaries and he belongs no more to Barbados than to Guyana, St Vincent or Jamaica. And to occupy that position more is demanded of him than cricketing ability. Sobers is insensitive to this … He made his choice as an individual but failed in his responsibility to the position he holds as captain of the West Indies cricket team.

Writing in the *International Journal* in 1988, author Brian Stoddart reflected, 'At a time when the anti-apartheid movement in sport was gaining strength this was ill-considered, at best. But when it is recalled that West Indian cricket authorities had for some time taken a consistently strong line against racism in South Africa, his action seemed inconceivable.' The criticism of Sobers, he argued, was a result of him 'losing sight of the political symbolism inherent in the Caribbean game'.[17]

As early as the time of his appointment as captain in 1964, there had been voices reminding Sobers that he would now be held to higher standards. CLR James told readers of *The Cricketer* that the sport provided the 'national identity' for most West Indians and with that came a moral responsibility. 'They will look at Sobers's appointment as a stage in their national development. His captaincy has an immense potential for the future of the game. Only a potential. But it will be able to do its best for cricket if the West Indians of all classes make him aware that his future success and achievements can mean much more than the winning of a series. It can play a role in national consolidation at home, and national consideration abroad.'[18]

That 'potential' was in danger of going unfulfilled. Even after his misjudgement had been pointed out and he had issued his letter of explanation, there was never any suggestion that Sobers might have considered issuing a condemnation of the Rhodesian regime. Instead, when he looked back on the episode more than three decades later, with the benefit of historical hindsight, he still felt that the 'affair had escalated out of control' and dismissed some of the criticism by saying, 'It was getting silly.' Such comments suggest that he maintained the view he had done nothing wrong. And with no hint of self-consciousness, he reiterated that Ian Smith was 'a very pleasant man'.[19]

Sobers appeared to believe it was sufficient defence to point out, 'I am a sportsman and have always judged people as I have found them. To me, the colour of your skin, or what country you come from, doesn't matter. I have found that sport forms a common bond between all peoples.'[20] Which, of course, is as it should be, but doesn't suggest any great understanding that he had allowed himself to be seen supporting those who held a very different view.

*　*　*

At the time of the incident, the autumn of 1970, the three black sportsmen most recognisable in large parts of the world – certainly outside Europe and North America – were Sobers, Pelé and Muhammad Ali. During the 40th anniversary celebrations of Sobers's Test debut in 1994, Barbados prime minister Owen Arthur would even link the trio by saying, 'In an era which saw contemporary international icons unique in their fields like Muhammad Ali and Pelé, it is quite impossible to measure the sense of pride which we as a people felt in knowing that a Barbadian colossus who rose from the poverty of the Bay Land stood alongside them at the pinnacle of international achievement and acclaim.'[21]

In the life of one of those contemporaries can be found an interesting parallel with Sobers, in the other a stark contrast.

Pelé, from a poor Brazilian background not dissimilar to that of Sobers in Barbados, had exploded on to the global stage around the same time. A few months after Sobers announced himself to the world with his record innings of 365, a 17-year-old Pelé was the star of Brazil's World Cup triumph in Sweden, captivating the world with what appeared to be a God-given talent that elevated him above all others in his sport. Sounds familiar.

During the English summer of 1970, while Sobers was reconfirming that he was still the greatest of all cricketers, so Pelé was reclaiming his place on top of the football world. Having been injured early in Brazil's successful campaign of 1962 and kicked out of the 1966 tournament, along with his team, he was the vibrant centrepiece of Brazil's beautiful World Cup-winning squad in Mexico.

Yet he and Sobers had more in common than environment, achievement and chronology. Pelé, too, was scrutinised for his lack of political astuteness, notably after meeting President Emílio Garrastazi Médici, the unpopular dictator leader of Brazil. 'A lot of people looked less at what he did on the pitch and more at what he did off it,' explained Brazilian journalist Paolo César Vasconcellos. 'Off the pitch he was known for his political neutrality. At that moment in history that worked against him.'[22] He could have been taking about Sobers.

Many felt Pelé allowed himself to be manipulated by Médici, keen to divert attention from the government's repressive policies. Yet Pelé, like Sobers, saw himself as a humble sportsman and was disinclined to use his position and power to speak out against injustice and inequality. Team-mate Paulo Cézar Lima told a Netflix documentary crew in 2020, 'I love Pelé but that won't stop me criticising him. I thought his behaviour was that of a black man who says, "Yes, sir". A submissive black man who accepts everything and doesn't answer back, question or judge ... Just one statement from Pelé would have gone a long way in Brazil.'[23]

A *Washington Post* article after the retirement of baseball great Willie Mays stressed, 'Mays was a black athlete. He ran black. Swung black. And caught black.' CLR James would wonder, 'Does Sobers bat, bowl and field black?'[24] The answer was that Sobers never appeared to consider himself a black cricketer, in the way of Viv Richards, for example, with his wristband in Rastafarian red, gold and green. Sobers considered himself a sportsman who happened to be black.

Caribbean writer and academic Maurice St Pierre argued in 1973, 'West Indian cricket fans were saying to Sobers that they who conferred on him the status of hero could therefore remove that status. In addition, they were saying that the hero role carries with it certain obligations, in this case not to betray the cause of non-white peoples.'[25]

When Sobers excelled on the symbolic stages of white privilege, such as Lord's, the impression was that he was happy to provide entertainment for patrons. Richards, who said that 'race was central to me', appeared to be ramming colonialism down their throats. 'I believe very strongly in the black man asserting himself in the world,' he explained.[26]

The same could be said of Ali, who had shed his 'slave' name of Cassius Clay and given up his world heavyweight boxing title rather than compromise his beliefs by joining the US military to fight in Vietnam (although the extent to which Ali was acting solely on his own free will or being coerced by others remains a matter of debate). While Sobers was trying to talk himself out of his Rhodesian mess, Ali was preparing to return to the ring against Jerry Quarry after being banned for three years because of his political stance.

It had certainly been quite something when Ali visited Sobers and team-mates in the Lord's dressing room in 1966 a few days before facing Henry Cooper at Highbury as part of a European tour enforced upon him by the US authorities' refusal to allow him to fight at home. He tried out a couple of bats in the visitors' dressing room and, as well as being photographed with Sobers, was pictured sipping tea on the pavilion balcony.[*]

---

[*] This meeting often gets incorrectly referenced as having been during the second Test match. In fact, it was earlier in the summer, during the West Indies tourists' match against MCC prior to the Test series.

It was, of course, a summer in which Pelé was in the country, too, as Brazil defended the World Cup. Ali departed after beating Cooper but was back to attend the final at Wembley ahead of battering another British fighter, Brian London. Brazil's early exit from the tournament meant that the three great men narrowly missed being in the country at the same time. It's delicious to wonder about the conversation had they ever found themselves in the same room,* much in the way Kemp Powers imagined events of a real evening shared by Ali, civil rights leader Malcolm X, NFL star Jim Brown and singer Sam Cooke – after Ali had beaten Sonny Liston in 1964 – in the play, later a movie, *One Night In Miami*.

Ali might have pressed home the views of civil rights campaigners that there was no room for anyone – certainly not those Malcolm X considered 'bourgeois negroes' – to be sitting on the fence, reluctant to speak out. He had risked imprisonment and lost the prime years of his career to make his stand. Pelé might well have argued, with justification, that taking up a position against his country's dictators had rarely ended well. 'He couldn't just turn his back on the president,' said journalist Juca Kfouri. 'Muhammad Ali knew that he would be arrested for draft evasion, but he also knew that he faced no threat of being hurt, of being tortured. Pelé didn't have that guarantee.'[27]

Imprisonment, torture, exile, suspension; none of these circumstances would have confronted Sobers had he turned down Rhodesian money and explained publicly the very good

---

* Ignoring the fact that Pelé spoke little English during his playing career.

reasons for doing so. Nor was he being asked to oppose his own government in the manner of the others.

Even one of the more reasoned voices throughout the argument, the *Barbados Advocate*, said, 'We are not in a world of sportsmen on one side and politicians on the other. We are in a world of human problems. One of these is "race". We have to face it. Whatever a man's activity, whatever his means of livelihood, there are not always times when he can turn his head and pretend that he just cannot see.'

Yet apparent ignorance of the political landscape was one mitigating circumstance Sobers could reasonably offer for accepting his invitation. Another was the imperative to maximise his earning potential. It would be unfair on him to underestimate the significance of that. At 34 years of age, with a dodgy shoulder and knees, he had no guarantees about how much of his career remained and little idea of what lay beyond it. The global explosion of televised cricket, and the jobs for former players that came with it, was still some way in the future. And although he would dabble in coaching, it was not yet a recognised post-playing career path – certainly not for one whose mastery of the sport was more inherent than tutored.

The amount offered, £600, might not seem a lot at half a century's distance, but it was the equivalent of a month's wages for a top First Division footballer in England; not the kind of sum typically offered to a professional cricketer for one weekend. He had married the previous year and he and Pru were discussing the family that would take shape from 1971 with the birth of son Matthew, followed by Daniel, and the later adoption of daughter Genevieve, a baby who was born in Colombia.

He was not one to put money away for the rainy days that might arrive once he finished playing. Gambling had accounted for earnings that might have been more safely invested, while his late-night lifestyle did not fund itself. And Trevor Bailey observed, 'When Garry sees something that appeals, he will buy it without counting the cost.'[28]

Bailey recalled that Weekes, someone Sobers looked up to, had long been stressing 'the dangers of Garry's easy-come, easy-go attitude to money and tried to make him a little more careful'. Bailey remembered Weekes 'having difficulty in making Garry understand the importance of having something put aside for the time when age slowed down that seemingly endless flow of runs and wickets, pointing out that although it was easy for Garry then to increase his standard of living it would be painful having to reduce it later.'[29]

Interviewed by journalist and former player Peter Walker in 1971, Sobers admitted his financial future was 'not as secure as it might be'. He explained, 'Before I got married I led a pretty full social life and it is no secret I enjoy a flutter on the horses. Yes, I've made a lot of money out of the game – not a vast sum by comparison with some other professional sports – and I must say I have been disappointed by a great deal of the financial advice and so-called guidance I have been given … At the moment I live very well, though the future outside the game is just beginning to concern me.'[30]

His bounteous nature towards others was also to his fiscal detriment. 'Garry Sobers would get my last penny,' said Clive Lloyd. 'Money came and it went. He was very generous to a lot of people, especially to myself and the youngers guys who came into the leagues when he was still playing.'[31]

Naivety and financial need aside, Sobers can also be cut some slack on the basis of his positive impact on the prestige of people from Barbados and the wider Caribbean. Pelé said before his death in 2022, 'I was no Superman. I didn't work miracles or anything. I was just a normal person whom God granted the gift of being a football player. But I am absolutely certain I have done much more for Brazil with football in my own way than many politicians who are paid to have done so.'[32]

Likewise, Sobers could highlight the place in the world he gave his people when others associated them with his region of origin; and the uplift in spirits his prodigious feats created for so many over the course of two decades. But perhaps the question will always remain of whether he could have done even more.

21

FINAL FLOURISHES

'Rage, rage against the dying of the light.'

Welsh poet Dylan Thomas

MELBOURNE CRICKET Ground and the Lord's. Great theatres of the sport that had made Garry Sobers famous, if not rich. Both might have thought they had seen the last of the most prodigious all-round talent that cricket had produced in the 20th century. Yet Sobers was not quite ready to go quietly into the night. He had one last virtuoso performance in store for each of them.

As the Rhodesia rumpus calmed, Sobers began his 1970/71 season by leading another World team – comprising mostly West Indians and Englishmen – in a four-day match against Pakistan in Karachi, where the home team were comfortable 226-run winners. Then, with the West Indies at home to India, there was a rare opportunity to play three Shell Shield matches for Barbados, with limited success, before the five-Test matches.

The series was memorable for Sobers becoming the first West Indian captain to be beaten by India – and for the emergence of one of the generation's most prolific performers, 21-year-old Sunil Gavaskar. Injured for the first Test, the diminutive opener racked up 774 runs at an average of 154.80. He eclipsed even Sobers, who scored 597 at almost 75, remaining his team's most reliable contributor.

With India 75 for 5 in rain-hit Kingston, Sobers seemed to have made the right move by inserting the opposition, but Dilip Sardesai scored a brilliant 212 to lead India to 387. Sobers scored a fluent 44 in a West Indies reply of 217, but there were suggestions that he had forgotten that the loss of the first day meant that the follow-on threshold was reduced to 150. *Wisden* said of Rohan Kanhai and Sobers, 'Believing the threat had passed, Kanhai chanced his arm, and was promptly caught. Shortly afterwards, Sobers was taken at short-leg and West Indies got into such a panic that their remaining five wickets went for only 15 runs.'[1] Sobers was said to have been surprised when Ajit Wadekar asked him to bat again, but the same two batsmen shared a partnership of 173 to ensure a draw, Kanhai making an unbeaten 158 and Sobers 93. Gavaskar was an enraptured spectator. 'Garry went out with the intention of showing the Indian bowlers where they really belonged,' he recalled. 'He just smashed everything.'[2]

West Indies again stumbled in the first innings in Port-of-Spain, bowled out for 214. Sobers seemed anxious to score quickly before running out of partners and was bowled sweeping for 29 by Srinivas Venkataraghavan. 'He bowled tight, flat off-breaks, pitching them on middle and leg,' explained Charlie Davis. 'One caught Garry in no-man's land but, since the bounce was uneven, the ball pitched and jumped over the off stump. The Indians knew that once they got Garry, who batted at six, they were home and dry. So in the next over Venkat brought the mid-on fielder to gully to force Garry into doing something stupid. He bowled the exact same ball and seemed to catch Garry again playing half-and-half. But at the last minute Garry got back and hit it to the mid-on boundary. He then came up to me and said, "This man must be mad to bowl to me without a mid-on." But that was Garry: he could do anything. Eventually Venkat bowled him to have the last laugh.'[3]

Sardesai reached three figures again and Gavaskar laid down a marker by occupying the crease for 260 minutes in scoring 65. India's innings of 352 was most remarkable, though, for the performance of off-spinner Jack Noreiga, who had made his debut in the first Test after spending eight years out of first-class cricket. Once Grayson Shillingford had removed opener Ashok Mankad, Noreiga, approaching his 35th birthday, took the other nine wickets.

A collapse early on the fourth day led to West Indies being dismissed for 261, Sobers bowled without scoring by Salim Durani. 'After pitching some deliveries outside off,' the bowler remembered, 'I pitched one on this rough spot just outside the off stump. It hit the spot nicely, turned a little, beat his defence, went between bat and pad and took the off stump. He couldn't believe it and walked back muttering, "Oh Jesus." I couldn't control my happiness and was jumping in jubilation.'[4]

Gavaskar finished undefeated on 67 as India completed their first Test win in the Caribbean by seven wickets. 'As usually happens, there was talk of dissension in the West Indies team,' Wadekar recalled. 'There were wild rumours that Sobers and Carew were not on talking terms. One radio commentator wanted Sobers sacked.'[5]

Georgetown hosted the third Test and the home crowd were enjoying local hero, Clive Lloyd, advance to 60 when he and Sobers collided while taking a second run. A dazed Lloyd departed after being run out and his captain batted for another half-hour with an injured neck before edging to slip. West Indies made it to 363, after which Gavaskar's first Test hundred gave his team a lead of 13. Sobers and Charlie Davis both scored second-innings hundreds to secure a draw. *Wisden* said that Sobers, whose 108 came in only 105 minutes with 14 fours and two sixes, 'batted with masterly confidence and aggression'.[6]

Sobers marked Barbados's victory against the tourists by scoring 135, before punishing their bowlers again in the fourth Test in Bridgetown. He recorded his third successive century against the Indians after four and a quarter hours at the crease, and then added a further 78 in even time, including hitting Bishan Bedi for two fours and a six off consecutive balls.

Sobers declared at 501 for 5, his 178 having included 19 fours and a six. Gavaskar remembered, 'The strokes were all there, the delicate late cuts off the off-spinners, the flick through midwicket off the front foot, back foot and off the left-hand spinners. Sobers was virtually standing, without moving his feet, and crushing Abid Ali on either side of the wicket as if to say, "I don't need footwork against your pace." For a 21-year-old like me it was a great education.'[7]

Sardesai's 150 ensured India avoided following on and the tourists were eventually set 335 to win in five and a quarter hours. Gavaskar was immovable, looking comfortable throughout his unbeaten 117. Sobers dismissed Wadeker and Gundappa Viswanath – his 200th Test wicket – early in the afternoon, but Gavaskar found the support he needed and India saved the game comfortably.

The series concluded with a six-day rematch in Trinidad, where India had taken their lead. Gavaskar scored another hundred in a score of 360, which was eclipsed by West Indies as Davis (105) and Sobers (132) mastered the spinners. Yet Gavaskar had saved his best until his last innings of his debut series, batting for the best part of nine hours, mostly while suffering severe toothache, to pile up 220. Sobers and his bowlers never came up with a counter-plan to his relentlessness. Davis was even quoted as saying, 'There were ridiculous ideas about getting him out. One expert said bowl a full toss at his chest and when he hits it hard it will be caught at square leg.'[8]

West Indies needed 262 in 145 minutes for a series-levelling win. A long shot became mission impossible when Sobers, coming in at 50 for 3, was bowled first ball by a shooter from Abid Ali. The game was drawn at 165 for 8 and India were left to celebrate only their second series win away from home.

West Indies' fourth successive series defeat – against a team they were used to beating – put Sobers under the microscope once more. The fact that his team had thrown a party on the night they lost in Trinidad – and even invited the Indian team – was seen as evidence that things were not being taken seriously enough. Never mind that the event had been planned by Davis to mark his return to his home country. As Mihir Bose noted in his history of Indian cricket, 'The victory led to scenes with which the Indians were very familiar: recriminations, accusations by the press about low morale, drastic changes in the team, with whispers being heard against the captain.'[9]

* * *

While Sobers was giving Nottinghamshire his undivided attention in the English 1971 season, the debate in Australia over South Africa's scheduled tour in the upcoming summer echoed the arguments heard in England a couple of years earlier. There was even another visit by that nation's rugby team taking place to provide a platform for protestors. And when the 1971/72 cricket tour suffered its inevitable cancellation, the solution to the empty schedule of international cricket was another World XI led by Garry Sobers – although he had to be persuaded by Sir Donald Bradman to accept the job rather than play a few matches for South Australia.

This time there was the construction of a full tour schedule of 12 first-class matches, including five internationals – the designation of Test matches having been ruled out from the start.[*] Australian crowds were more responsive than those in England had been, even though the strength of the World XI was several notches down from the superstar team that

---

[*] *Wisden*, which had originally championed Test status for the England–Rest of the World series, did not even include match reports for the Australia–World XI series, merely printing a series summary and scorecards.

344

beat England. Of the new faces, Indians Gavaskar and Bedi were good additions, but New Zealand and Pakistan seamers Bob Cunis and Asif Masood were hardly likely to scare the Australian batsmen.* Nor would an English contingent of uncapped Tony Greig and marginal players Richard Hutton, Norman Gifford and wicketkeeper Bob Taylor. The cricket proved to be less memorable than in England and the whole endeavour might have been quickly forgotten but for an innings for the ages by Sobers.

A draw in Brisbane was notable for first-innings hundreds by Keith Stackpole and Australian skipper Ian Chappell, and World duo Hylton Ackerman, a South African, and Kanhai. Chappell reached three figures again in the second innings. Australia then won by an innings in Perth, where Dennis Lillee was rampant on his home ground, taking 8 for 29 – including a burst of five wickets in nine balls – as the World team were blitzed for 59.

Sobers, who delayed his entry until 46 for 5, remembered, 'Because they had put the tarpaulins on overnight [the wicket] had sweated. And the Perth wicket was so hard that the sweat remained on top of the wicket.' As the ball began flying, he was visited by team-mates advising him on which number they should bat. 'Gentlemen,' he replied, 'you can bat at whatever position you like, but you're not batting at mine, which is number seven.'[10] He eventually arrived at the crease with

---

* Perhaps Sobers's regard for those two can be gauged by him referring to them in his 2002 autobiography as 'Tunis and a fellow named Masoo from India who had never played Test cricket'.

'eyes flashing', according to Stackpole.[11] Seeing wicketkeeper Rodney Marsh 25 yards back, Sobers admitted that it was 'the only occasion in my career when I felt a little anxious about my physical wellbeing'.[12] When he edged to Marsh for nought, 'Sobey was off before the umpire could put up his finger,' said Stackpole. 'Not that he was frightened, but the greatest left-hander in the world wasn't that keen on sticking around.'[13] Sobers rated Lillee on that Perth pitch as the fastest bowler he faced in his career.

Another defeat, another inquest. 'I was getting a lot of stick as well for my own lack of form and we were being told that we didn't care; that we were on a joy ride,' Sobers recalled.[14] According to Gavaskar, 'That accusation was very unfair because Garry was really concerned about the team's performances.'[15]

Yet Stackpole believed that 'Sobers was the wrong man to lead the group, some of whom regarded the trip as a carefree holiday'. The Aussie batsman also heard stories that tour manager Bill Jacobs was having problems with Kanhai, who 'seemed bitter at having lived so long in the shadow of Sobers'. Jacobs even had to drag one player out of bed drunk ten minutes before a team bus was due to depart for a match.[16]

There was criticism from within the World camp itself. Taylor, an assuming presence on so many England tours before World Series Cricket gave him a chance to emerge from the shadow of Alan Knott, explained that 'we had no team spirit, no team room'. Indians and Pakistanis mixed easily while their countries engaged in conflict, yet Taylor argued, 'Early in the tour, the whites couldn't get through to the non-whites. We just never saw them other than at grounds. They took taxis together, socialised together and kept away from us. Even Garry Sobers ... took no part in socialising with the white members of his team.'[17]

For Sobers, such behaviour was not, as evidenced by previous tours, anything to do with colour. He simply chose to spend spare time away from the team and away from cricket. Australia's John Benaud, for example, remembered a round of golf at the Victoria Club in Melbourne, where Sobers landed a one-iron on the green of the par-four first hole, 'which was just unheard of. He had that tremendous natural talent.'[18]

What Taylor and others might not have realised was that he was going through a rocky patch in his marriage to Pru, who was threatening to take their young son, Matthew, and leave because of a letter Sobers had received 'from a girl I knew'.[19]

In the end, Taylor, Hutton and Gifford instigated a 'Saturday Night Club', at which attendance was compulsory. At the first meeting players had to dress in only a jock strap and one white sock. Sobers 'laughed himself silly at the scene', according to Taylor. The ice was broken. 'It turned out to be a happy, harmonious tour,' the wicketkeeper recalled years later, 'but to this day I don't know why it started off on the wrong foot.'[20]

In Tasmania, Sobers cracked 134 against the state team and reached 25,000 first-class runs in the course of a match against a Combined side. Yet it didn't translate into better form in the internationals. Rain had begun falling from a dark sky over the MCG on New Year's Day as, at 26 for 3, Sobers faced Lillee, who had proved he was not afraid to bowl short at the great man. He edged a nasty, rising first ball to Stackpole. According to Australian leg-spinner Kerry O'Keeffe, 'Everybody liked Garry and there was genuine sadness that his marriage was under strain, but perhaps we had benefited from his restless state of mind in his first-innings failure.'[21]

Yet Sobers seemed pretty focused when the teams met for their usual post-stumps beer. Different accounts have Sobers delivering his warning directly to Lillee or via skipper Chappell, but the gist of the message is always the same: 'I can bowl fast and I can bowl bouncers, too. But I can bat better than you.'

The World XI had been dismissed for 184 and an unbeaten 115 by Greg Chappell gave Australia a lead of 101. Sobers had made true on his promise by flinging down a fast bouncer at Lillee, who skied a catch to Bedi shortly afterwards. Lillee's bat arrived through the dressing-room door a few seconds before its owner appeared, uttering, 'That little bastard.'[22]

By the time Sobers came in at 146 for 3 on the third day Australia still held the upper hand, but O'Keeffe noticed that 'his mood seemed relaxed'.[23] It was time for Sobers to give one of the finest batting exhibitions of his career. Good enough for Sir Donald Bradman to say, 'I believe Garry Sobers's innings was probably the best ever seen in Australia. The people who saw Sobers have enjoyed one of the historic events of cricket. They were privileged to have such an experience.'

According to Greg Chappell, 'Sobey hadn't been very serious about the series,' and he was also upset that 'Dennis had the temerity to bowl short at him'.[24] Bristling with intent,

Sobers was soon racing towards three figures off only 129 balls, his first hundred at the MCG. 'Batting as nobody else can, Sobers instantly took command,' said Australian writer Ray Robinson. By the close of play, Sobers had reached 139 not out in just over three and a half hours, hitting 21 fours, and his team were on top at 344 for 7. 'It was an unforgettable display, combining such elegance of stroke play, power and aggression that the crowds responded ecstatically,' *Wisden*'s TL Goodman recorded. 'It was a throwback to the dominance of Sobers in other years.'[25]

He cut fiercely and drove elegantly. When slashing the ball square, his front knee jerked up towards his chest under the effort of the shot; when piercing the covers, his feet made only minimal movement in the process of execution. 'Having been canned for his lackadaisical attitude he certainly needed to redeem himself,' said Stackpole. 'At one stage I was fielding at gully and O'Keeffe was at third man. Sobers was slashing the ball past us so savagely that by the time I turned it had crashed into the fence. On what's probably the biggest ground in the world, that demonstrated his power.'[26]

Lillee explained, 'I had a man at square on the point boundary and he was hitting the ball behind and in front at will. I asked Ian Chappell for someone finer, just behind square, and he pierced that gap as well and continued to play in front of square until I asked Ian for another man in front of point – and he still hit it between those three fielders several times.'[27]

The second new ball produced another burst of boundaries. 'I attempted to bowl a big inswinging yorker,' Lillee recalled.

'He leant into it with great power. I went down in my follow-through to try to stop it; by the time I was down, I was looking back and the ball had bounced back off the fence. I have never witnessed a shot of such power and grace.'[28]

When the Australian players went into the opposition dressing room at the end of the day, Chappell found his former South Australian team-mate sitting alone in a corner. 'That was a surprise to me because Garry was normally in the thick of things, chatting about cricket or whatever.' Sobers beckoned Chappell to sit next to him.

'Mate, Pru's left me,' he said softly. Chappell responded with what he remembered as 'dark humour'.

'Garry, if that's what's pissing you off, give me her phone number and I'll ring her up and tell her to come home immediately.'

Sobers didn't laugh or smile. 'I thought, hmm, this is quite serious,' Chappell recalled.* 'But it didn't stop him taking it out on us when he went out to bat again.'[29]

According to Greig, Sobers had told him, 'If I have to do it all by myself I shall make sure we win this match.'[30] So when he resumed his innings after the rest day, he quietly played himself back in before targeting O'Keeffe, who ended up bowling 27 wicketless overs for 121 runs. Sobers greeted one over by launching the first two balls beyond long-off and long-on. 'A defensive push to extra cover would have been nice,' said the bowler. 'Did they deserve to go 110 metres into a baying crowd?'

---

* The couple remained together on this occasion.

Recalling the end of his spell, he added, 'I needed more than a rest, I needed counselling.'[31]

Ian Chappell remembered, '[Garry] hit a straight drive and Kerry sort of ducked and the thing just kept going and sort of went like a plane taking off and it went for six. That shot has always stayed with me.'[32] Stackpole reckoned Sobers's performance 'was so machine-like it finally became boring'. It sounds a little ungracious, but even he could not help gasping at that same shot off O'Keeffe. 'Sobers had no respect for his spin, playing him like a medium-pacer.'[33]

The shedding of his sleeveless sweater was the only hint of exertion and Sobers reached both the 200 and 250 landmarks with the silkiest of drives. When he finally chipped Greg Chappell lazily to mid-on, he had scored 254 in six hours and 16 minutes, facing 324 balls and hitting 35 fours and two sixes. 'I'll say no more,' went the TV commentary as the MCG rose to acclaim Sobers. 'Just listen to that crowd.'

Bradman's assessment for a video in which he broke down Sobers's performance in great detail was, 'It was an incredible innings, full of the most savage power, the most brilliant shots, the most brilliant placement. Some of his footwork was absolutely perfect.'[34] And Robinson stated, 'I believe Sobers's 254 shares the blue riband [with South African Graeme Pollock] for the best double-century against Australia since the war and perhaps within living memory.'[35]

But the artificial, subjective ranking of the innings means less than the place it occupies in the folklore of the game and the memories of those present. Bradman was not wrong when he said it 'will live in the minds of all who saw it as long as life shall last'.

Cricket writer and broadcaster Jarrod Kimber tells the story of his father, Peter, then 25, who was working as a barman at the MCG while studying. Of all the cricket he attended, Sobers's innings was the only thing he talked about. 'He has no real memory of who was on either side,' Kimber wrote. 'Part of this is down to age. Partly it is to do with the way Sobers has taken over that game in the memory of anyone who was there.'

Kimber senior left his post when Sobers went out to bat and his description of the innings was, 'Forwards, backwards, front foot, back foot, he had every shot in the book. He was just a genius; over the top, along the ground, he just did it.' His son added, 'In my dad's story, Sobers isn't Sobers, but Batman with Superman's powers.

'My dad is not a big talker. I know nothing about the moment he met my mother or how he proposed ... Yet this Sobers story has been told to me a hundred times. He always tells it the same way, like he won a prize that day ... I know everything I need to know about that innings simply by looking at his face and listening to his voice.'[36]

The magnificent contribution by Sobers took the World XI to a total of 514. They completed a 96-run win by dismissing Australia for 317 after Doug Walters had counter-attacked to score 127, including a century before lunch.

Australia could have regained the lead in the series had play been possible on the final day of the fourth match in Sydney, a match in which Bob Massie, destined to capture 16 wickets on his Test debut later in the year at Lord's, took 7 for 76 and Greg Chappell amassed 197 in the second innings.

The series concluded with a nine-wicket World XI victory in Adelaide, giving them an overall 2-1 win. As in the equivalent series in England, Graeme Pollock finally discovered his touch in the last match, his 136 being the highlight of the contest. Greig took six wickets in the first innings and Ian Chappell's unbeaten century was the only resistance in the second.

Greig believed that Sobers's role in steering the World XI from one-down to win the series was under-appreciated. 'Perhaps the most remarkable thing of all was that Sobers managed to keep his team together,' he said. 'As captain, he had strong and numerous critics. I can only speak from the experience of one tour, but I would have chosen no one else to lead such a side.' Referring to the ongoing war between Pakistan and India, Greig added, 'Somehow the spirit of the team never faltered and Sobers must take a large part of the credit for that.'

He concluded, 'He could at times be deeply casual, almost lazy in his attitudes, but there was never any doubt who was in control. He was in constant demand for public appearances, autographs, match tickets and a hundred other chores but he managed it all capably.'[37]

* * *

Sobers was quickly into another five-match series, his last as West Indies captain, as New Zealand embarked on their first Caribbean tour. Every match was drawn, which, according to Henry Blofeld's summary in *Wisden,* 'was little short of a disaster for the West Indies'. He added, 'Sobers's captaincy was not as sharp or as far-sighted as it might have been; there was an epidemic of dropped catches; and at the moment there are no genuine fast bowlers in the Caribbean.'[38] It was the sadly familiar story of West Indies' last years under Sobers.

The series was dominated by the bat, even though 300 runs in a day was never achieved. Neither side possessed the depth of bowling needed to force victory. The home side at least managed to discover two new batting talents. Jamaican Lawrence Rowe delighted his home crowd by scoring 214 and an unbeaten 100 in the first Test, the first player to achieve that feat on debut. In the fourth Test in Georgetown, Guyanese left-hander Alvin Kallicharran also scored a debut century on his home ground. In both matches, New Zealand's response was led by opener Glenn Turner, who scored an unbeaten 223 in Kingston and 259 at Bourda, where he shared an opening partnership of 387 with Terry Jarvis (182). 'Seldom has a more boring, pointless cricket match been played in the West Indies,' said Tony Cozier of that game.[39]

Wisden criticised the way Sobers handled Turner in the first Test, especially when he was joined by the lower order. 'Sobers made no attempt to keep Turner away from the strike and so he was able to shield his partner with impunity.'[40] In the second Test in Trinidad, New Zealand recovered from 99 for 6 in the first innings thanks to poor West Indies catching and the home team's chance to push for a win was wasted.

It was West Indies who were in trouble in Barbados, 52 for 6 after Sobers won the toss and was surprised at how much the ball seamed on the green pitch. They were 289 behind on first innings with more than two days remaining. Sobers's entry was delayed until five wickets were down for 171 on the fourth afternoon, walking out with 'his head erect as if sniffing the scent of battle', according to DJ Cameron in his chronicle of the tour.[41] Sobers settled in to accompany Davis to a century partnership by the close of play and he was seen, unusually for him, practising before the next day's play began in front of a packed crowd.

Dropped on 87, Sobers reached his first century against New Zealand after 248 minutes as he and Davis batted their team to safety. Davis was eventually run out for a ten-hour 183 and Sobers launched into an assault on Cunis late in his innings to reach 142. It was his 25th and penultimate Test hundred, his first and his only notable effort of the series.

After the bore of Bourda, Sobers decided not to enforce the follow-on in the final Test, back in Port-of-Spain, after Kallicharran scored another century and left-arm spinner Inshan Ali helped shoot out the tourists cheaply with five wickets. Sobers was left regretting his decision when rain wiped out most of the final day's play.

It seemed suitably appropriate that Sobers's time as captain should end with a calculated gamble that went wrong. 'He had shown a capacity to lead a strong side effectively but he had not shown the capacity to lift a weak or ageing side beyond performances which came naturally,' was Michael Manley's sign-off to the reign of Sobers in his West Indies history.[42]

The series had been mostly dull but signified a triumph for an injury-hit New Zealand team with little pedigree in Test cricket. Sobers was less than effusive in discussing their achievement in its immediate aftermath. 'They set out to do a job and they did it adequately,' he said, suggesting that their batsmen needed to play more expansively. 'Until they start doing this I don't think New Zealand cricket will improve in the way it should.'[43]

Ironically, Sobers made that remark in a foreword to the tour book written by Cameron, whose suggestion on how West Indies could improve included an apparent dig at Sobers. 'What they need is the drive and spirit with which the New Zealanders foiled them in the Test series,' he said. 'These things will only come when the West Indies are properly selected, and properly led.'[44]

Meanwhile, Tony Cozier observed accurately, 'Sobers, labouring under the handicap of an unsettled team, had clearly become disinterested in the captaincy and, indeed, the game as a whole.'[45]

To make things worse, the condition of his 36-year-old left knee was becoming critical. He might have been delighted to find, upon returning to Nottinghamshire in 1972, that Trent Bridge was among the cricket grounds to have installed betting facilities, but his season was not even halfway through when it came to a premature end. With bone rubbing against bone in his joint, the only solution was surgery.

Knowing that he could not guarantee being fit enough for the Australian tour of the West Indies early the following year, he wrote to the WICBC. He told them it would not be fair to accept the Board paying for his flight back to the Caribbean, as they usually did, when he could not be sure he could play. 'In the circumstances, I resign as captain,' he added, a low-key manner in which to end one of cricket's most important and deeply scrutinised appointments.[46]

When asked for his opinion, he named David Holford, the Barbados skipper, as his preferred successor, followed by Clive Lloyd, who had recovered from a serious back injury suffered when playing for the World XI in Australia, and Rohan Kanhai. Sobers was realistic enough to know that recommendation of his cousin was unlikely to be accepted, even though he genuinely believed he was the best captain in the Caribbean. Kanhai, for so long seen as Sobers's great rival, got the job.

By the time the first Test had been drawn the following February, Sobers was keen to be considered for selection. He felt his recent experience of facing the Australian attack would be an asset – although the much-feared Lillee had just suffered a back injury that would threaten his career. He hoped an appearance in the Shell Shield against Trinidad would prove his fitness, bowling eight wicketless overs in each innings and being dismissed twice in the 20s. It was enough to convince himself he could survive a five-day Test.

Before the second Test, Australia were due to play Barbados. Jeff Stollmeyer, former West Indies captain and now a selector, asked Sobers if he intended to play. Sobers suggested it would be better to give a younger player the experience, to which Stollmeyer replied that if he didn't play in the warm-up game he would not be considered for the Test.

'If that's the way it is, that's the way it is,' Sobers responded angrily. 'You can say whatever the hell you like, do what you like, because I won't be playing.'

His mood darkened even more when Clyde Walcott, chairman of selectors, suggested he play in a two-day game with the West Indies squad in St Vincent to prove his health. Sobers told him that 'he and Stollmeyer could go and jump in the Caribbean'.[47] He was no longer the man who would be asked to play when injured because the selectors insisted he was better on one leg than anyone else on two. Now nobody would believe him when he said he was fit. He felt hurt, insulted and betrayed.

The importance of Sobers's place in Caribbean life was evidenced by the public debate that surrounded his subsequent exclusion from a series that West Indies ended up losing 2-0. 'Some of us went for a walk in Bridgetown, where the locals sat under trees playing dominoes,' Greg Chappell recalled. 'They were constantly arguing about Sobers. One guy said, "His eyes are gone." Another guy retorted, "You think God has trouble with his eyes?"'[48]

Even politicians were getting involved. Trinidad's prime minister, Eric Williams, said in a speech that the former captain had been treated as though 'we were discarding at the roadside an old car that had been smashed up in a road accident'. A group of 64 sports people petitioned Williams to have the matter discussed at the region's Head of Government Conference in Guyana. 'It was a fraught time for me and the selectors,' Walcott remembered.[49]

Sobers's only significant cricket in the remainder of the Caribbean season came in two one-day games staged at Kensington Oval as part of his benefit season, sponsored by Banks Breweries. Sobers recalled that the fund amounted to 'a most welcome' BD$85,000.[50]

* * *

Criticism of the West Indies selectors after the latest defeat and the fact that the team was now returning to England, where Sobers boasted a long record of achievement, meant that he was not a forgotten man. In fact, it now appeared that the WICBC was prepared to go out of its way to accommodate him.

Conscious that the clock was ticking on his career and feeling guilty about how little time he'd been able to devote to Nottinghamshire, Sobers was reluctant to commit to the full West Indies tour that would occupy the second half of the English season. Instead, he told WICBC chairman Cecil Marley that if he was needed for the three Test matches he would make himself available.

Marley gratefully accepted the offer, so Sobers was surprised when, early in the tour, he received a call from manager Esmond Kentish asking him if he wanted to play in the Tests. 'What kind of question is that?' he replied. 'I already told the selectors I am available.'[51] He admitted that there was nothing in his current form to make him an automatic selection. He had not scored a fifty for Nottinghamshire until the final few days of June and had added only two more by the time of the first Test at The Oval in late July. He was surprised to be picked.

And yet *Wisden* editor Norman Preston would end up writing of the subsequent 2-0 victory against England, 'There can be no two opinions that the presence of Garfield Sobers was the main cause for West Indies regaining their former glory.'[52]

Lloyd's brilliant century in the first innings set the stage for West Indies to achieve a 158-run lead after Essex all-rounder Keith Boyce, in his first Test in England, took five wickets. Sobers, his new-ball partner, bowled quickly and accurately, weighing in with three wickets and conceding only 27 in 22 overs. Sobers then made 51 in a second-innings total of 255, the same score for which England were bowled out second time around. Lancashire's Frank Hayes reached a century on his debut, but Boyce took the honours with six more wickets and the West Indian fans who had turned out in huge numbers were able to celebrate their team's first Test victory for four years.

The second Test at Edgbaston was an altogether different occasion, killed by the tourists' approach and beset by unpleasantness. West Indies batted as though avoiding defeat was the sole ambition, scoring only 198 on the first day. But it was after they had been dismissed for 325, Roy Fredericks contributing 150, that things turned nasty. Geoffrey Boycott was given not out by Arthur Fagg after Boyce appealed for a catch to the wicketkeeper and for two hours Kanhai and some of his colleagues made no effort to hide their anger.

Sobers, who placed great value on sportsmanship, was unimpressed, saying that Kanhai 'went too far in showing his displeasure'. He added, 'It shouldn't have happened. He was captain and it was his responsibility to see that decisions were accepted in the right spirit.'[53]

Fagg demanded an apology and threatened to withdraw from the match. In fact, Alan Oakman took his place for the first over of the third day while he concluded talks with Kentish and England's chairman of selectors, Alec Bedser. In the end a statement from Kentish that his team were 'fully satisfied with Mr Fagg's umpiring' was enough to ensure that he resumed duties in time to preside over a stream of bouncers by Boyce and Bernard Julien. The game progressed to its inevitable draw, with Sobers, whose discovery of form had continued with an unbeaten hundred against Derbyshire, making a second-innings 74.

Sobers arrived at Lord's for the third Test in the knowledge that this would be, barring a knockout final appearance for his county, his last big game at cricket's headquarters. For most players, it would have been good reason to ensure full nights of sleep in order to be as sharp as possible. But Sobers was unlike most cricketers. When he ended the first day 31 not out after Kanhai's brilliant unbeaten 156 led West Indies to 335 for 4, he decided not to go to bed at all.

Instead, he met former West Indies and Jamaica off-spinner Reg Scarlett and set off for central London in search of food, drink and merriment. It was 5 a.m. when they returned to the hotel, too wired to sleep. After giving up the fight, Scarlett drove Sobers to Lord's.

'I wasn't seeing the ball too clearly,' Sobers would admit, telling himself to 'just play straight' as Bob Willis pounded in at him.[54] *Wisden* recorded that 'there was a quiet period at the start when Sobers played within himself', without being aware of the circumstances.[55]

Even in defence, though, his batting was worthy of the praise of EW Swanton. 'He needed no luck in the way of chances and, for one who has had such vast success for so long, his application was extraordinary,' he wrote in *The Daily Telegraph*. 'He treated Willis and [Geoff] Arnold with the respect they deserved and when doing so his long flowing defensive back-strokes were as much a joy to the connoisseur as all the splendid, flamboyant stuff that followed.'

By the time he had advanced beyond his half-century, the indulgences of the previous night were catching up with him. His stomach was churning, causing enough pain to have him considering retiring ill. Fearful that he might not be able to recapture momentum if he interrupted his work, and driven by a desire to show the selectors what they had been missing in the Caribbean a few months earlier, he stepped up the pace of his innings.

Twice he drove Ray Illingworth for four, taking his team's total past 400, and when he hit Willis for four with a front-foot flourish, BBC commentator Jim Laker gasped, 'You'd really have to see a lot of cricket to see a better shot than that.' He pushed Arnold for a single to reach his century. But shortly after a bludgeoning hook off Arnold brought him another four, he admitted to umpire Charlie Elliott, 'I am not feeling well. Can I go off?' When asked for a reason, Sobers replied, 'I can't say,' and beat a hasty path to the dressing-room toilets. Kanhai, who still referred to Sobers by his former title, knew his colleague well enough to call for an instant remedy. 'Bring the captain a brandy and a port to settle his stomach,' he told the 12th man, repeating the order when the first dose was downed.[56]

At 604 for 7, Kanhai asked Sobers to rejoin Julien, who had reached his first Test century. 'A laugh greeted Sobers's reappearance,' Swanton recorded in the *Telegraph*. 'My word, they are putting us through it, was the thought.' Returning at 132, Sobers whipped Willis off his legs for two more fours. When he pushed a two into the outfield to reach 150, Kanhai declared at 652 for 8. Sobers had faced 227 balls and hit 19 fours. Preston would comment, 'I have seen Sobers tear an attack apart in many of his wonderful batting displays, but for a well-controlled and disciplined exhibition of brilliant strokes coupled with sound defence that 150 at Lord's portrayed the true master.'[57]

And *The Cricketer Quarterly* stated, 'Of the three West Indian centuries, that which probably gave the most pleasure was the 150 not out by Sobers – this great cricketer, because of physical handicap supposed to be beyond his best, showing that even on one leg he remains among the greats.'[58]

England lost crucial wickets late on both the second and third days as they were bowled out for 233 and 193 to lose by an innings and 226 runs – a defeat that ultimately cost captain Illingworth his job. Sobers equalled what was then a Test record for a non-wicketkeeper by taking six catches in the match. Saturday's play went down in history when the match was halted by a telephoned bomb threat that led to most of the 26,500 crowd being evacuated – although, famously, some took refuge on the field while umpire Dickie Bird sat on guard on the covers. The call ended up being a hoax, but no one was taking any chances at the end of a week that had seen a spate of IRA letter bombs in London.

Sobers played his last West Indies game in England when he made what would be his only one-day international appearance in the Prudential Trophy at Headingley. He was caught behind sixth ball without scoring and, having taken one wicket, had the winning runs struck off him by Bob Willis in the final over. Sobers sat out the other match in the series – won by West Indies by nine wickets at The Oval – but was on hand to be presented with a cheque for hitting the most boundaries in the Test series, 41. Accepting his prize, he enjoyed a little dig at the selectors when he said, 'As a Test discard with no legs, I have to hit boundaries.'

22

SIR GARFIELD DEPARTS

'He was a true, a perfect gentle-knight.'

The Canterbury Tales: The Knight's Tale
(Geoffrey Chaucer, 1387)

HAD WEST Indies been playing anywhere but in the Caribbean during 1973/74, the international career of Garry Sobers might well have been over. What better way to bow out than with an unbeaten 150 at Lord's? But with a home series against England coming up, Sobers made himself available. He wanted a grand farewell, in particular one more Test in front of the Jamaican crowds that meant so much to him and, of course, on his home ground in Barbados.

Selected for the first Test in Trinidad, he took five wickets across two innings of a seven-wicket West Indian win. But his bigger contribution might have been in saving Tony Greig from the mob after he ran out Alvin Kallicharran as he headed to the pavilion at the close of the second day. 'Greigy nearly got us lynched,' England bowler Geoff Arnold recalled. 'The crowd went mad and I thought we were not going to get out of Trinidad alive. It was a legitimate wicket because I don't think the umpire had called "over", but probably only Greigy would have run him out like that.'[1]

A large group of fans remained behind after play with the intent of confronting Greig. It was only when Sobers offered to drive him back to the England team hotel that it was safe for him to emerge from the dressing room, knowing that the company of his revered opponent would guarantee safe passage. Kallicharran was eventually reinstated – a decision Sobers disagreed with – but the tone of another tetchy series had been established.

Dennis Amiss said that England's matches against the West Indies at that time 'were not pleasant affairs' and featured 'an undercurrent of bad feeling'.[2] England spinner Pat Pocock remembered, 'There was a horrendous atmosphere, the worst I have ever known between two cricket teams. It only stopped when Garry Sobers walked in. Then, no one said a word. It would have been like swearing at the Pope. He was held in awe by every cricketer.'[3]

England, bowled out for 131 in the first innings, looked as though they might be safe when 328 for 1 in the second. But then Mike Denness was run out and Amiss, on 174, was removed by Sobers, whose efforts prompted a charming description from Christopher Martin-Jenkins. 'This afternoon the emperor of all-round cricketers felt like a bowl,' he wrote. 'It was a bit hot for his quicker stuff, so, since bowling of any kind to Sobers is second nature, he decided to try a little spell of orthodox left-arm spin. Walking one pace into his delivery stride, he achieved all that was necessary with absurd ease: perfect length, excellent direction, a trajectory difficult to attack, and considerable turn off the pitch.[4] Sobers added two more wickets in his next 14 deliveries.

It was with the ball that Sobers had greater success in his last Test series. A final tally of 14 wickets at 30.07 was hardly the stuff of his legend, but there were plenty of occasions when he looked the most threatening component of the attack. He managed only 100 runs at an average of 20 and it was in the second Test in Jamaica, where he took three first-innings wickets, that he played his one significant innings, 57 in a mammoth West Indies total. Amiss saved the game for England with an epic 262 not out in the second innings.

Sobers's final Test on his home ground could hardly have been less auspicious. He took one wicket with his medium pace in an England innings dominated by 148 by Greig, whom he dropped at second slip. Then, with Lawrence Rowe marching towards 302, Sobers was caught third ball off Bob Willis for a duck. It was a spectacular effort by Greig, who took six wickets to add to his century, confirming that he had assumed Sobers's mantle as the world's premier all-rounder. After West Indies declared just short of 600, Keith Fletcher produced a match-saving effort with an unbeaten 129.

The possibility of Sobers having ended his Test career with a duck loomed when he announced that he needed a rest and would not play in the fourth Test in Guyana, although in the meantime he had the energy to play in a golf tournament in Barbados. 'Those who knew him well thought that the real reason for his absence was that he was simply not interested in playing,' said Martin-Jenkins.[5]

The selectors were not going to deny him what most people assumed would be his last Test match, naming him for the finale back in Trinidad after a rain-hit draw in Georgetown meant that England were still hanging on in the series. He took one wicket early in England's total of 267, but troubled Boycott, on his way to 99, when he took the second new ball. 'Sobers showed what a superb artist he is,' Martin-Jenkins recorded. 'Sobers was at once causing Boycott difficulties with late inswing and the occasional ball flying away across the batsman towards the slips.'[6]

When Sobers appeared at the top of the pavilion steps to bat in West Indies' first innings a great roar erupted around Queen's Park Oval. The England players joined in the applause and it was a beaming Sobers who arrived at the crease, where Jack Birkenshaw helped him hitch up his shirt sleeve. He pushed forward to his third ball, bowled by Greig in his experimental off-spin style, and edged to gully, where Birkenshaw took the catch. Two consecutive three-ball ducks. Surely that was not how his great Test career was to end?

Greig's eight wickets restricted the West Indies lead to 38, after which Boycott scored 112 in England's 263. Sobers yorked Arnold with his arm ball and took his 235th and final Test wicket with a full toss that struck Knott's pad. West Indies needed 226 to win, but had reached only 84 for 4 when Sobers came out to bat. Greig, on his way to another five wickets, immediately caught Clive Lloyd brilliantly off his own bowling.

'Sobers began to play some of those easy, graceful, classical stokes which had established him as one of modern cricket's most elegant stylists,' said Martin-Jenkins.[7] The crowd buzzed excitedly at the promise of one final match-winning knock from their hero as he and Deryck Murray added 50 for the sixth wicket. But then Derek Underwood gave the ball a little more flight and Sobers missed his attempted drive. He threw his head back as the ball struck the off stump. Bowled for 20. 'I was disappointed to throw away my wicket,' he admitted. 'I was feeling good.'[8] West Indies were all out for 199 and Sobers's Test career had ended as it began, with a home defeat to England.

Sobers, now almost 38, returned to Nottinghamshire with an announcement that it would be his final year with the county. He did not specifically refer to it as a retirement from first-class cricket – as reported by many journalists – because he was still considering playing for Barbados, even if he took some time off to play golf in the meantime. He ended the season against Lancashire at Old Trafford, where he scored an unbeaten 132 in the first innings and was denied signing off with two hundreds when he was out for 77 to the occasional left-arm spin of David Lloyd.

'He must have been caught in Stretford,' laughed Lloyd when reminded that he was the last man to dismiss Sobers in first-class cricket. In fact he was bowled. 'There was never any bat-throwing with Garry. I imagine he just went back to the pavilion and carried on reading *The Sporting Life*.'[9]

Sobers was done with first-class cricket. There were no more games for Barbados. 'The travelling and the hassle had taken their toll,' he admitted. 'It was time to go. Golf, with its different, more private, pressures, had taken over.'[10]

He would return to England in 1975, however, to reappear in the Central Lancashire League. He had hoped to turn out again for Radcliffe, but as they already had commitments to a professional he signed with Littleborough, a club based in Rochdale. When fitness allowed, Sobers was still able to record three-figure scores and five-wicket hauls, surpassing 1,000 runs and taking 68 wickets. He recalled Littleborough as 'a lovely club' and was grateful to their former professional, Barbadian Duncan Carter, for continuing to play as an amateur and 'still doing the bulk of the work'.[11]

And why wouldn't people want to help him out? After all, by this time he was Sir Garfield.

* * *

The first step in the process of making Sobers a knight of the realm was an October 1974 meeting of the sports committee of the Civil Service Department in Whitehall, at which it was decided to float with the Foreign and Commonwealth Office the idea of recognition in the Queen's Honours List in the summer of 1975. 'The committee would wish, I feel sure, to recommend him for CBE, or even knighthood,' recorded Stuart Milner-Barry.[12]

The initial response from WE Hall, of the FCO's Honours Section, expressed potential concerns. Posing the question of whether the honour would be more appropriately bestowed by his own country from their usual allocation,* he pointed out

---

* Sobers had previously held dual Barbadian and UK citizenship, his UK passport having been issued in 1964 but invalidated two years later when Barbados became an independent state.

that Frank Worrell, knighted 'as a West Indian' in 1964, was 'a more popular and successful captain of the West Indian XI than Sobers'. He continued, 'Feeling in Barbados about Sobers has been ambivalent. He is generally regarded as "The Greatest" (as a player) but has not been popular with the middle-class (cricket) oligarchy; some would say he has not shown much interest in his own country since becoming famous; others might add that he has not been very successful as captain of the West Indies. Errol Barrow, PM of Barbados, is a cricket devotee but not perhaps a Sobers fan.'

Presumably, Hall was referring to the manner in which Sobers had put Barrow's nose out of joint with his post-Rhodesia 'apology'. Hall concluded by suggesting that as Colin Cowdrey had only ever been appointed a CBE any knighthood would be better coming from Barbados, which appointed three knights every five years.[13]

After seeking the opinion of the British High Commissioner in Barbados, fears about how an honour would be received locally proved unfounded. According to CS 'Stuart' Roberts, Barrow 'warmly welcomed the suggestion that [Sobers's] name should go forward in our own prime minister's list. Nothing, he assured me, would give the people of Barbados greater pleasure.' Barrow also suggested that including Sobers in the upcoming New Year's Honours offered the opportunity for the Queen to conduct the ceremony during her visit to the island in February.

Roberts concluded, 'Cricket has the standing of a religion here in Barbados and Garry is its high priest.'[14]

After initial resistance to the idea of expediting Sobers's award, the FCO wrote to Buckingham Palace asking informal approval from the Queen for a Knight Bachelorhood to be bestowed out of the Diplomatic and Overseas Service List, the Prime Minister's List having been fully spoken for.[15] A flurry of telegrams confirmed Her Majesty's approval, Sobers's acceptance and confirmation of a February investiture. The only dissenting note was from the Governor General of Barbados, Sir Arleigh Winston Scott. According to Roberts, he was 'a bit huffed' to have heard the news only when the public announcement was made on New Year's Day.[16]

The Garrison Savannah racecourse, a short walk from the streets where Sobers had been raised, was selected for the ceremony. On 19 February, more than 10,000 were estimated to have seen Sobers mount a platform for the Queen to place her sword on his shoulder. 'Who would have thought that a poor boy from a wooden house in Walcott's Avenue would end up like this?' he said.[17] Sobers was particularly pleased that the investiture should take place, not at Buckingham Palace, but at a location that had such meaning to him. Given that whenever he had met the Queen at previous events conversation had revolved round horse racing, the setting was doubly appropriate.

According to former England bowler Pat Pocock, it was a memorable occasion for Her Majesty. Introduced to her during the 1976 Lord's Test against West Indies, Pocock ventured, 'Have you ever watched a match in the West Indies, ma'am?'

'No, I suppose the closest I ever came to it was when I knighted Sobers,' was the reply, causing Pocock to recall, 'For a couple of irreverent seconds, I almost suspected the Queen of name-dropping.'[18]

The knighthood opened the door for another honour. Only those who watched British television in the 1960s, '70s and '80s can fully appreciate the magnitude of presenter Eamonn Andrews ambushing celebrities with a red book and the words, 'This is your life.' Based on a 1952 American series, *This Is Your Life* was regularly drawing more than 20 million viewers on ITV. To be its subject was considered one of the great honours, as tributes were paid and unexpected guests were flown in from all corners.

The show's producers had targeted Sobers for years, but his busy schedule made it unachievable. But when they heard that the Barbados High Commission in London was planning an event to mark his knighthood on 29 April, they pounced. First, they had to get an agreement to hijack the event; then they needed to ensure Sobers attended. High Commissioner Cameron Tudor took care of both, informing Sobers that Princess Margaret would be present, making the invite by royal command.

Having then acquired the approval of Sobers's wife, the producers discovered through the office of Bagenal Harvey that Trevor Bailey was visiting him in Barbados to discuss his forthcoming biography. While Bailey kept Sobers busy in reminiscence, members of the production team interviewed Pru and Sobers's mother, Thelma, to get the details of his life. Thelma even agreed to board an aeroplane for the first time and fly to London for the show. 'She felt that this was going to be the biggest night of her son's life,' recalled producer Jack Crawshaw.[19]

Not everything went to plan. On the day of the recording, Sobers arrived at the High Commission too early and a quick-thinking Tudor told him to leave because it would be against protocol to arrive before the princess. 'Nearly six years of waiting and we had lost him,' Crawshaw feared.[20]

Sobers sat for 20 minutes in the Hilton Hotel on Park Lane before walking to the reception. When he arrived it was television royalty in the shape of Andrews that greeted him. 'It amazed me that I could live with Pru and not know what was going on,' he said.[21]

His biggest surprise was when his mother walked into the Euston Road Studios once recording began later that evening. Brothers, sisters, sons, team-mates, opponents and friends, including early influences Everton Barrow, Wilfred Farmer and Garnett Ashby, helped make it a memorable occasion. The programme was broadcast a week later and also aired in Barbados.

Sobers looked set to be on screens around the globe a few more times when the inaugural cricket World Cup was staged in England in June. In April, he had been named in West Indies' 14-man squad, despite his retirement from Test cricket, his lack of experience in ODIs and the fact that he was now only playing league cricket. But with the eight teams assembling in England for the two-week festival of 60-over contests, Sobers withdrew after straining a groin muscle playing for Littleborough. 'It might have healed in the intervening two weeks,' he explained. 'I did not believe it was worth taking the risk."*

West Indies, now under the captaincy of Clive Lloyd, named veteran Rohan Kanhai as his replacement. He ended up playing a vital supporting innings to Lloyd's match-winning century against Australia in a memorable Lord's final, suggesting that Sobers might well have had a significant role in the tournament rather than just making up the numbers. He would finally make the tournament eight years later, in the most unlikely of roles.

---

* Interestingly, Sobers announced that he was missing out on one final hurrah on the same day that Pelé, in many ways his footballing counterpart, was explaining that he was coming out of retirement to play for New York Cosmos in the North American Soccer League in a reported £2 million, three-year deal.

23

BEYOND THE BOUNDARY

'The secret of genius is to carry the spirit of the child into old age, which means never losing your enthusiasm.'

Author Aldous Huxley

THE 1983 World Cup created a tidal wave of change. A shock defeat of twice-winners West Indies in the final meant that India, a nation that already loved cricket, developed a passion for the one-day format that transformed the sport's economics for all time.

But cricket was already in the throes of an evolution that had begun when Australian media magnate Kerry Packer announced in 1977 that he had signed the world's greatest players to take part in his own 'Supertests' – an act of retaliation against the Australian Cricket Board's refusal to consider a bid to secure television rights for his Channel 9 network. Players who could not understand why they saw so little of the vast sums being generated by packed crowds for Australian Test matches – and those who played for national boards who had no means of competing with Packer's salaries – eagerly signed up for three years of 'pirate' cricket, as John Arlott was the first to call it.

Packer had no doubt that his cricket would be both compelling and brilliantly televised. History would prove him right on both counts. But what it needed up front was gravitas. An Australian team taking on West Indians and a World XI while wearing yellow caps on makeshift grounds had to compete for credibility against the baggy greens facing India and England in official Tests in traditional arenas. Richie Benaud's presence as cricket consultant and the face of the broadcasts was, therefore, an undoubted coup.

Tony Greig, who had forfeited the England captaincy to lead Packer's World team and recruit talent, persuaded his new boss that Garry Sobers, his hero, had the global popularity and stature to be the ideal statesman for World Series Cricket. Packer went as far as deciding that his Australia and West Indies teams would compete for the Sir Garfield Sobers Trophy and offered the man himself a place on the top table when he and the team captains met the media ahead of the first match. Sobers conducted the toss for the first Supertest, in front of near-empty banks of seats at the Melbourne football stadium, VFL Park.

Sobers could see how Packer was improving the lot of professional cricketers, especially those from his own region, and would have had no hesitation in signing for WSC had he been a few years younger. He also bonded with him on the golf course, where Packer, who played off a handicap of eight, asked Sobers to help improve his swing.

He remained close enough to the Packer organisation after WSC's first season to be invited by Greig, in September 1978, to co-captain a World all-star team, including Greg Chappell, Mushtaq Mohammad, Majid Khan, Bishan Bedi and John Snow, against an American equivalent at New York's Shea Stadium. In front of 8,000 spectators – mostly expat West Indians – Sobers's team lost by seven wickets. Australian David Hookes had been excited at the chance to bat with Sobers. 'From the non-striker's end I watched him block two balls, then I got out first ball at the other end,' he remembered. 'So that was my great partnership with Sobers.'[1]

Living in the Melbourne suburb of Mount Waverley, Sobers would play half a dozen games with limited success, for North Melbourne in the Victoria Cricket Association season of 1979/80, the summer that marked the beginning of the post-Packer truce in world cricket. Driven by floodlit cricket, the securing of iconic arenas such as the Sydney Cricket Ground and an aggressive campaign to win the hearts of the cricket public, Packer had made enough progress in his second season to persuade the ACB to give him the broadcast rights he desired, at which point he handed his players back to the establishment.

Despite having been part of Packer's coterie, Sobers would not gain a place on the roster of former professionals in the commentary box for Channel 9's coverage of an expanded schedule of international cricket. He had decided after some radio work that broadcasting did not interest him. He had never been a great watcher of cricket once it became his profession, and the joy of spending a couple of hours at a match was in meeting friends rather than scrutinising events on the field. A full day at the cricket – even if he was being paid – was a waste of time that could be spent on the golf course.

Instead, he made an unlikely and incongruous entry into the world of coaching. Daryl Raggat, president of East Malvern Cricket Club in the Melbourne suburb, had bumped into Sobers at the Olympic Park greyhound track. The pair got on so well that, after a subsequent lunch, Sobers accepted Raggat's invitation to coach his team, even though it didn't even play in the highest grade of Victorian club cricket.

Beginning in 1981/82, Sobers spent two summers at East Malvern, earning a 'very modest' fee, according to Raggat. Additionally, his contract specifically stipulated that he would not be given any concessions at the bar. 'We were a bit dubious,' remembered former player John Russell, 'and we thought, "Will he actually turn up to training?" But he did the first night.' The influx of good players eager to learn from a legend meant that the club's first three elevens all won their league championships in Sobers's first season. Russell remembered their coach as 'a funny, humble, courteous, loving sort of guy, just a brilliant bloke', adding, 'Cricket-wise, he was good, helped us a lot. We were scrubbers, ordinary blokes trying to play cricket, and he was never ever critical or a smart Alec, nothing like that.'[2]

Sobers's coaching career now moved in a surprising direction: from the Victoria Junior Cricket Association to that game-changing World Cup.

Part of the eight-team line-up since the inaugural tournament in 1975, Sri Lanka had achieved Test-playing status in 1982 under the leadership of Gamini Dissanayake. A

MAESTRO

lawyer from a wealthy family, Dissanayake had been a member of parliament since 1971 and was passionate about cricket, serving as chairman of the Sri Lanka Cricket Board. Having seen his country celebrate its new place in world cricket by hosting – and losing to – England in its first Test, Dissanayake was determined that Sri Lanka should be able to hold their own. Of their first seven Test matches, they had lost five and managed two draws. Who better, he reasoned, to help them compete with the best in the world than a man who had himself been the best in the world? It mattered little to him that Sobers had no experience of top-level coaching. Besides, the role was still a developing one in international cricket so there was not the pool of viable, battle-tested candidates that would exist in later years.

Dissanayake knew Sobers would not offer his services cheaply, but with access to the chequebook of Raja Mahendran, the wealthy businessman who served as vice-president of the SLCB, he was able to come up with a tempting offer. Early in 1983, it was confirmed that Sobers would coach Sri Lanka in the four one-day internationals and one Test match that formed the basis of Australia's tour. He would then travel to England as coach, under manager Tambyah Murugaser, for the World Cup. His fee, it was reported, was $140,000 for three months – a huge cricketing salary for the time and, at the equivalent of around $425,000 in the 2020s, comparable to an Indian Premier League head coach for a similar period of time.

'I came here to watch an under-25 festival last year and saw some amazing talent,' Sobers said after accepting the job. 'Kids who learned their cricket on the beaches and in the streets, the same as in the West Indies.'

Peter McFarline of the *Melbourne Age* was in Colombo when Sobers arrived to begin work and noted, 'To the western mind, it is hard to imagine that even the reappearance of Buddha would have had more impact here than the presence of Sir Garfield Sobers.' He described Sobers going into the bar of a leading hotel, where 'the entire staff became rigid with nervous admiration'.

Sobers was no great technical theorist and therefore did little coaching in the practical sense. He was not one to work with batsmen on keeping a high elbow or drill the bowlers on their mechanics, although he did his share of net bowling. Rather, his contribution was more in the role of adviser, sharer of experience and sprinkler of gold dust by his mere presence. 'He just inspired you because of who he was,' batsman Sidath Wettimuny told author Nicholas Brookes. 'You wanted to try and do well to make sure he thought you were a decent player.'[3]

According to Wettimuny, 'With Sir Garry around, we felt like we were behind a king,'[4] while Duleep Mendis, skipper at the time, recalled, 'He gave invaluable tips by talking about the tactical side of the game, analysing our game, teaching us how to bat in different conditions, how to exert pressure on the batsmen and different stages. He taught the bowlers how to dictate terms to the batsmen and how to set the appropriate field.'[5]

Sobers reckoned that 'a very good coaching structure' existed in Sri Lanka and told reporters a few weeks into his job, 'When I saw the quality of their players I couldn't understand what I was doing there. Their technique was so good it looked as though they had already enjoyed the best coaching.' He recalled later that his job was 'to brainwash people that they can face fast bowlers without much trouble. Well, I knew they had the technique, perhaps they lacked self-belief.'[6]

Sri Lanka's performance in one-day cricket had been a source of optimism, ever since they acquitted themselves with honour in defeat against Australia in the first World Cup. In 1979 they beat India and, thanks to rain against West Indies, lost only one match – to New Zealand.

In their pre-World Cup series against Australia, which followed an innings defeat in the Test, Sri Lanka won the only two matches to be completed, both low-scoring run chases. Having restricted Australia to 207 for 5 in the second game, Sri Lanka lost their top four batsmen with 100 still required. 'No panic – this game can still be won,' Sobers told Ranjan Madugalle as he went out to join Arjuna Ranatunga. The duo turned the match with a partnership of 69 in seven overs.

Ranatunga had been the first young Sri Lankan to catch the eye of Sobers when he'd visited ahead of their inaugural Test match a year earlier. 'I was immediately entranced,' he explained. 'What a beautiful little player he was – still a teenager but so accomplished. When you see a youngster of that age playing with that technique, not afraid of anybody and not afraid to hit the ball, it is a great thrill, whatever nationality he may be.'[7]

Sobers saw much of his young self in Ranatunga and, remembering the support of the West Indies selectors as he made his early tentative steps in international cricket, was shocked to discover that the 18-year-old all-rounder had been dropped after some low scores. Attending a selection meeting as an observer, Sobers could not contain himself when Ranatunga's name was dismissed for the matches against Australia. Interrupting the discussion, Sobers announced, 'He must play.' Reminded that he had no say in selection, Sobers retorted, 'If this cricketer isn't in the side, I will be speaking to the president about it.' Ranatunga was duly selected. 'I pulled rank and it worked,' Sobers admitted.[8]

Having gone on to captain his country for 11 years, including winning the 1996 World Cup, Ranatunga never tired of citing the influence of Sobers. 'What I am today is mainly because of Sir Garry,' he said. 'The first thing he told us when he came to Sri Lanka was that our techniques were good and that there was nothing much left for him to do. He asked us to be positive always. He helped to develop my bowling a lot. He brought a two-coloured ball. I hadn't seen anything of that nature before and the first person to teach me to swing the ball was Sir Garry.

'Working with Sir Garry was a treat. Everyone in cricket respected him and looked up to him. When he was with us, he wasn't a West Indian, but a Sri Lankan. He loved his rice and curry. Once, he told me that he likes to speak some Sinhalese and if he's able to do that, he would be the best Sri Lankan ambassador. He could adapt his nature. He could be a coach one moment and after some time he was your best friend.'[9]

Mendis said after the ODI series against Australia, 'We didn't realise how many mistakes we were making until Sobers came along. His coaching was so useful to us.' And having gained from the experience of working with him at home, the Sri Lankans were now to discover to joys of touring with him as they travelled around England. Denied the opportunity to be part of the first World Cup, Sobers was determined to enjoy the tournament, which saw the number of group games doubled to six.

'That was a memorable tour, he was something else,' said Wettimuny. 'He was fabulous on and off the cricket field. He had the most amazing number of stories about cricket and whenever we travelled from one county to another he would just entertain us.' Wicketkeeper-batsman Ranjit Fernando added, 'He never changed his ways: he liked to have a cigarette, he would have his drink with the boys.'[10]

The players sensed that Sobers conferred increased status upon them. 'Sri Lanka didn't have an identity,' explained opening bowler Ashantha De Mel, among the leading wicket-takers in the tournament. 'Where we went, we got a lot of respect from everyone because of his name; he was like a brand ambassador.'[11]

They also discovered that Sobers, famously modest in his manner, could brandish his name on their behalf when necessary. In Leeds, the squad were stuck in their hotel lobby because of a delay in the delivery of room keys. The reception-desk telephone rang. 'Call for Mr Sobers!' bellowed across the lobby, where Sobers sat motionless. As the pause continued, team manager Murugaser approached. 'Sir Garry. I think there's a call for you.'

The boy from the Bay Land, Garry Sobers, aged 18 – already a Test match player

The crowd at Sabina Park in Kingston, Jamaica, rush to celebrate with Sobers as he beats Len Hutton's Test-record score of 364

Sobers and Tom Dewdney at the inquest into the death of West Indies team-mate Collie Smith, who was killed in a car crash while Sobers was at the wheel

Having begun his Test career as a slow bowler, Sobers became one of the world's greatest batsmen, yet his ability to deliver in three different styles ensured that his bowling remained an important part of his game

Sobers at the head of his West Indies touring team at Worcester in 1966. Back row: Basil Butcher, Jackie Hendricks, Joey Carew, Rawle Brancker, Peter Lashley, Seymour Nurse, Joe Solomon. Front row: Rohan Kanhai, Wes Hall, Garry Sobers, Conrad Hunte, Lance Gibbs

A meeting of the greats. Sobers is visited in the Lord's dressing room by world heavyweight boxing champion Muhammad Ali during West Indies' 1966 tour match against MCC

Sobers, who was at the peak of performance throughout the 1966 series against England, pulls to leg on his way to a century at Lord's

Sobers tosses the coin for England captain Colin Cowdrey before the infamous Trinidad Test in 1968. He blamed Cowdrey's negative tactics for forcing him into a declaration that cost him the match and brought his captaincy into question

Rohan Kanhai walks out to bat with Sobers during the fifth Test against England in Bridgetown in 1968. There were constant rumours of a rivalry between the two during their Test careers

As wicketkeeper Arnold Long waits in vain for an edge, Sobers hits out against Surrey during his first season in county cricket for Nottinghamshire, a campaign memorable for his six sixes against Glamorgan

Sobers marries Australian-born Pru Kirby at a ceremony in Nottingham in September 1969

Sobers takes a typically sharp catch off Lance Gibbs to dismiss Australia's Ian Chappell at Adelaide, but the unhappy 1968-69 tour brought his captaincy under close scrutiny

Sobers and Ray Illingworth at the toss before the 1970 England-Rest of the World contest at a sparsely populated Lord's. It took the public time to get behind the series

Sobers on the attack for Rest of the World at Lord's, leaving England wicketkeeper Alan Knott to watch admiringly. Sobers re-established himself at the top of his sport during a triumphant summer

Sobers with South Africa's Eddie Barlow before the double-wicket competition in Rhodesia that plunged him into the middle of a political storm

Arise, Sir Garfield. Queen Elizabeth II knights Sobers in February 1975 at Garrison Savannah racecourse, only a short walk from where he grew up

Sobers congratulates Brian Lara on his Test-best 375 against England in Antigua in 1994. There was no one else he would rather have seen break his world record

Golf gradually overtook cricket as the love of Sobers's sporting life and he ended up wishing he'd discovered it earlier

Allen Stanford greets Sobers at Lord's at the launch of his controversial $20 million Twenty20 match. Sobers was among the many leading figures and organisations in cricket who were taken in by the Texan fraudster

Sir Garfield Sobers rings the time bell at Lord's during a visit to England in 2016

Sobers remained seated. Again, a voice was raised. 'Call for Mr Sobers.' The female receptionist was able to identify her man by the looks being directed at him. 'Are you Mr Sobers? There's a call for you.'

He rose from his chair and approached the desk. 'I am not Mr Sobers. I am Sir Garry Sobers. I didn't ask for it. Your Queen gave it to me. So you better call me Sir Garry Sobers.'

The silence in the lobby was broken only by the sound of room keys being hastily distributed.

Sobers was able to offer more than an expedited check-in. His experience of local conditions was especially helpful. 'We were struggling at Headingley during practices,' said Ranatunga. 'The ball was seaming around. Ashantha was bowling fast and none of us could face him. We were all getting beaten. Sir Garry was looking from behind the stumps and asked for my right glove and the front pad. He took the middle stump and faced Asantha with that stump. He didn't miss a single ball. We were all in total admiration of him.'[12]

According to Wettimuny, 'His knowledge of wickets was phenomenal. We went to play one of these initial games on a rain-affected wicket. It was not even against a county – it was against a combined league team or something. He walked up to Duleep and he said, "What do you want to do?" So we said we want to field first because it looked so damp. He said, "If I were you I would bat on this." We were amazed. He said, "Look, if you bat second on this wicket it is going to get much tougher because the dents will have hardened and the ball will start jumping around. In the morning it may be soft but you won't have physical danger." So we followed his advice and, true to his word, Ashantha hit a couple of guys.'[13]

Yet Sobers could not work miracles with a team who were no match for the others in Group A, losing both games against England and Pakistan. 'We never lacked confidence,' said Wettimuny. 'Maybe sometimes we were impetuous or didn't quite have that pro attitude.' They salvaged some pride by winning one of their matches against New Zealand at Derby.

Wettimuny's conclusion that 'we were relaxed, enjoying ourselves, we had a great time' perhaps hints at the truth that Sobers's nature was never suited to the disciplined, detailed and technical requirements that would characterise the role of the modern coach. As a captain at least he could grab the ball or hit a few fours to influence matters. His individual mentoring; his ability to impart his own experiences; his tales of the past on long bus trips; none were enough to rescue a developing group of players when the required run-rate was mounting or bowlers were being dispatched into the stands.

Speculation followed later in the year that Sobers would continue his coaching career in Australia, assisting former Test batsmen Ian Redpath and Keith Stackpole in guiding Victoria. Sobers killed that story by stating a desire to spend the 1983/84 season with the Sri Lankan team. 'I've had no contact with the VCA [Victoria Cricket Association] whatsoever,' he said. 'Even if Redpath or the VCA approached me now, I wouldn't be very interested.' Sobers had told the VCA he was available for a coaching role before they decided to advertise and subsequently appoint Redpath, and he felt disinclined to be seen to be touting for a role with an organisation that had overlooked him. As it turned out, his days with Sri Lanka were over, too, and a role outside of his sport beckoned.

* * *

Cricket had not made Sobers anywhere near rich enough to be free of financial concerns, especially given the free-and-easy manner in which he liked to live and the lack of solid fiscal guidance he had received. 'I had made more money out of the game than anybody else at that time, but my future was far from secure,' he admitted.[14]

At least the sport had given him a name that could generate income. Typical of the various gigs he accepted was an ambassadorial role with CARICOM (Caribbean Community), the organisation working to unite the various regions economically and politically.

One job that didn't materialise was as manager of the West Indian team travelling to South Africa to play a series of 'rebel' Test matches. When news broke in the first days of 1984 that Sylvester Clarke, Wayne Daniel, Collis King, Lawrence Rowe and other fringe or former Test players had signed up, the Caribbean News Agency named Sobers as manager. From Australia, wife Pru said she was 'surprised and shocked' at the report and issued a statement on her husband's behalf that he was not participating. He would have sympathy with those who chose to go, even though many of them were eventually ostracised by the Caribbean cricket community. 'They found themselves in the same position that I had been in in 1970 – putting cricket first and politics second,' he claimed.[15]

It was a job opportunity arising later that year that proved to be the final factor in the break-up of his marriage. Since 1980, Sobers had been working for several months each year for the Barbados Tourist Board (now known as Visit Barbados), based on his home island and focusing on supporting the ministry of tourism and sport. When he was asked to make it a year-round commitment, Pru made it clear that he was on his own.

According to his own accounts, there were a number of elements in the break-up of a relationship that had survived the rocky days of 1971/72. His gambling habits had never sat well with Pru, and he had been a regular in the casinos of Sri Lanka in the absence of close friends and anything else to do with his spare time. He'd not spent so much time in such establishments since playing blackjack until the early hours in Manchester while engaged in league cricket. 'If something went wrong I would just say to hell with it and back I went,' he said of his attempts to cut down on gambling. 'At the time, I had nothing to replace it.'[16]

The Sobers family home had been in Australia since 1978, but when the opportunity arose to return to Barbados permanently he was keen to move. With her own career as a writer taking off at a time when she was becoming increasingly frustrated with her husband's lifestyle, Pru chose not to go with him. The couple became officially separated and the formalities of the divorce were completed in 1990. 'There was no malice or envy and the children hardly noticed we had broken up with me having been away travelling so much anyway,' Sobers would insist years later.[17]

So Sobers was back in Barbados, where his children would all end up being based for at least part of their adult lives. Older son Matthew completed his schooling and achieved a degree in accounting on the island, while Daniel moved there after completing a degree in graphic arts in Australia. Genevieve, too, having initially remained in Australia with Pru, also later found her way there.

Having witnessed former West Indies team-mate Ron Headley, son of a West Indies cricket legend, becoming fed up with constantly being introduced as 'George's son', Sobers made no effort to persuade his children to take cricket seriously and was relieved when they showed no inclination to follow his career path. As a now-committed golfer, he would eventually take pride in seeing Matthew qualify to play in the Caribbean inter-island tournament, the Hoerman Cup, in 2001. Sobers, who got his handicap down to four, had been a good enough player to feature in the competition several times.

Sobers was still in demand on the cricket field, playing for a World team in 1984 against a combined India and Pakistan side at Bombay's Wankhede Stadium as part of a benefit for ex-India wicketkeeper Farokh Engineer. Former England captain Tony Lewis remembered that Sobers 'could only walk with difficulty because of arthritic knees', but continued, 'He had not forgotten how to bat. What struck me first was his absolute concentration, as if it was second nature. He laughed and joked between balls but never once toyed with the great game itself. He had too much respect for it. In one stroke he produced a thunderclap of a reminder of how superb he was. He flicked a ball from [Ravi] Shastri, with the spin, off middle and leg through midwicket for four. His bat scarcely made a sound. It was all eye and timing.' Lewis said there was 'a ghostly perfection' to the shot. Sobers took his innings into the 40s and was cheered from the field. 'I did not miss one drop of the old Sobers mix of ferocity and grace,' said the man who'd been the opposition captain on the day of the six sixes.[18]

His last prolonged experience as a cricketer came in 1991 when he accepted the invitation of Wes Hall to play as a 'ringer' for a team of parliamentarians touring England. 'They just expected me to carry them when things went wrong,' Sobers complained. 'Not even playing against England at Lord's did I have the same pressure to perform.' The unsatisfactory experience further cemented golf as the sport now closest to his heart.[19]

As a sports consultant for Barbados, Sobers's responsibility was to help organise sponsorship and use sport to attract tourists, a role in which his name and patronage was the biggest asset. At the suggestion of travel agent friend Don Golding, the Sir Garfield Sobers International Schoolboys Tournament was established, initially recruiting teams from England. Featuring a final at Kensington Oval, the competition developed quickly to attract sides from around the world and would feature future West Indies Test players, including Brian Lara, and many county cricketers.

After a five-year hiatus, the tournament returned to the calendar in 2024, reflecting the continuing influence of Sobers on his island's landscape. Competitions in sports ranging from golf to table tennis have carried his name; while the Sir Garfield Sobers Sports Complex opened in Wildley in 1992 and, along with a 5,000-seat arena that stages major sport and music events, hosts the island's big football matches and all manner of recreational activities.

His name on the walls of sports venues never paid the bills, though, and he was grateful when, in 1994, a group of friends and supporters executed a year-long 40th anniversary of his Test debut. The idea, first promoted by Barbados Tourist Board director Tony Arthur and discussed with government officials, was a series of celebrations that included lectures, dinners and other fundraisers. Publications raised additional money, with the contents of the lectures collated in book form in *An Area of Conquest: Popular Democracy and West Indies Cricket Supremacy.*

Under the chairmanship of former team-mate Rawle Brancker, the organising committee arranged what amounted to a county cricketer's benefit year. Events even spread to Toronto, where Clive Lloyd chaired a night of celebration attended by close to 1,000 people. With Sobers's track record for spending money as quickly as he earned it, a group of trustees – chaired by a friend, Philip Greaves, and including WICB* president Peter Short and Barbados attorney general David Simmons – ensured that the proceeds went into a trust fund to provide a pension. 'I shall not forget the generosity of the Bajan people,' said Sobers,

---

* The words 'of Control' would be dropped from the organisation's title in 1996.

who reckoned that BD$300,000 (worth around £100,000 at the time) had been raised.[20]

Recognition outside the sporting arena also came his way. In 1992, he was celebrated by the University of West Indies in Barbados with an Honorary Doctorate in Laws. Sir Henry Fraser, professor emeritus, declared in his citation, 'Sir Garry has done more to bring Barbados to the attention of the world's thinking population than any other born Bajan.' A similar honour came his way in 1998 from the University of Nottingham.

In the same year, the government of Barbados introduced the Order of National Heroes Act, with Sobers one of the original ten people to be honoured, earning him the title The Right Excellent. Only one more National Hero has been created since, pop singer Rihanna in 2021. At the time of writing she and Sobers are the only living recipients of the award.

Also in 1998 was the bestowal of The Order of the Caribbean Community, an award given to 'Caribbean nationals whose legacy in the economic, political, social and cultural metamorphoses of Caribbean society is phenomenal.' Lloyd, Viv Richards and Lara have also received the Order.

Discussion of a Sobers statue on the island began seriously in 1977 when Maurice Foster, a former Barbados Cricket Association opponent, suggested the bottom of Broad Street, the main road leading into Bridgetown, as a suitable site. Despite receiving encouraging initial feedback, Foster was eventually told by the Barbados government that it would not change its policy of not erecting statues of those still alive. It was not until

2002 that a bronze likeness of himself clubbing the ball down the ground appeared on the Sir Garfield Sobers Roundabout in Wildley. Created by Barbados artists and sculptors Karl Broodhagen and son Virgil, the statue was unveiled by prime minister Owen Arthur and Sobers himself, the inscription on the plinth citing his 'invaluable contribution to cricket and sport in general in Barbados, the region and the world'. Ahead of the 2007 World Cup, the statue was relocated outside Kensington Oval.

In 2003, Sobers was among the first inductees in the Hall of Fame for West Indies Cricket, while the ICC decided in 2004 that the Sir Garfield Sobers Trophy was the appropriate honour to be given to its Men's Cricketer of the Year. The name had been chosen on the recommendation of Richie Benaud, Sunil Gavaskar and Michael Holding, who were instructed to select 'an individual with whom to honour cricket's ultimate individual award'.

Even a man as modest as Sobers could not help being touched by such acts of recognition. 'People say that I have been a role model, an icon even, for the way I have behaved,' he said. 'I have always been happy to carry the flag for my country and for my sport. I am sure that people like me are awarded honours such as these to show how the general public feel about you.'[21]

24

HIS MASTER'S VOICE

'I knew I was going to have a life as long outside cricket as I had within it. If you keep trying to live the game after you've left, it is not good for your health. You've got to move on, enjoy it while you are there. It was consuming but some people get so wrapped up and involved in it, it's all they've known. I didn't sleep, eat, drink it.'[1]

Sir Garfield Sobers

GOVERNMENTAL AND sporting recognition, cultural citations, physical tributes, fundraising events. Yet for decades one thing was missing from the post-playing life of Garry Sobers: an official role on behalf of West Indian cricket.

Rawle Brancker was correct in saying in 1994, 'It is only fitting that all Barbadians should be involved in the 40th anniversary celebration of Sir Garfield Sobers's Test debut. Sir Garfield is, after all, easily the most famous and most popular of all Barbadians.'[2] Yet he might also have asked whether the wider region, notably the WICB, should have taken on responsibility for such an occasion. Or offered Sobers the kind of position that made a benefit unnecessary.

No meaningful role as statesman, selector, coach, manager or adviser came his way until he was 30 years removed from the field, by which time it felt like a token, an afterthought. Certainly there was nothing approaching the status offered to Clive Lloyd, who, admittedly, enjoyed far greater success as captain than Sobers when he presided over one of the greatest West Indies sides. Lloyd ended up as team manager, WICB director and chairman of selectors at various times, and in 2024 was commissioned, along with former team-mate Deryck Murray, to lead a study entitled 'The Way Forward for West Indies Cricket'.

'It remains one of the most inexplicable acts of neglect and omission committed by the West Indies Cricket Board that Sobers's obviously invaluable input has never before been officially utilised,' wrote renowned Caribbean journalist Vaneisa Baksh.[3] Tony Cozier, in 1984, had called it 'a matter of regret that Sobers, a true West Indian hero, has been lost to West Indies cricket and that he has been passing his knowledge and experience to Australians and Sri Lankans in recent times.'[4]

As is frequently the case in examining the life of Sobers, what he thought about the situation can be difficult to gauge, given the different views he expressed over the years. In 2002 he said he had never fulfilled a formal role for the WICB because 'they haven't asked me'. In 1984, he recalled, he had received an informal approach to coach the West Indies team but felt he had been away from the country too long to know the players and suggested they waited a couple of years. 'I'm still waiting.'[5]

Yet in his 1996 book, *The Changing Face of Cricket*, he'd not only said that he received other approaches from the WICB but had effectively accepted that any meaningful role was outside his scope. 'I have never had any particular desire to manage a West Indies party on tour and consequently have turned down several invitations to do so,' he said. Most self-damningly, he admitted, 'I do not have the aptitude to be an administrator, or the patience to be a selector, umpire or team manager.'[6] And, as confirmed by comments such as that at the top of this chapter, he was no longer consumed by the sport anyway.

So whether or not he was genuinely expecting, or desirous of, a role in the region's cricket is unclear. Perhaps he felt, not unreasonably, that his achievements merited some sort of formal offer, even if he didn't wish to accept. Being asked was perhaps what mattered most. He was certainly too proud to go campaigning on his own behalf.

It is not hard to find reasons why some in the WICB hierarchy might have felt Sobers was unsuitable. For a start, his retirement from cricket came while memories of the furore over his involvement with Rhodesia were still fresh. And, for all his years as captain, there had been various run-ins with the Board; over money and, in the latter part of his career, selection. When former chairman of selectors Clyde Walcott went on to become WICB chairman such rifts appeared even wider. Not forgetting, either, that his lifestyle, even when captain, had made few concessions to expectations of propriety.

Attention to administrative detail was not his thing, while his dabbling in coaching had not exactly marked him down as a natural. And as that profession continued to develop, he had no desire to achieve the kind of paper qualifications that he felt were becoming too important. 'Many of the people who hold the certificates are well educated rather than having a true cricket background,' was his view. 'They can read a manual, listen to a clinic and pass exams.'[7]

Ian Chappell enjoys telling the story of Sydney club Mosman looking for a coach and their president telling Sobers they would love to employ him 'but you haven't got the qualifications'. Sobers offered a terse reply. 'What do you think I got my knighthood for?'[8]

He might have been merely an observer of West Indies cricket, but it never ceased to matter dearly to him. 'I have never made a run for me,' he would say tearfully at a press conference in London late in 2015 during another promotional visit on behalf of Barbados. 'It was such a pleasure and joy to be able to do that. I have always played for the West Indies team. You know, records meant nothing; the team was important. I don't think we have that kind of person in West Indies cricket any more. And that hurts.'

The WICB might not have wanted his experience or knowledge, but Sobers was frequently in demand when media outlets needed an opinion about the decline of Caribbean cricket, which accelerated from the mid-1990s onwards. His view that the WICB was backward-looking, too unwilling to give young players a chance, and that 'there are some officials who don't know what they are doing' would have won him few friends within influential circles.[9]

It was a mystery to many why the esteem in which Sobers was held in Caribbean cricket could not have been put to greater use in some kind of mentoring, advisory role with the younger generation of players. According to former Test team-mate Cammie Smith, serving as vice-president of the Barbados Cricket Association, 'Many of us who have had the privilege to hear him speak to cricketers who have played after his time marvel at the ease with which he can impart his knowledge of the game,' adding that he was 'especially outstanding when demonstrating to the youth'.[10]

Instead, for many years any close and meaningful connection to a new generation of West Indian cricketers was limited to his relationship with one particular player, a young left-hander from Santa Cruz, in Trinidad and Tobago. He first saw Brian Lara during one of the school tournaments in Barbados, since when the 15-year-old had considered Sobers a 'father figure'. When observers remarked that the youngster was too small, Sobers was in their ears, insisting, 'Just give him a little bit of time.' When Lara returned to the tournament for a second season Sobers was encouraged to see how much he had grown. 'Right away I thought, "There is going to be a great player."'[11]

Enough of a bond had been formed that Lara would phone Sobers to ask, 'You been watching me?' and would request that he found time to give him tuition. Lara, who Sobers came to consider his protégé, promised his teacher that he would break his records. As his career developed – a Test debut in 1990 and a first Test century in 1993 when he scored 277 in Sydney – Sobers kept press clippings and eagerly predicted great feats to anyone who would listen.

Former Hampshire player Andrew Murtagh, who became head of cricket at Malvern College, recalled Sobers visiting in the early 1990s at the invite of the school's professional coach, ex-England batsman Roger Tolchard. The former Leicestershire wicketkeeper grabbed his gloves and urged, 'Come on, Garry. Show us your bag of tricks.' Murtagh recounted, 'Garry picked up any old ball and proceeded to bowl an inswinger, an outswinger, a Chinaman, a googly and an orthodox slow left-arm. And then for good measure, he bowled a bouncer that sailed over Roger's head. He also told the boys to look out for a young West Indian left-handed batsman who would soon be breaking all records. His name? Brian Lara.'[12]

Sobers was watching during Lara's breakthrough innings against Australia, calling him in the dressing room during a break for rain, when Lara was in the 30s, to assure him it was going to be his day. And when Lara found himself 320 not out overnight against England in Antigua in 1994, Sobers was at the ground the next day. 'You've got a chance, don't throw it away,' he told Lara before play began.

On 365, Lara pounced upon a short ball by Chris Lewis and hooked it for four to break the single-innings Test record. Sobers made his way to the middle for a photo opportunity that, although clearly stage-managed, was a genuinely heartfelt moment of shared joy. Sobers hugged Lara and told him how proud he was. 'I'm very happy for you,' he said. 'I knew you could do it, son. You were always the one.'[13]

Keith Fletcher, the England manager at the time, said of the delay to the match, 'You can forgive Sir Garry anything. He was the most generous of individuals in his playing days and regarded Lara … as a worthy batsman to beat his record. The reality, though, is that there is no comparison. Sobers was the finest cricketer I ever saw.'[14]

As well as joy for his protégé, Sobers felt some relief that the weight of being record-holder had been lifted. No longer, when any batsman reached a double-century overnight, would he be disturbed by reporters wanting to know if he thought his 365 was about to be eclipsed. The fact that it was Lara who eased him of such a burden, eventually advancing to 375, made it all the more satisfactory.

Sobers was happy to be asked by WICB president Peter Short to address the West Indies team before the 1996 World Cup in Asia, where they ended up beaten semi-finalists, even though he doubted he would make much impression on the senior players. It was when Lara served as West Indies captain, a position he first took in 1998, that Sobers believed he might be asked to support him as manager. But the WICB delayed their call.

* * *

By the end of 2004 the WICB was ready to change direction, despite the team coached by Gus Logie having won the ICC Champions Trophy in England. The role of West Indies head coach had been reserved for prominent on-field figures in the region's history: such as Rohan Kanhai, Malcolm Marshall, Roger Harper and Logie. Now the Board looked to Australia and decided that their man was 39-year-old Bennett King, a former rugby league player who was leading Australia's cricket academy after a successful stint in charge of Queensland.

It was, in fact, the same decision that had been made a year earlier when King, who had formed a connection with CEO Roger Brathwaite through some coaching he'd done in Grenada, was originally asked to apply for the role. 'I did an interview,' King recalled, 'and they announced I had got the job before we had even discussed remuneration. I thought that is a poorly run organisation and I pulled out. A year later, they were advertising again. I had another crack and they did it properly and I was offered the position. When I was considering it they got Sir Garry to phone me and he spoke to me about the possibilities. I think they used him – not that it swayed me.'

Having accepted the job, King found that Sobers came with it. The WICB had finally given him an official role, that of 'technical consultant' to the team. 'It wasn't something I did,' King clarified. And while generous in his appraisal of Sobers's contribution, King added, 'I thought it was just a show from the cricket board that they were getting the former greats involved. And he had been the greatest of them all.'[15]

There is no doubt that it was a good public relations move by the WICB, who were seen to be embracing Sobers and were managing to offset a little of the parochial opposition to a non-West Indian running the team. The view of many would be voiced by Tony Becca of the *Jamaica Gleaner* when eventually King was succeeded by another Australian, John Dyson. Calling it 'an insult' to all West Indians, he wrote, 'West Indies cricket is good enough to find a coach from among those West Indians who have played the game and to go outside to find one is a waste of money – money that is so needed at the grassroots level of the game at that. The Board has no faith in its own people.'[16]

The official WICB announcement said that Sobers would 'work with specific individuals' and 'assist with coaching and tactical strategies in collaboration with the coach'. Sobers looked forward to 'the opportunity to give back' and added, 'I hope that whatever contribution I make will assist in making this team a well-rounded championship unit.'

There were a couple of printed side-swipes at Sobers for taking the role after being a vocal opponent of having a foreign national coach, but few in the Caribbean took serious issue with their hero accepting some kind of official recognition. And King, who learnt quickly that Sobers shared a lot of his own outlook on the game, picked up no hint of resentment from his new colleague over that long wait for a job. 'Sir Garry doesn't speak badly of too many people,' he laughed. 'I think you just felt his belief that West Indies could always do better.'

King explained, 'He had a strong affiliation with Australia, and I think he always liked the way Australia played their cricket to win. When he was captain of the West Indies team, he did some unusual things to try and conjure up some wins. He wanted them to win games and be entertaining, rather than playing boring cricket. That resonated with me. For example, I hated negative leg-side bowling and tried to get it out of our style. We had to be trying to get guys out, rather than being negative and waiting for the inevitable to happen. Every time I went to Barbados, we would have dinner and have a good chat about the game.'

To King's frustration, he discovered that Sobers's involvement was limited by budget. 'It would have been nice for Sir Garry to come away for international matches. But we didn't have a lot of money. When we went to New Zealand we had to ask the cricket board there for balls because we couldn't afford any. He was mainly just there for training camps but we didn't have a lot of them.'

King gave Sobers a free hand to contribute where he felt he could be most useful. 'He came in as an observer and then spoke to players. I gave him a lot of autonomy. We would discuss what he had spoken about with the players so I could reinforce things, that sort of stuff. He was really good. My role was helping them technically with improvements, but Garry certainly had a good eye. I could talk to him about what I saw and what he saw, and then I could go about making some of those changes. It was quite refreshing when you spoke to Garry on that technical side to find that we had similar views.

'Game situation was a very strong point, his tactical approach. He would talk to players when they came off the field after games about what they were seeing and we used to do some game-sense training. His biggest asset for us was that knowledge of the game and what he saw through his eyes.

He saw it a little bit differently to other people. He was just a competitive man.'

Being an icon of the region's sport also helped King in his attempts to make the players more aware of the legacy of which they were now custodians. 'I did my due diligence on West Indies cricket,' he said. 'I read *Beyond the Boundary*, learned the history. Some of the players didn't have that knowledge. They didn't know who George Headley was. I thought there was an opportunity to give them greater knowledge of West Indies cricket, instil some history into them, and that was a great role for Garry. Some of his stories were important to our game. We even had quiz nights.'[17]

Before leaving his role following West Indies' disappointing display in the World Cup on home soil in 2007, King sent the WICB a written report on Sobers's contribution, observing that 'his presence brought inspiration and gravitas to the West Indies team during his consultancy'. He felt that 'Sir Garry's role was complementary to my leadership' and he emphasised 'Garry's role as a mentor, guiding younger players'. He concluded, '[His] presence reinforced the cultural and historical significance of West Indies cricket, inspiring players to embody the spirit of the game. Tangible results weren't immediate but were a crucial step in building long-term foundations.'[18]

Two decades on, he summarised Sobers's stint with the team by recalling, 'It would have been good if he could have come away with us on tours. It was a shame that we didn't use him a great deal. I felt that we could have made more use of him. It was not because we didn't want to.'[19]

With King's departure, Sobers ended his first official role with the West Indies team. But someone else was soon to come calling.

* * *

Allen Stanford, a Texas-born banker, had settled in Antigua in 1990. Sole shareholder of the Stanford Financial Group, he earned a knighthood from the local government in 2006 after bankrolling a local hospital, rebuilding a marina and becoming one of the island's major employers. He had also poured millions of dollars into Caribbean cricket, establishing the Stanford 20/20, played at his own stadium and featuring 19 teams that he ensured were well-funded.

In 2008, he approached the England and Wales Cricket Board (ECB) about a $20 million winner-takes-all match between England and what was effectively an unofficial West Indies team, the Stanford Superstars. Eager to give its players a financial incentive to remain in England colours instead of playing in the newly launched and highly lucrative Indian Premier League, the ECB accepted eagerly. When Stanford landed his helicopter on the nursery ground at Lord's to announce the match in a gaudy press conference, one of the first men to greet him with a handshake and a hug in the manner of a lifelong friend was Garry Sobers.

As in the days of Kerry Packer, Sobers had been happy to accept an invitation to become a spokesman and lend respectability to a cricketing outsider. He and several other West Indies cricket legends, including the likes of Viv Richards and Everton Weekes, were reportedly being paid $100,000 for their advice and endorsement. No one could begrudge him the opportunity to make some easy money in such a harmless way.

But, to the embarrassment of all concerned, federal agents in the United States established that Stanford's money had come from an elaborate Ponzi scheme, where nothing was being done to grow customers' investment. Instead, Stanford was using funds deposited in his banks or entrusted to his wealth management company to finance his whims and lavish lifestyle. Charged in February 2009 with fraud amounting to around $8 billion, he was eventually sentenced to 110 years in prison.

Sobers, who in 2009 was one of the inaugural inductees into the ICC Hall of Fame, was slower than others to distance himself from Stanford. After Stanford's December 2009 court appearance in Houston, *The Times* reported Sobers insisting that the Texan's money had been good for Caribbean cricket and he was quoted as saying, 'I know some are pretending that they never trusted him, but I could never do that. I did and still do. I've seen pictures of him in chains, which they don't seem to do to other people accused of crimes. I hope that he is cleared.'

Generously, one can applaud Sobers for his loyalty towards his benefactor. And there is no doubt that the money Stanford invested in cricket helped create a structure that led to West Indies' triumphs in the 2012 and 2016 T20 World Cups. But Sobers appeared to miss the point that it was at the expense of those who had been swindled out of their savings. Sobers was in no way an uncaring man but, as shown in the Rhodesian affair, he could present himself as naïve and unworldly, suggesting that his horizon extended no further than the boundary. What was it that CLR James asked about those 'who only cricket know'?

* * *

In his later years, Sobers has lived only a couple of miles from his birthplace in the parish of St Michael's. Close to his home is the Church of Nazarene, Collymore Rock, and when *Indian Times* writer K. Shriniwas Rao visited the area he reported, 'As blasphemous as this may sound, and as locals here don't mind putting it, the God lives on the other side of the road.' Even those born several decades after Sobers last held a cricket bat were able to advise Rao, 'Sir Garry? That's his house.'[20]

Like many people advancing through their decades, he had his share of health issues, including a detached retina in his left eye requiring surgery in Miami in 1992, followed by an uncomfortable recovery period and somewhat impaired depth perception on the golf course. He felt fortunate that the problem had not occurred earlier in life and affected his career.

Then, in 1993, he suffered from septicaemia in his troublesome knee while in London for the World Travel Market. It became so swollen that doctors forbade him to fly and ordered an operation which required a four-week stay in hospital, much of it spent on a drip.

Yet life, he always maintained, was for living. Making no concession to age or ailments, he remained a regular golfer throughout his ninth decade, with former opponent Pat Pocock recalling late in 2024, 'I played golf with him about three years ago at my club and he was still a ten-handicapper. He had rocket hands on the golf course. I remember once when Garry rocked up with a girl I knew who had played squash for England, but never played golf in her life. After about three years' guidance from Garry she was playing off a four handicap.'[21]

As well as long hours on the golf course, retirement had allowed him to further indulge his love of horse racing, but no longer as a mere punter. His success as a cricketer had seen him progress from roadside spectator to the VIP enclosure at Garrison Savannah. He owned horses with his friend and former team-mate, Wes Hall, whose son Sean initially rode and later trained for the duo. Sobers wrote proudly of the success they achieved with a two-year-old called Cruise Missile.

His routine continued to include frequent visits to England, often with his partner, Jackie White. Close friend and former Nottinghamshire team-mate Basharat Hassan, effectively acting as his manager, would arrange and oversee speaking engagements and appearances – at cricket clubs, golfing societies and the like – which maintained an additional income as well as allowing him to run into familiar faces. If he attended matches, it was usually as someone's guest and always it was the pleasure of the company that meant more to him than the action on the field.

He was rarely short of people seeking him out at home either. 'I used to holiday a lot in Barbados,' said David Lloyd. 'I knew Garry played golf at the Royal Westmoreland and liked to tee off at 1.35 p.m. I would try to make sure I was waiting in the clubhouse when he finished his round.'[22]

'He is a very humble guy,' said Roger Davis, former opponent at Glamorgan. 'I was in awe of him as a player and

I would let him talk to the senior players at the bar. But when I went over to Barbados to play golf at Sandy Lane, he was playing there every day and he spent time with me and my friend asking about all the players I played with. Which was lovely really. He was such a sociable guy, a lovely man.'[23]

When those conversations about cricket advanced beyond pure reminiscence, Sobers was never one to lament his bad luck to have played in a less lucrative era, or to begrudge modern stars their good fortune, or to begin each sentence with, 'In my day ...' Lloyd remembered one of the few elements of the modern game he took issue with. 'He could hold his own in a debate,' he said. 'And the one thing that he wouldn't have at all was reverse swing. He said the ball swung this way or that and, "There's no such thing as reverse swing."'[24]

Sobers became patron of the Cerebral Palsy Sport charity and in 2022 he even announced the launch of his own charity, the Sir Garry Sobers Foundation, aimed at supporting young, under-privileged cricketers around the world. Its publicity stated an ambition to establish hubs in the UK, West Indies, India, Australia and South Africa, an initiative supported by Bravia Capital, a private investment firm based in New York – although at the time of writing, the foundation's website address, *sirgarrysobers.org*, was still announcing, 'Coming Soon'.

Sobers's 80th birthday in 2016 had been cause for more national celebration and fundraising in Barbados, including a celebrity match between a Sobers XI and a Lara XI at Kensington Oval on his big day; a gala dinner at the Lloyd Erskine Sandiford Centre the following day; and an invitational golf tournament at his beloved Sandy Lane Golf and Country Club. The Caribbean Premier League honoured him at the Barbados Tridents' match against the Trinidad and Tobago Knight Riders.

He was back in the headlines in 2021 when he stated his disappointment at Barbados becoming a republic, with an elected head of state rather than the UK's royal figurehead. As unusual as it was for Sobers to comment politically, it was hardly surprising that the knighthood he'd received from Queen Elizabeth II gave him a monarchist leaning. 'It will be very sad for a lot of us,' he said. 'The Queen was very highly appreciated here. It was a bit of a shock.'

As this book went to press, Sobers's 90th birthday was approaching. All being well, as another century hoves into view, there will be more celebrations. The tributes and anecdotes will amount to love letters from his sport and his nation. The expressions of admiration and affection will mean more to him than the numbers in the averages columns. The approval or disapproval of his captaincy will matter less than the memories of him as an honest, giving man. Tony Lewis's description of him as 'generous and modest' could apply to him on or off the field and has been duplicated by almost everyone with any connection to him.[25]

'I learnt a lot from Garry Sobers, who was a very modest and approachable man, always willing to talk about the game and share his experience,' was the memory of Pakistan's Younis Ahmed, an International Cavaliers team-mate.[26] Derek Randall, who played alongside Sobers at Nottinghamshire, said, 'It sometimes seemed unfair that any one man should be blessed with so much talent and yet manage to remain a thoroughly nice man.'[27]

Former Australia captain Greg Chappell remembered sharing the field with Sobers as one of the highlights of the time he spent with Somerset. 'Having known Ian in Adelaide he was very kind to me, looking after me at the bar and taking us out for dinner. For someone who had been my idol, he was a wonderfully humble, down-to-earth man.'[28]

And so on. Testimonies such as those are what he cares about, not people's willingness or not to understand his Rhodesia visit.

'It makes me proud that those I have played with and against have described me as one of the most honest and gentlemanly people in cricket,' he said during one of his most recent visits to England. 'I was born that way. I achieved everything as a common man.'

A common man who came to represent royalty to the Caribbean. Whose brilliance lifted people into the light of his achievements. People such as journalist Angela MacGeoch, who grew up only a mile from Bay Land. 'It is hard for us, West Indians, to see greatness in our midst,' she explained. 'This is largely because our colonial background encouraged us to believe we were insignificant.'

The conquests of Sobers helped to change that. When, during a six-month spell in Australia, locals discovered that MacGeoch's accent was Barbadian, Sobers was all they wanted to talk about. One butcher even gave her several pounds of beef by way of his own tribute to the man he insisted was the greatest cricketer in history. 'I had travelled thousands of miles across the world and had been told with no uncertainty that one man was the best,' she remembered. 'We were, after all, a people of significance. Garry Sobers has filled our hearts not only with joy and excitement, but with a pride that encourages us to hold our heads high wherever we go and to proclaim to all, "We are West Indian. We're as good as the rest and sometimes we're the best in the world."'[29]

A common man who played cricket like a god yet retained the human touch. Who could make someone feel ten feet tall with a smile and a few minutes of conversation. Someone such as Dorian Bryan, who remembered his trepidation as a young *Barbados Advocate* reporter at Queen's Park Oval when a player invited him into the pavilion to meet Sir Garry. 'I went in and was introduced at the door only to hear a booming voice saying, "Bring a chair and come and sit down."' It was Sobers who engaged in conversation, asking Bryan what he thought the bowler should be doing and congratulating him when his suggestions brought a wicket a few balls later. 'The great man smiled at me and said that proved I watched the game. It was a highlight of my time in sports journalism.'[30]

A common man who made his fans dream. Fans such as Guyson Meyers, who became one of Barbados's leading lawyers. 'All the youngsters with whom I grew up walked to the batting crease with upturned collar and a distinct lean,' he said. 'No, we were not all deformed. We were simply emulating the great man who made these features popular. We did not have his talents, but emulation was the closest we could come to worshipping him.'[31]

A common man whose own dreams of what was achievable on the field frequently defied logic and the longest of odds. Whose feats inspired poetry and prose, music and lyrics. A common man who became, as The Merrymen would have it, a maestro.

STATISTICS

Career record of Garry Sobers

TEST MATCHES

Batting	M	Inn	NO	Runs	HS	Ave.	100	50	Catches
	93	160	21	8,032	365*	57.78	26	30	109

Bowling	Balls	Mdn	Runs	W	BB	Ave.	Econ	S/Rate	5wkt	10wkt
	21,599	974	7,999	235	6-73	34.03	2.22	91.91	6	-

UNOFFICIAL TEST MATCHES (England v Rest of World 1970; World XI in Australia 1971/72)

Batting	M	I	NO	Runs	HS	Ave.	100	50	Catches
	10	18	3	929	254	61.93	3	3	11

Bowling	Balls	Mdn	Runs	W	BBI	Ave	5wkt	10wkt
	2,450	111	886	30	6-21	29.53	1	-

FIRST-CLASS CRICKET

Batting	M	I	NO	Runs	HS	Ave	100	50	Catches
	383	609	93	28,314	365*	54.87	86	121	405

Bowling	Balls	Mdn	Runs	W	BBI	Ave	Econ	S/Rate	5wkt	10wkt
	70,778	2,894	28,941	1,043	9-49	27.74	2.45	67.86	36	1

ONE-DAY INTERNATIONALS (1 match)

Batting: 10 runs. *Bowling:* 10.3-3-31-1. *Fielding:* 1 catch

LIST A CRICKET

Batting	M	I	NO	Runs	HS	Ave.	100	50	Catches
	95	92	21	2,721	116*	38.32	1	18	41

Bowling	Balls	Mdn	Runs	W	BB	Ave	Econ	S/Rate	4wkt	5wkt
	4,423	122	2,426	109	5-43	22.35	3.29	40.57	4	1

TEST CENTURIES

365* v Pakistan, Kingston, 1957/58
125   v Pakistan, Georgetown, 1958/59
109* v Pakistan, Georgetown, 1958/59
142* v India, Bombay, 1958/59
198   v India, Kanpur, 1958/59
106* v India, Calcutta, 1958/59
226   v England, Bridgetown, 1959/60
147   v England, Kingston, 1959/60
145   v England, Bridgetown, 1959/60
132   v Australia, Brisbane, 1960/61
168   v Australia, Sydney, 1960/61
153   v India, Kingston, 1961/62
104   v India, Kingston, 1961/62
102   v England, Headingley, 1963
161   v England, Old Trafford, 1966
163* v England, Lord's, 1966
174   v England, Headingley, 1966
113* v England, Kingston, 1967/68
152   v England, Georgetown, 1967/68
110   v Australia, Adelaide, 1968/69
113   v Australia, Sydney, 1968/69
108* v India, Georgetown, 1970/71
178* v India, Bridgetown, 1970/71
132   v India, Port-of-Spain, 1970/71
142   v New Zealand, Bridgetown, 1971/72
150* v England, Lord's, 1973

TEST 5-WICKETS

5-120 v Australia, Melbourne, 1960/61
5-63 v India, Kingston, 1961/62
5-60 v England, Edgbaston, 1963
5-41 v England, Headingley, 1966
6-73 v Australia, Brisbane, 1968/69
5-42 v England, Headingley, 1969

FIRST-CLASS CAREER RECORDS

Highest Score: 365*, West Indies v Pakistan, Kingston, 1957/58

Highest Season First-Class Batting Average: 143.85 (1957/58)

Most Runs in First-Class Season: 1,742 (1970)

Most Centuries in First-Class Season: 7 (1970)

1,000 Runs in First-Class Season: 14 times

Best Bowling: 9-49, West Indians v Kent, Canterbury, 1966

Most Wickets in First-Class Season: 84 (1968)

Most 5-wickets in First-Class Season: 5 (1968)

Highest One-day Score: 116*, Nottinghamshire v Worcestershire, Newark-on-Trent, John Player League, 1971

Best One-day Bowling: 5-43, Nottinghamshire v Derbyshire, Chesterfield, John Player League, 1969

HONOURS

Knighted by HM Queen Elizabeth II, 1975

Wisden Cricketer of the Century, 2000

Wisden Cricketer of the Year, 1975

Indian Cricketer of the Year, 1958/59

Cricket Society Wetherall Award (Leading All-Rounder in English season), 1970

Walter Lawrence Trophy (Fastest Century in English season), 1974

West Indies captain, 1964–72

Nottinghamshire captain, 1968–73

This Is Your Life, 1975

Barbados Order of National Heroes, 1998

The Order of the Caribbean Community, 1998

Hall of Fame for West Indies Cricket, 2003

ICC Hall of Fame, 2009

ACKNOWLEDGEMENTS

WHEN THE subject of your work completed his playing career half a century before you type your first word, you are obviously indebted as an author to much written material that has gone before. Fortunately, in the case of Garry Sobers, very few of his contemporaries – the majority of whom are no longer with us – failed to include their recollections and opinions of the game's greatest all-rounder in their memoirs. And in addition to extensive newspaper and magazine coverage, most of Sobers's Test cricket was played in an era when comprehensive tour chronicles were published after most major series. Such publications have been invaluable and are referenced throughout the pages of this book, along with interviews and other sources.

There are a few other people I need to thank for their contributions to this book. At the risk of omissions: Charles Dagnall, Brett Heyward, Andrew Hignell, Simon Lister, Andrew Murtagh, Daniel Nice and Tom Rawlings. I am indebted to the staffs at the following organisations: The Barbados Museum and Historical Society in Bridgetown, in particular Cherrie Paris-Bourne, for access to the Sobers family archives; the Legends of Cricket Museum in Bridgetown; the MCC Library at Lord's; and the National Archives in London.

Richard Whitehead has been as insightful, knowledgeable and sympathetic as ever in his role as copy-editor, while my agent, David Luxton, and his staff at DLA Associates continue to support my endeavours with great professionalism. My thanks go out to all at Pitch Publishing, including Jane Camillin, Duncan Olner, Graham Hales and Dean Rockett.

This book always felt like a project that would not benefit greatly from the involvement of its subject, especially with his various autobiographies providing source material where necessary. Without influence from Garry Sobers himself I felt more able to place his feats and flaws in proper context. I hope he and his family would feel that I have achieved the goal set out in this book's introduction.

My own family continue to sustain me with their love and encouragement, including daughters Amy, Sarah, Laura and Karis, grandsons Jacob and Oscar and granddaughter Heidi. My wife, Sara, is the great all-rounder of my team and, like Sobers, willingly carries a far heavier load than she ought to. I can never thank her enough.

NOTES ON SOURCES

Where not referenced below or identified within the main text, quotations are sourced from contemporaneous press interviews and reports in national and local media:

INTRODUCTION

1 *Wisden Cricketer's Almanack*, 2000
2 Dennis Lillee, *Menace: The Autobiography* (Headline, 2014)
3 *The Cricketer*, March 1972
4 Interview with author
5 TheGuardian.com, 28 July 2016
6 Clyde Walcott with Brian Scovell, *Sixty Years on the Back Foot; The Cricketing Life of Sir Clyde Walcott* (Victor Gollancz, 1999)
7 Michael Manley, *A History of West Indian Cricket* (Andre Deutsch, 1988)
8 Hilary Beckles, *The Development of West Indies Cricket: Vol. 1 The Age of Nationalism* (University of the West Indies Press, 1998)
9 Garry Sobers, *The Changing Face of Cricket* (Ebury Press, 1996)
10 *Wisden Cricket Monthly*, February 2002
11 Sunil Gavaskar, *Idols* (Allen and Unwin, 1984)
12 Sir Garfield Sobers, *My Autobiography* (Headline, 2002)
13 TheGuardian.com, 25 November 2001

1: LIFE AFTER DEATH: BOY FROM THE BAY

1 *The Times*, 30 January 1942
2 *The Gazette* (Montreal), 24 February 2007
3 Sobers, *My Autobiography*
4 *Barbados Advocate*, 8 August, 2017
5 Charlie Griffith, *Chucked Around* (Pelham Books, 1970)
6 Mary Chamberlain, *Empire and Nation-Building in the Caribbean: Barbados, 1937–66* (Manchester University Press, 2010)

7 Keith AP Sandiford, *Sir Garfield Sobers: The Bayland's Favourite Son* (JW McKenzie, 2019)
8 Sir Garfield Sobers with Brian Scovell, *Sobers: Twenty Years at the Top* (Macmillan London Limited, 1988)
9 Sobers, *Twenty Years at the Top*
10 Sobers, *My Autobiography*
11 Trevor Bailey, *Sir Gary: A Biography* (Collins, 1976)
12 Bailey, *Sir Gary*
13 Sandiford, *The Bayland's Favourite Son*
14 Sobers, *Twenty Years at the Top*
15 Sobers, *My Autobiography*
16 Sobers, *My Autobiography*
17 *The Nightwatchman*, Barbados Special Edition, 2016
18 Ernest Eytle, *Frank Worrell: The Career of a Great Cricketer* (Hodder and Stoughton, 1963)
19 Sobers, *My Autobiography*
20 *Cricket's Greatest: Garry Sobers* (Pitch International, 2015)
21 The Official Programme of the Sir Garfield Sobers 40th Anniversary Committee (1994)
22 Gary Sobers with Tony Cozier, *Gary Sobers' Most Memorable Matches* (Stanley Paul, 1984)
23 Sobers, *Twenty Years at the Top*
24 Sobers, *My Autobiography*
25 *New Society*, 6 June 1983
26 Sobers, *Twenty Years at the Top*
27 Banks Breweries Souvenir Programme for Garry Sobers Benefit (1973)
28 Sobers, *Most Memorable Matches*
29 Banks Breweries Souvenir Programme
30 Eytle, *Frank Worrell*
31 Sobers, *Most Memorable Matches*
32 Official Programme of 40th Anniversary
33 Sobers, *My Autobiography*
34 *Banks Breweries Souvenir Programme*
35 Official Programme of 40th Anniversary
36 Official Programme of 40th Anniversary

2: COMING OF AGE

1 Sobers, *My Autobiography*
2 Gary Sobers, *Cricket Crusader* (Pelham Books, 1966)
3 Sandiford, *The Bayland's Favourite Son*
4 Sobers, *Most Memorable Matches*
5 Sobers, *Most Memorable Matches*

6 Sobers, *Most Memorable Matches*
7 Sobers, *Cricket Crusader*
8 Jim Laker, *Cricket Contrasts: From Crease to Commentary Box* (Stanley Paul, 1985)
9 Sobers, *My Autobiography*
10 Sobers, *My Autobiography*
11 Sobers, *Most Memorable Matches*
12 Sobers, *My Autobiography*
13 *The Cricket Monthly*, ESPNCricinfo, July 2016
14 Sobers, *Most Memorable Matches*
15 Bailey, *Sir Gary*
16 Bailey, *Sir Gary*
17 Michael Manley, *A History of West Indies Cricket* (Andre Deutsch, 1988)
18 Jeff Stollmeyer, *Everything Under the Sun: My Life in West Indies Cricket* (Stanley Paul, 1983)

3: LIVING THE DREAM

1 Sobers, *Most Memorable Matches*
2 Sobers, *My Autobiography*
3 Landsberg, Pat, *The Kangaroo Conquers: West Indies v Australia, 1955* (Museum Press, 1955)
4 Landsberg, *The Kangaroo Conquers*
5 Landsberg, *The Kangaroo Conquers*
6 Landsberg, *The Kangaroo Conquers*
7 Stollmeyer, *Everything Under the Sun*
8 Manley, *A History of West Indies Cricket*
9 Sobers, *My Autobiography*
10 Sobers, *Most Memorable Matches*
11 Landsberg, *The Kangaroo Conquers*
12 Sobers, *Most Memorable Matches*
13 Bailey, *Sir Gary*
14 Landsberg, *The Kangaroo Conquers*
15 Landsberg, *The Kangaroo Conquers*
16 Banks Breweries Souvenir Programme
17 Sobers, *Cricket Crusader*
18 Barry Knight with Andrew Leeming, *Beyond the Pavilion: Reflections on a Life in Cricket* (Amberley Publishing, 2022)
19 Sobers, *Twenty Years at the Top*
20 Harris, Bruce, *West Indies Cricket Challenge 1957* (Stanley Paul, 1957)
21 Harris, *West Indies Cricket Challenge*
22 Sobers, *Most Memorable Matches*

23 Tony Cozier, *The West Indies: Fifty Years of Test Cricket* (Angus & Robertson, 1978)
24 Graveney, Tom, *Cricket Through the Covers* (Frederick Muller, 1958)

4: RECORD BREAKER

 1 Manley, *A History of West Indies Cricket*
 2 Sobers, *My Autobiography*
 3 Sobers, *My Most Memorable Matches*
 4 Sobers, *Twenty Years at the Top*
 5 EW Swanton, *West Indies Revisited: The MCC Tour 1959-60* (*William Heinemann,* 1960)
 6 Sobers, *Twenty Years at the Top*
 7 Sobers, *Twenty Years at the Top*
 8 Sobers, *Twenty Years at the Top*
 9 Hanif Mohammed: *Playing for Pakistan: An Autobiography* (Hamdard Press, 1999)
10 Sobers, *Twenty Years at the Top*
11 Manley, *A History of West Indies Cricket*
12 Sobers, *Twenty Years at the Top*
13 *Cricket's Greatest*
14 Sobers. *My Autobiography*
15 Sobers, *Twenty Years at the Top*

5: GIANT AMONG MEN

 1 *The Nightwatchman*, Barbados Special, 2016
 2 *Manchester Evening News*, 15 April 1958
 3 *Manchester Evening Chronicle*, 18 April 1958
 4 *The Cricketer Spring Annual*, 1952
 5 *Manchester Evening News*, 15 April 1958
 6 Sobers, *My Autobiography*
 7 *Bury Times*, 21 September 2006
 8 *Manchester Evening Chronicle*, 24 April 1958
 9 *Manchester Evening News*, 15 May 1958
10 Basil D'Oliveira, *Time to Declare* (WH Allen & Co, 1980)
11 Sobers, *My Autobiography*
12 Sobers, *My Autobiography*
13 *Bury Times*, 21 September 2006
14 *The Nightwatchman*, Barbados Special, 2016
15 *The Nightwatchman*, Barbados Special, 2016
16 Sobers, *My Autobiography*
17 Sobers, *My Autobiography*
18 Bill Alley, *Standing The Test of Time* (Empire Publications, 1999)

19 Piesse, Ken, *Pep: The Story of Cec Pepper, The Best Cricketer Never to Represent Australia* (cricketbooks.com.au, 2018)
20 *Wisden*, 1965
21 Scott Oliver, *Sticky Dogs and Stardust: When the Legends Played in the Leagues* (Fairfield Books, 2023)
22 Oliver, *Sticky Dogs and Stardust*
23 Oliver, *Sticky Dogs and Stardust*
24 Oliver, *Sticky Dogs and Stardust*
25 *Coventry Telegraph*, 14 August 2023
26 Interview with author

6: LIFE AFTER DEATH: PLAYING FOR COLLIE

1 Simon Lister, *Worrell: The brief but brilliant career of a Caribbean cricket pioneer* (Simon & Schuster, 2024)
 2 Sobers, *My Autobiography*
 3 Sobers, *Twenty Years at the Top*
 4 Banks Breweries Souvenir Programme
 5 Sobers, *My Autobiography*
 6 Sobers, *My Autobiography*
 7 Sobers, *Cricket Crusader*
 8 Sobers, *Cricket Crusader*
 9 Sobers, *Cricket Crusader*
10 Sobers, *Cricket Crusader*
11 Sobers, *Cricket Crusader*
12 Gavaskar, *Idols*
13 Alf Gover, *The Long Run: An Autobiography* (Pelham Books, 1991)
14 Vaneisa Baksh, *Son of Grace: Frank Worrell, A Biography* (Fairfield Books, 2023)
15 Sobers, *My Autobiography*
16 Bailey, *Sir Gary*
17 Sobers, *My Autobiography*

7. MASTERING HIS ART

1 Swanton, *West Indies Revisited*
 2 Sobers, *My Autobiography*
 3 Alan Ross, *Through the Caribbean: England in the West Indies, 1960* (Hamish Hamilton,1960)
 4 Ross, *Through the Caribbean*
 5 Swanton, *West Indies Revisited*
 6 Swanton, *West Indies Revisited*
 7 Ross, *Through the Caribbean*
 8 Sobers, *My Autobiography*
 9 Ross, *Through the Caribbean*

10 John Arlott (editor), *The Great All-Rounders* (Pelham Books, 1969)
11 Swanton, *West Indies Revisited*
12 Swanton, *West Indies Revisited*
13 Sobers, *My Autobiography*
14 Ross, *Through the Caribbean*
15 Ross, *Through the Caribbean*
16 Ross, *Through the Caribbean*
17 Ross, *Through the Caribbean*
18 *Wisden Cricketers' Almanack*, 1961
19 Swanton, *West Indies Revisited*
20 *Wisden*, 1962
21 *Calypso Summer* (Australian Broadcasting Corporation, 2000)
22 *Calypso Summer*

8: ON THE RISE DOWN UNDER

1 Ray Illingworth, *Spinner's Wicket* (Stanley Paul, 1969)
2 *Britain's Forgotten Slave Owners* (BBC, 2015)
3 Manley, *A History of West Indies Cricket*
4 Learie Constantine, *Cricket in the Sun* (Stanley Paul, 1946)
5 Lister, *Worrell*
6 Manley, *A History of West Indies Cricket*
7 Ross, *Through the Caribbean*
8 *Calypso Summer*
9 Stollmeyer, *Everything Under the Sun*
10 Sobers, *My Autobiography*
11 *Caribbean Quarterly*, Spring 1973
12 AG Moyes, *With the West Indies in Australia, 1960-61* (William Heinemann, 1961)
13 *Calypso Summer*
14 *Calypso Summer*
15 *Calypso Summer*
16 Richie Benaud, *Anything But An Autobiography* (Hodder & Stoughton, 1968)
17 *The Tied Cricket Test* (ABC Sports, 1984)
18 Sobers, *Most Memorable Matches*
19 *The Tied Cricket Test*
20 *ESPN Legends of Cricket* (ESPN, 2002)
21 Ken Mackay, *Slasher Opens Up* (Pelham Books, 1964)
22 Eytle, *Frank Worrell*
23 Mackay, *Slasher Opens Up*
24 *Calypso Summer*
25 Norman O'Neill, *Ins and Outs* (Pelham Books, 1964)
26 Moyes, *With the West Indies in Australia*

27 *The Tied Cricket Test*
28 *The Tied Cricket Test*
29 Ian Meckiff, *Thrown Out* (Stanley Paul, 1961)
30 *Calypso Summer*
31 *Calypso Summer*
32 Sobers, *My Autobiography*
33 *Calypso Summer*
34 Sobers, *My Autobiography*
35 Mackay, *Slasher Opens Up*
36 Neil Harvey, *My World of Cricket* (Hodder & Stoughton, 1963)
37 *Calypso Summer*
38 *Calypso Summer*
39 Moyes, *With the West Indies in Australia*
40 Sobers, *My Autobiography*
41 ESPN Cricinfo, October 2009
42 Alan Davidson, *Fifteen Paces* (Souvenir Press, 1963)
43 *Calypso Summer*
44 *Calypso Summer*
45 Manley, *A History of West Indies Cricket*
46 Meckiff, *Thrown Out*
47 *Calypso Summer*
48 *Calypso Summer*

9: SHIELD OF STRENGTH

 1 Moyes, *With the West Indies in Australia*
 2 Sobers, *Cricket Crusader*
 3 Michael Sexton, *Three Summers of Sobers* (Sportswords.com.au, 2022)
 4 Sexton, *Three Summers of Sobers*
 5 Sexton, *Three Summers of Sobers*
 6 Official Programme of 40th Anniversary
 7 Sexton, *Three Summers of Sobers*
 8 Sobers, *Cricket Crusader*
 9 Knight, *Beyond the Pavilion*
10 Richard Sayer, *David Larter, Bowling Fast: The Highs and Lows* (Albert Publications 2021)
11 Paul Akeroyd, *Answering the Call: The Extraordinary Life of Sir Wesley Hall* (JW McKenzie, 2022)
12 Akeroyd, *Answering the Call*
13 *The Guardian*, 10 June 2002
14 Neil Hawke, *Bowled Over* (Rigby, 1982)
15 *ESPN Legends of Cricket*
16 Ian Chappell, *Chappelli: Life, Larrikins and Cricket* (Ebury Press 2012)

17 Interview with author
18 Favell, *By Hook or by Cut*
19 Interview with author
20 Interview with author
21 Chappell, *Chappelli: Life, Larrikins and Cricket*
22 Arlott (editor), *The Great All-Rounders*
23 Sobers, *Cricket Crusader*
24 Sobers, *Cricket Crusader*

10. WORRELL'S FINAL TRIUMPH

1 Ian Wooldridge, *Cricket, Lovely Cricket: The West Indies Tour 1963* (Robert Hale, 1963)
2 JS Barker, *Summer Spectacular, The West Indies v England, 1963* (Collins 1963)
3 Paul Akeroyd, *Answering the Call: The Extraordinary Life of Sir Wesley Hall* (JW McKenzie, 2022)
4 Sobers, *Cricket Crusader*
5 Wooldridge, *Cricket, Lovely Cricket*
6 Barker, *Summer Spectacular*
7 Sobers, *Twenty Years at the Top*
8 Barker, *Summer Spectacular*
9 Wooldridge, *Cricket, Lovely Cricket*
10 Wooldridge, *Cricket, Lovely Cricket*
11 Barker, *Summer Spectacular*
12 Barker, *Summer Spectacular*
13 Wooldridge, *Cricket, Lovely Cricket*
14 CLR James, *A Majestic Innings: Writings on Cricket* (Aurum Press, 2006)
15 Wooldridge, *Cricket, Lovely Cricket*
16 Wooldridge, *Cricket, Lovely Cricket*
17 Wooldridge, *Cricket, Lovely Cricket*
18 Barker, *Summer Spectacular*
19 Sobers, *My Autobiography*
20 Lister, *Worrell*
21 *Wisden Cricketers' Almanack*, 1964
22 *Wisden Cricketers' Almanack*, 1964
23 Wooldridge, *Cricket, Lovely Cricket*
24 *Wisden Cricketers' Almanack*, 1964
25 Cozier, *The West Indies: Fifty Years of Test Cricket*

11: SONGS OF PRAISE

1 Sobers, *My Autobiography*
2 Gary Sobers, *Cricket, Advance!* (Pelham Books, 1965)

NOTES ON SOURCES

3 Sobers, *My Autobiography*
4 David Lemmon (editor), *Cricket Heroes* (Queen Anne Press, 1984)
5 Sobers, *My Autobiography*
6 Knight, *Beyond the Pavilion*
7 Interview with author
8 Interview with author
9 Erapalli Prasanna, *One More Over* (Rupa, 1977)
10 Derek Underwood, *Beating the Bat* (Stanley Paul, 1975)
11 Peter Walker, *Cricket Conversations* (Pelham Books, 1978)
12 Gavaskar, *Idols*
13 Interview with author
14 Walker, *Cricket Conversations*
15 D'Oliveira, *Time to Declare*
16 Interview with author
17 *Wisden*, 1967
18 Mike Brearley, *On Cricket*
19 Interview with author
20 Griffith, *Chucked Around*
21 Len Hutton, *Fifty Years in Cricket* (Stanley Paul, 1984)
22 Colin Shindler, *Barbed Wire and Cucumber Sandwiches: The Controversial South Africa Cricket Tour of 1970* (Pitch Publishing, 2020)
23 Prasanna, *One More Over*
24 Interview with author
25 Interview with author
26 *The Cricket Monthly*, ESPNCricinfo, July 2016
27 Interview with author
28 Mallett, *Hitting Out*
29 Tom Graveney, *The Heart of Cricket* (Arthur Baker 1983)
30 Sobers, *My Autobiography*
31 Alan Knott, *It's Knott Cricket: The Autobiography of Alan Knott* (Macmillan, 1985)
32 D'Oliveira, *Time to Declare*
33 Interview with author
34 Graveney, *The Heart of Cricket*
35 www.bbc.co.uk/sport
36 Knight, *Beyond the Pavilion*
37 Roger Knight, *Boundaries: A Memoir* (JW McKenzie, 2021)
38 Knight, *Beyond the Pavilion*
39 Sobers, *My Autobiography*
40 Chappell, *Chappelli: Life, Larrikins and Cricket*
41 *ESPN Legends of Cricket*

427

12: A QUESTION OF LEADERSHIP

1 Sobers, *Cricket Crusader*
2 Sobers, *Cricket Crusader*
3 Sobers, *Cricket Crusader*
4 Sobers, *Cricket Crusader*
5 Sobers, *Cricket Crusader*
6 *The Cricketer*, July 1964
7 *Caribbean Quarterly*, Spring 1973
8 Sobers, *Twenty Years at the Top*
9 Baksh, *Son of Grace*
10 Sobers, *Cricket Crusader*
11 Geoff Boycott, *The Autobiography* (Macmillan, 1987)
12 *The Nightwatchman*, 2015
13 Sobers, *My Autobiography*
14 Stollmeyer, *Everything Under the Sun*
15 Richie Benaud, *The New Champions: Australia in the West Indies, 1965* (Hodder & Stoughton, 1965)
16 Benaud, *The New Champions*
17 https://betweenwickets.com/fifty-years-reminiscences-1965-caribbean-tour
18 Benaud, *The New Champions*
19 *The Cricketer*, April 1965
20 *The Cricketer*, April 1965
21 Benaud, *The New Champions*
22 https://betweenwickets.com/fifty-years-reminiscences-1965-caribbean-tour
23 Benaud, *The New Champions*
24 Benaud, *The New Champions*
25 Bill Lawry, *Run-Digger* (Souvenir Press, 1966)
26 Benaud, *The New Champions*
27 Rohan Kanhai, *Blasting for Runs* (Souvenir Press, 1966)
28 Sobers, *Cricket Crusader*
29 *Wisden*, 1966
30 Sobers, *Most Memorable Matches*
31 Sobers, *Most Memorable Matches*
32 *The Cricketer*, April 1966

13: MAN FOR ALL SEASONS

1 David Hepworth, *Uncommon People* (Bantam Press, 2017)
2 *Wisden Cricketers' Almanack*, 1967
3 Ken Barrington, *Playing It Straight* (Stanley Paul, 1968)
4 Sobers, *King Cricket*
5 Sobers, *King Cricket*

6 John Clarke and Brian Scovell, *Everything That's Cricket: The West Indies Tour 1966* (Stanley Paul, 1966)

7 Christopher Sandford, *Keeper of Style: John Murray – The King of Lord's* (Pitch, 2019)

8 Sobers, *King Cricket*

9 Stollmeyer, *Everything Under the Sun*

10 Stollmeyer, *Everything Under the Sun*

11 *The 1966 West Indian* Tour, official film available on YouTube

12 Clarke and Scovell, *Everything That's Cricket*

13 Colin Milburn, *Largely Cricket: An Autobiography* (Stanley Paul, 1968)

14 Sobers, *King Cricket*

15 Sobers, *King Cricket*

16 Griffith, *Chucked Around*

17 Sobers, *King Cricket*

18 Knight, *Beyond the Pavilion*

19 Sobers, *King Cricket*

20 Clarke and Scovell, *Everything That's Cricket*

21 Sobers, *Most Memorable Matches*

22 *The 1966 West Indian Tour*

23 Sobers, *My Autobiography*

24 Sobers, *Most Memorable Matches*

25 Boycott, *The Autobiography*

26 D'Oliveira, *Time to Declare*

27 Stollmeyer, *Everything Under the Sun*

28 Sobers, *King Cricket*

29 Sobers, *King Cricket*

30 *The 1966 West Indian Tour*

31 Sobers, *King Cricket*

32 Sobers, *King Cricket*

33 Sobers, *My Autobiography*

34 Griffith, *Chucked Around*

35 Stollmeyer, *Everything Under the Sun*

36 Sobers, *King Cricket*

37 Stollmeyer, *Everything Under the Sun*

38 *Wisden*, 1967

39 Stollmeyer, *Everything Under the Sun*

40 Sobers, *King Cricket*

14: FUN, LOVE AND MONEY

1 *Cricket's Greatest*

2 Trevor McDonald, *Clive Lloyd: The Authorised Biography* (Grafton Books, 1985)

3 Simon Lister, *Supercat: The authorised biography of Clive Lloyd* (Fairfield Books, 2007)
4 The Nawab of Pataudi, *Tiger's Tale: The Story of One of India's Great Cricketers* (Stanley Paul, 1969)
5 Sobers, *My Autobiography*
6 *The Times of India*, 4 March 2007
7 Prasanna, *One More Over*
8 *Playfair Cricket Monthly*, March 1967
9 Sobers, *My Autobiography*
10 Pataudi, *Tiger's Tale*
11 Sobers, *My Autobiography*
12 Sobers, *King Cricket*
13 TheGuardian.com, 25 November 2001

15: A GAMBLE TOO FAR

1 JS Barker, *In The Main, West Indies versus MCC 1968* (Pelham Books, 1968)
2 Henry Blofeld, *Cricket in Three Moods* (Hodder & Stoughton, 1970)
3 *The Cricketer*, 8 September, 1967
4 *Wisden Cricketers' Almanack*, 1969
5 Graveney, *The Heart of Cricket*
6 Manley, *A History of West Indian Cricket*
7 Barker, *In The Main*
8 Barker, *In The Main*
9 Blofeld, *Cricket in Three Moods*
10 Brian Close, *The MCC Tour of West Indies, 1968* (Stanley Paul, 1968)
11 Close, *The MCC Tour of West Indies, 1968*
12 Colin Cowdrey, *MCC: Autobiography of a Cricketer* (Hodder & Stoughton, 1976)
13 Sobers, *Twenty Years at the Top*
14 Graveney, *The Heart of Cricket*
15 Close, *The MCC Tour of West Indies, 1968*
16 Cowdrey, *MCC*
17 Manley, *A History of West Indian Cricket*
18 Barker, *In The Main*
19 Banks Breweries Souvenir Programme
20 *Playfair Cricket Monthly*, April 1968
21 Barker, *In The Main*
22 Barker, *In The Main*
23 Rob Kelly, *Hobbsy: A Life in Cricket* (Von Krumm, 2018)
24 Interview with author
25 Blofeld, *Cricket in Three Moods*

26 Interview with author
27 Barker, *In The Main*
28 Kelly, *Hobbsy*
29 Cowdrey, *MCC*
30 Close, *The MCC Tour of West Indies, 1968*
31 Cowdrey, *MCC*
32 *Wisden*, 1969
33 Sobers, *My Autobiography*
34 McDonald, *Clive Lloyd*
35 Blofeld, *Cricket in Three Moods*
36 McDonald, *Clive Lloyd*
37 Manley, *A History of West Indian Cricket*
38 D'Oliveira, *Time to Declare*
39 John Edrich, *Runs In The Family* (Stanley Paul, 1969)
40 Close, *The MCC Tour of West Indies, 1968*
41 Sobers, *My Autobiography*
42 Bailey, *Sir Gary*
43 Manley, *A History of West Indian Cricket*
44 Manley, *A History of West Indian Cricket*
45 Barker, *In The Main*
46 Close, *The MCC Tour of West Indies, 1968*
47 Close, *The MCC Tour of West Indies, 1968*
48 Sobers, My Autobiography
49 Barker, *In The Main*
50 *Wisden*, 1969
51 Sobers, My Autobiography
52 Blofeld, *Cricket in Three Moods*
53 Sobers, My Autobiography
54 Barker, *In The Main*

16: CAPTAIN UNDER PRESSURE
1 Manley, *A History of West Indies Cricket*
2 Sobers, *Twenty Years at the Top*
3 Barker, *In The Main*
4 Blofeld, *Cricket in Three Moods*
5 Banks Breweries Souvenir Programme
6 Blofeld, *Cricket in Three Moods*
7 Lister, *Supercat*
8 *ESPN Legends of Cricket*
9 Barker, *In The Main*
10 Blofeld, *Cricket in Three Moods*
11 Interview with author
12 McDonald, *Clive Lloyd*

13 Lister, *Supercat*
14 Bailey, *Sir Gary*
15 John Snow, *Cricket Rebel* (Hamlyn, 1976)
16 Pat Pocock, *Percy: The Perspicacious Memoirs of a Cricketing Man* (Clifford Frost Publications, 1987)
17 Phil Tressider, *Captains on a See-Saw: The West Indies Tour of Australia, 1968-69* (Souvenir Press, 1969)
18 Tressider, *Captains on a See-Saw*
19 Cozier, *West Indies: Fifty Years of Test Cricket*
20 McDonald, *Clive Lloyd*
21 Manley, *A History of West Indies Cricket*
22 Keith Stackpole, *Not Just for Openers* (Stockwell Press, 1974)
23 Blofeld, *Cricket in Three Moods*
24 Tressider, *Captains on a See-Saw*
25 Bailey, *Sir Gary*
26 *Playfair Cricket Monthly*, April 1969
27 Tressider, *Captains on a See-Saw*
28 Manley, *A History of West Indies Cricket*
29 Manley, *A History of West Indies Cricket*
30 Interview with author
31 Blofeld, *Cricket in Three Moods*
32 Manley, *A History of West Indies Cricket*
33 Tressider, *Captains on a See-Saw*
34 Bailey, *Sir Gary*
35 *Playfair Cricket Monthly*, February 1969
36 *Caribbean Quarterly*, Spring 1973
37 Interview with author
38 Lemmon (editor), *Cricket Heroes*
39 *ESPN Legends of Cricket*
40 Blofeld, *Cricket in Three Moods*

17: JOINING THE COUNTY SET

1 *Playfair Cricket Monthly*, January 1968
2 Interview with author
3 Interview with author
4 Nottinghamshire CCC Handbook, 1968
5 *Wisden*, 1968
6 *Playfair Cricket Monthly*, March 1968
7 Interview with author
8 *Playfair Cricket Monthly*, July 1968
9 Underwood, *Beating the Bat*
10 Interview with author
11 Tony Lewis, *Playing Days* (Stanley Paul, 1985)

12 TrentBridge.co.uk, June 2020
13 YouTube interview on the Ben Seebaran channel, 2013
14 Interview with author
15 TrentBridge.co.uk
16 YouTube interview on The Analyst channel, 2018
17 Interview with author
18 YouTube, Seebaran
19 YouTube, The Analyst
20 Walker, *Cricket Conversations*
21 Interview with author
22 Lewis, *Playing Days*
23 Interview with author
24 YouTube, The Analyst
25 Interview with author
26 YouTube, Seebaran
27 Interview with author
28 Interview with author
29 Interview with author
30 YouTube, Seebaran
31 YouTube, The Analyst
32 YouTube, The Analyst
33 Walker, *Cricket Conversations*
34 TrentBridge.co.uk
35 YouTube, The Analyst
36 *Playfair Cricket Monthly*, October 1968
37 Interview with author
38 *Playfair Cricket Monthly*, October 1968
39 *Wisden*, 1969
40 Nottinghamshire CCC Handbook, 1969
41 Sobers, *Twenty Years at the Top*
42 Interview with author
43 Interview with author
44 *The Cricket Monthly*, ESPNCricinfo, July 2016
45 Interview with author
46 Pocock, *Percy*
47 Peter Wynne-Thomas, *The History of Nottinghamshire County Cricket Club* (Christopher Helm, 1992)
48 Derek Randall, *The Sun Has Got His Hat On* (Collins Willow, 1984)
49 @EssexCricket on X, 8 December, 2024

18: DECLINE AND FALL

1 Tressider, *Captains on a See-Saw*
2 Tressider, *Captains on a See-Saw*

3 *Melbourne Age*, 9 September 1969
4 Sobers, *My Autobiography*
5 Blofeld, *Cricket in Three Moods*
6 *Playfair Cricket Monthly*, February 1969
7 Blofeld, *Cricket in Three Moods*
8 *Playfair Cricket Monthly*, March 1969
9 Blofeld, *Cricket in Three Moods*
10 Lemmon (editor), *Cricket Heroes*
11 Sobers, *My Autobiography*
12 Blofeld, *Cricket in Three Moods*
13 Sobers, *Twenty Years at the Top*
14 Tressider, *Captains on a See-Saw*
15 *Wisden*, 1970
16 Cozier, *West Indies: Fifty Years of Test Cricket*
17 Cozier, *West Indies: Fifty Years of Test Cricket*
18 *Wisden*, 1970
19 *Playfair Cricket Monthly*, July 1969
20 Official Programme of 40th Anniversary
21 *The Cricketer*, 11 July 1969
22 *Wisden*, 1970
23 *Wisden*, 1970

19: BACK ON TOP OF THE WORLD

1 *The Cricketer*, August 1970
2 *Playfair Cricket Monthly*, 1970
3 *Playfair Cricket Monthly*, 1970
4 *The Cricket Monthly*, ESPN Cricinfo, July 2016
5 *The Cricketer*, August 1970
6 *The Cricketer*, September 1970
7 Interview with author
8 *The Cricketer*, September 1970
9 *Playfair Cricket Monthly*, September 1970
10 Interview with author
11 *Wisden*, 1971
12 *Playfair Cricket Monthly*, October 1970
13 *The Cricket Monthly*, ESPNCricinfo, July 2016
14 *The Cricketer*, October 1970
15 Snow, *Cricket Rebel*
16 Mike Procter, *Caught In The Middle: Monkeygate, Politics and Other Hairy Issues* (Pitch Publishing, 2017)
17 Eddie Barlow, *The Autobiography* (Tafelburg Publishers, 2006)
18 *The Cricketer*, October 1970

20: 'AFRO-SAXON': THE RHODESIA AFFAIR

1 Procter, *Caught in the Middle*
2 Manley, *A History of West Indies Cricket*
3 Manley, *A History of West Indies Cricket*
4 Rodney Hartman, *Ali: The Life of Ali Bacher* (Viking Penguin, 2004)
5 Ian Smith, *The Great Betrayal: The Memoirs of Ian Douglas Smith* (John Blake Publishing, 1997)
6 Manley, *A History of West Indies Cricket*
7 Manley, *A History of West Indies Cricket*
8 Beckles, *The Development of West Indies Cricket*
9 Memo from Barbados High Commission to the Foreign and Commonwealth Office, 14 October, 1970
10 Documents held in the National Archives, London. Ref: FCO 36/324
11 Sobers, *My Autobiography*
12 Manley, *A History of West Indies Cricket*
13 Blofeld, *Cricket in Three Moods*
14 Official Programme of 40th Anniversary
15 Manley, *A History of West Indies Cricket*
16 Letter from Barbados High Commission to the Foreign and Commonwealth Office, 30 October 1970
17 *Caribbean Cricket: the role of sport in emerging small-nation politics* (*International Journal*, Autumn 1988)
18 *The Cricketer*, July 1964
19 Sobers, *My Autobiography*
20 Sobers, *Most Memorable Matches*
21 Speech at book launch during 40th anniversary celebrations, November 1994
22 *Pelé* (Netflix, 2021)
23 *Pelé*
24 CLR James, *Cricket and Race* (*Cricket,* 1975)
25 *Caribbean Quarterly*, Spring 1973
26 Viv Richards, *Hitting Across the Line* (Headline, 1991)
27 *Pelé*
28 Bailey, *Sir Gary*
29 Bailey, *Sir Gary*
30 Walker, *Cricket Conversations*
31 *ESPN Legends of Cricket*
32 *Pelé*

21: FINAL FLOURISHES

1 *Wisden*, 1972
2 Gavaskar, *Idols*

3   ESPNCricinfo, 21 December 2008
4   ESPNCricinfo, 21 December 2008
5   Ajit Wadekar, *My Cricketing Years* (Vikas Publishing, 1973)
6   *Wisden*, 1972
7   Gavaskar, *Idols*
8   Mihir Bose, *A History of Indian Cricket* (Andre Deutsch, 1990)
9   Bose, *A History of Indian Cricket*
10 *Wisden Cricket Asia, 2002*
11 Stackpole, *Not Just for Openers*
12 Sobers, *Twenty Years at the Top*
13 Stackpole, *Not Just for Openers*
14 Sobers, *Most Memorable Matches*
15 Gavaskar, *Idols*
16 Stackpole, *Not Just for Openers*
17 Bob Taylor, *Standing Up, Standing Back* (Willow Books, 1985)
18 *The Cricket Monthly*, ESPNCricinfo, July 2016
19 Sobers, *My Autobiography*
20 Taylor, *Standing Up, Standing Back*
21 Kerry O'Keeffe, *According to Skull* (ABC Books, 2004)
22 West Indies Cricket Videos YouTube channel
23 O'Keeffe, *According to Skull*
24 Greg Chappell, *Fierce Focus* (Hardie Grant Books, 2011)
25 *Wisden*, 1973
26 Stackpole, *Not Just for Openers*
27 Lillee, *Menace*
28 Lillee, *Menace*
29 *Ian Chappell's XI Greatest Centuries* (ESPNCricinfo, 2012)
30 Tony Greig, *My Story* (Stanley Paul, 1980)
31 O'Keeffe, *According to Skull*
32 *Chappell's XI Greatest Centuries*
33 Stackpole, *Not Just for Openers*
34 Lord's Cricket Ground YouTube channel
35 *The Cricketer*, March 1972
36 Ryan, Christian (editor), *Australia: Story of a Cricket Country* (Hardie Grant Books, 2011)
37 Greig, *My Story*
38 *Wisden*, 1973
39 *The Cricketer*, June 1972
40 *Wisden*, 1973
41 DJ Cameron, *Caribbean Crusade: New Zealand Cricketers in the West Indies* (Hodder & Stoughton, 1972)
42 Manley, *A History of West Indies Cricket*
43 Cameron, *Caribbean Crusade*

44 Cameron, *Caribbean Crusade*
45 Cozier, *The West Indies: Fifty Years of Test Cricket*
46 Sobers, *Twenty Years at the Top*
47 Sobers, *My Autobiography*
48 Chappell, *Fierce Focus*
49 Walcott, *Sixty Years on the Back Foot*
50 Sobers, *Twenty Years at the Top*
51 Sobers, *Twenty Years at the Top*
52 *Wisden*, 1974
53 Sobers, *Twenty Years at the Top*
54 Sobers, *Twenty Years at the Top*
55 *Wisden*, 1974
56 Sobers, *Most Memorable Matches*
57 *Wisden*, 1974
58 *The Cricketer Quarterly*, Autumn 1973

22: SIR GARFIELD DEPARTS

1 Interview with author
2 Interview with author
3 Interview with author
4 Martin-Jenkins, Christoper, *Testing Time: MCC in the West Indies 1974* (Macdonald and Jane's, 1975)
5 Martin-Jenkins, *Testing Time*
6 Martin-Jenkins, *Testing Time*
7 Martin-Jenkins, *Testing Time*
8 Sobers, *My Autobiography*
9 Interview with author
10 Sobers, *Twenty Years at the Top*
11 Sobers, *My Autobiography*
12 Memo to John Curle, Foreign and Commonwealth Office Protocol and Conference Department, 7 October 1974
13 Memo by WE Hall, FCO Honours Section, 10 October 1974
14 Letter to John Curle, FCO, 6 November, 1974
15 Letter from John Curle, FCO, to the Queen's Private Secretary, 6 December, 1974.
16 Memo to John Curle, FCO, 10 January, 1975.
17 Sobers, *Twenty Years at the Top*
18 Pocock, *Percy*
19 www.bigredbook.info
20 www.bigredbook.info
21 Sobers, *My Autobiography*

23: BEYOND THE BOUNDARY

1 Gideon Haigh, *The Cricket War: The Inside Story of Kerry Packer's World Series Cricket* (The Text Publishing Company, 1993)
2 CodeSports.com.au, 30 December 2021
3 Nicholas Brookes, *Island's XI: The Story of Sri Lankan Cricket* (The History Press 2022)
4 Speaking at unveiling ceremony of the Sobers-Tissera Trophy, to be contested in Sri Lanka-West Indies Test series, on 21 October, 2015 (Note: Michael Tissera was a former Sri Lanka captain)
5 *Indian Express*, 22 March 1987
6 Sobers-Tissera ceremony
7 Sobers, *My Autobiography*
8 Sobers, *My Autobiography*
9 *ThePapare.com*, 1 March 2018
10 Brookes, *Island's XI*
11 Brookes, *Island's XI*
12 *ThePapare.com*, 1 March 2018
13 Brookes, *Island's XI*
14 Sobers, *The Changing Face of Cricket*
15 Sobers, *The Changing Face of Cricket*
16 Sobers, *My Autobiography*
17 Sobers, *My Autobiography*
18 Lewis, *Playing Days*
19 *The Guardian, 10 June, 2002*
20 Sobers, *The Changing Face of Cricket*
21 Sobers, *The Changing Face of Cricket*

24: HIS MASTER'S VOICE

1 *The Guardian*, 10 June 2002
2 Official Programme of 40th Anniversary
3 ESPNCricInfo, 30 August 2005
4 Lemmon (editor), *Cricket Heroes*
5 Sobers, *My Autobiography*
6 Sobers, *The Changing Face of Cricket*
7 Sobers, *My Autobiography*
8 *The Cricket Monthly*, ESPNCricinfo, July 2016
9 Sobers, *My Autobiography*
10 Official Programme of 40th Anniversary
11 'Evening With the Stars', Barbados Hilton, 14 September 2016
12 Email to author
13 Lara, Brian with Brian Scovell, *Beating The Field: My Own Story* (Partridge Press, 1995)

14 Keith Fletcher, *Ashes to Ashes: The Rise, Fall and Rise of English Cricket* (Headline, 2005)

15 Interview with author

16 *Jamaica Gleaner*, 23 October 2007

17 Interview with author

18 Bennett King written report for WICBC, 2007

19 Interview with author

20 *Times of India*, 29 June 2011

21 Interview with author

22 Interview with author

23 Interview with author

24 Interview with author

25 Lewis, *Playing Days*

26 Younis Ahmed, *Lahore to London* (Chequered Flag Publishing, 2016)

27 Randall, *The Sun Has Got His Hat On*

28 Chappell, *Fierce Focus*

29 Official Programme of 40th Anniversary

30 *Barbados Advocate*, 7 July 2023

31 *Barbados Advocate*, 8 August, 2017

INDEX